FREEDOM OF PRESS
The Rise of People's Journalism

FREEDOM OF PRESS

The Rise of People's Journalism

Kishore Sharma

CENTRUM PRESS
NEW DELHI-110002 (INDIA)

CENTRUM PRESS
H.O.: 4360/4, Ansari Road, Daryaganj,
New Delhi-110002 (India)
Tel: 23278000, 23261597, 23255577, 23286875
B.O.: No. 1015, Ist Main Road, BSK IIIrd Stage,
IIIrd Phase, IIIrd Block, Bangalore-560085 (INDIA)
Tel: 080-41723429
Email: centrumpress@gmail.com
Visit us at: www.centrumpress.com

Freedom of Press: The Rise of People's Journalism

First Edition, 2010

ISBN 978-93-80836-17-1

PRINTED IN INDIA

Printed at Mehra Offset Press, Delhi

Contents

Preface

Journalists should always remember that freedom is about choice, and choice is about making 'right' or 'wrong' decision. In other word, the freedom of the press is precisely about the freedom to make a mistake. The best way to show the importance of ethics in the profession is to adhere to a set of guidelines or code of conduct. Take privacy, for example. A journalist might have the highest regard for the right to privacy, but claim that some information about a politician doesn't qualify for his protection. The question then arises: does the end justify the means? A code of conduct, with regulations and guidelines by the journalists themselves is probably the solution.

Proprietors invariably seem to safeguard their position through the appointment of an editor who shares or accepts their opinions on general policy. The same applies in the relationship between newspapers and the state. The task of a good editor is to allow journalists to write without any conflict with their own principles or knowledge of the facts. This is editorial independence, and it sometimes means independence of complaint. There is never a good reason for not reporting a story simply because of reader or viewer complaint. However, as the battle for circulation increases and money gets tighter pressures on editors increase to erode journalistic standards on matters of truth, accuracy and ethical acceptability.

Commercial decisions of marketing and the publisher's responsibility easily overlap with editorial requirements. Even democracy is an ethical, moral term, since it is concerned with the right or the best form of social and political organisation. Ethics is inseparable from journalism, the problem with ethics as a governor of the procession is that it can be used for control.

Chapter 1

Introduction

THE FIRST AMENDMENT AND ITS HISTORY

PRELUDE

Freedom of the press is undoubtedly one of the most important freedoms in a democratic society. Although influencers or threats, such as business, advertising, and specific organized groups, among others, exist, the biggest influence or threat is unquestionably the government. Media actions that contribute to heightening this particular form of threat will be examined exclusively.

THE HISTORY OF THE FIRST AMENDMENT

This amendment was not the most important item on the agenda when the fifty-five founding fathers drew up the U.S. Constitution in 1787. In fact, when James Madison's journal of the secret proceedings was published fifty-three years later, it revealed only one reference to press freedom - a motion by delegates from Massachusetts and South Carolina "that the liberty of the press should be inviolably observed".

As Michael Emery pointed out, "most delegates agreed with the argument that 'it is unnecessary. The power of Congress does not extend to the press.' The motion died, seven states to four."

When the framers of the U. S. Constitution finished their document there was no Bill of Rights. When state conventions met to ratify the U. S. Constitution they asked that amendments be added so that power would not be abused.

The state of Virginia had a Declaration of Rights from which twelve amendments were proposed. Eventually, ten were submitted to the states for ratification. These ten became the Bill of Rights.

As Emery mentioned, "The press freedom clause went through various forms, some of which would have applied to the states, or to all branches of government, not just Congress." The First Amendment, which had been worked out by Madison and others in a House-Senate conference committee, provided:

Congress shall make no law respecting an establishment of religion, or prohibiting the free exercise thereof, or abridging the freedom of speech, or of the press, or the right of the people peaceably to assemble, and to petition the government for a redress of grievance.

Thomas I. Emerson claimed that the purpose of the First Amendment "was to support the principles of an open and self-governing society. More specifically, it was intended to protect speakers who criticized the government, to forbid censorship of the press and to permit assemblies in the public halls or demonstrations on the street."

But how free was the press?

Within nine years after the ratification of the Bill of Rights, freedom of the press became a question rather than a statement of fact. With the passage of the Alien and Sedition Acts in 1798, it was a federal offense to "write, utter or publish...any false, scandalous or malicious writing...against the government of the United States, or either house of Congress...or the President".

The Alien and Sedition Acts did not include the Vice President, who was Thomas Jefferson, the political opponent of President Adams. Thus, proFrench, pro-Jefferson editors were "fair game."

Fortunately, the sedition law died in 1801 and remained dead until World War I. Nonetheless, it had been applied, even to the press, and as a result "awakened many persons to the freedom issues involved". The press saw other crises, however. During the 1830s, mobs condemned abolitionist editors, killing Elijah Lovejoy in 1837. Over the next two decades several states passed laws prohibiting anyone from subscribing to newspapers opposed to slavery.

The Civil War presented another crisis. News reports, especially those sent by telegraph, were first checked by secretary of War Edwin Stanton's office personnel. Then sometimes these were delayed or stopped. During World War I the Espionage and Sedition Acts were passed, and about 100 newspapers were banned from the mails.

In 1919-1920, the "Red Scare"caused newsmen to be accused of being communistic if they did not speak against the Bolshevik Revolution in Russia or the Industrial Workers of the World (IWW) movement in America. Similarly, in the early 1950s, newsmen were accused of being soft on communism or "pink"if they attacked Senator Joseph McCarthy and his "Red Scare".

The 1960s and early 1970s presented another crisis for the press. The Vietnam War, which was supported by the press in the early years partly because it was pressured into accepting the administration's interpretation of the conflict, helped ignite a battle over press freedom. In 1971, in the Pentagon Papers case, for the first time in American history, the government encouraged the courts to impose prior restraint; consequently, four newspapers were ordered to halt publication concerning the Pentagon Papers. Later, the order was lifted.

The press was not alone. The broadcasting industry was attacked, too, especially by the Nixon administration. For instance, Frank Stanton, president of CBS, refused to release certain materials used in making the documentary, "The Selling of the Pentagon,"and was subsequently threatened with contempt of Congress.Former Vice-President Agnew made vigorous attacks on the fairness of the press.

These attacks were used by former President Nixon on October 26, 1973, as the Watergate scandal was discrediting him and his White House staff. After he charged the media of distorted reporting, Patrick Buchanan, his aide, pressed for legal action to break the power of ABC, NBC, and CBS.

Even the dean of broadcasters, Walter Cronkite, was criticized for his role in reporting Watergate. Although other presidential administrations complained about the press, President Reagan's administration eliminated the press from the military invasion of Grenada.

When Bill Clinton was president, the press was criticized for its reliance on unidentified sources, its investigative leaks, and its emphasis on Clinton's sex scandal.

President Bush's administration has criticized the press for its coverage of the War on Terrorism although some of the press cooperated with the administration by not publishing or broadcasting certain stories whenever the stories were considered questionable or possibly causing additional acts of terrorism.

GOVERNMENT CONTROLS

Wilson Dizard, Jr., wrote, "The First Amendment's prohibitions against political interference with media remain a formidable barrier against direct government intervention. It is, however, by no means a guarantor against more indirect kinds of interference".

Even though the First Amendment guarantees freedom of the press, one must remember that freedom is never absolute. As pointed out, freedom of the press has had limitations and stipulations attached to it.

John L. Hulteng and Roy Paul Nelson mentioned, "the liberties and freedoms of a people weaken and die when access is cut off to a continuing flow of honest and uncensored news about what is happening in the state, the nation, and the world".

Rulers of countries know this; in order to establish an authoritarian or totalitarian society, the media are usually controlled first. Once the press is under control, the people no longer are exposed to anything other than the doctored propaganda the state permits them to read or hear.

The media of information thus constitute the jugular vein of a democracy: strike there decisively and the wound is mortal. The importance of the information media to the survival of democratic freedoms stems from the basic concept of a representative system of government: if the people are fully and accurately informed, they will be able to choose their governors wisely.

Freedom of the press is important in a democratic society. But what does freedom of the press mean? Unfortunately, Supreme Court justices have not come up with a definitive answer. For example, Hugo L. Black and William O. Douglas argued that the First Amendment meant exactly what it said, that it was absolute, subject to no restrictions.

However, Chief Justice Burger insisted that the Supreme Court had not provided the press with special privilege. He claimed that the framers of the Constitution had merely added the clause regarding the press so that written speech would be protected along with oral speech. Thus, one can understand why freedom of the press has suffered from infractions. If the Supreme Court justices cannot decide on what the founding fathers meant, who can?

CENSORSHIP

Printed media have been banned by the Post Office Department more than once. As mentioned, numerous newspapers were banned during World War I. Books and magazines have been banned, too. In 1978, for example, the Postal Service won eleven convictions against pornographic material.

Paul Gilbert claimed that censorship should not play a major role in democratic societies. He wrote, "In democratic societies the only area in which it is openly accepted that censorship has a part to play is in the field of military security".

Nonetheless, even the film industry, which has a movie rating system, has been censored, more by states and municipalities than by the federal government, especially in cases involving indecency.

But the industry as a whole has tested obscenity restrictions by producing more movies of a questionable nature. Even so-called hard-core films have flooded the market; some, such as "Deep Throat" and "Anyone But My Husband," have been removed from theaters, however.

Radio and television broadcasting, since both are under the continuing regulation of the Federal Communication Commission, have seen frequent attacks and threats of censorship. However, since the early 1980s, when the FCC's budget was dramatically curtailed by the Reagan administration, broadcasters, especially the major networks, have enjoyed more freedom, particularly in regard to their programming.

Nonetheless, local stations are supposed to operate in the public interest and meet community needs in order to have their licenses renewed. Thus, both radio and television stations are limited in what can be broadcast.

LIBEL

The First Amendment, according to the courts, "does not render the publisher immune from responsibility after the fact of publication, if what he has published injures other well-established and safeguarded rights".

The press is under control, the people no longer are exposed to anything other than the doctored propaganda the state permits them to read or hear. The media of information thus constitute the jugular vein of a democracy: strike there decisively and the wound is mortal.

The importance of the information media to the survival of democratic freedoms stems from the basic concept of a representative system of government: if the people are fully and accurately informed, they will be able to choose their governors wisely.

Freedom of the press is important in a democratic society. But what does freedom of the press mean? Unfortunately, Supreme Court justices have not come up with a definitive answer. For example, Hugo L. Black and William O. Douglas argued that the First Amendment meant exactly what it said, that it was absolute, subject to no restrictions.

However, Chief Justice Burger insisted that the Supreme Court had not provided the press with special privilege. He claimed that the framers of the Constitution had merely added the clause regarding the press so that written speech would be protected along with oral speech.

Thus, one can understand why freedom of the press has suffered from infractions. If the Supreme Court justices cannot decide on what the founding fathers meant, who can?

CENSORSHIP

Printed media have been banned by the Post Office Department more than once. As mentioned, numerous newspapers were banned during World War I. Books and magazines have been banned, too. In 1978, for example, the Postal Service won eleven convictions against pornographic material.

Paul Gilbert claimed that censorship should not play a major role in democratic societies. He wrote, "In democratic societies the only area in which it is openly accepted that censorship has a part to play is in the field of military security".

Nonetheless, even the film industry, which has a movie rating system, has been censored, more by states and municipalities than by the federal government, especially in cases involving indecency.

But the industry as a whole has tested obscenity restrictions by producing more movies of a questionable nature. Even so-called hard-core films have flooded the market; some, such as "Deep Throat" and "Anyone But My Husband," have been removed from theaters, however.

Radio and television broadcasting, since both are under the continuing regulation of the Federal Communication Commission, have seen frequent attacks and threats of censorship. However, since the early 1980s, when the FCC's budget was dramatically curtailed by the Reagan administration, broadcasters, especially the major networks, have enjoyed more freedom, particularly in regard to their programming.

Nonetheless, local stations are supposed to operate in the public interest and meet community needs in order to have their licenses renewed. Thus, both radio and television stations are limited in what can be broadcast.

LIBEL

The First Amendment, according to the courts, "does not render the publisher immune from responsibility after the fact of publication, if what he has published injures other well-established and safeguarded rights".

Although there is no such thing as a federal law of libel, all of the fifty states have statutes that define it: a publication that damages the reputation of an individual or group of individuals. Donna A. Demac wrote, "Libel is defined as communication - words or pictures - that tends to expose someone to public ridicule, shame, or contempt, or otherwise damages a person's reputation".

In the first definition, the term publication embraces not only the print media, but radio and television broadcasting. Therefore, the media as a whole may, in certain circumstances, be accountable.

As Demac wrote.

Television newscasts, editorials, history books, biographies, and even novels and cartoons have been subjected to libel suits brought by public officials, celebrities, and others who find themselves depicted in ways that displease them. Suits against student publications are also on the rise.

There have been several developments, however, that have made the media more vulnerable to libel suits and have made the libel suits more damaging. According to Eve Pell,

Among these developments are increases in the number of libel suits filed, sky-high legal expenses, the risk of losing hundreds of thousands or millions of dollars in damage verdicts, a more hostile attitude toward the press in the courts, particularly on the part of juries, and a strong public perception that the press is not fair and ought to be made so.

According to Pell, punitive damages have been the major problem for the news media. She wrote, "No insurance can be purchased that is guaranteed to cover these damages;

several states have laws stating that punitive damages cannot be paid by insurance, and in those states insurance companies have refused to pay punitive awards".

Also, as Demac pointed out, even when libel suits are decided in favour of the defendants, the energy and expense involved to prepare a defence has a chilling effect on future coverage. Alan U. Schwartz, in "Using the Courts to Muzzle the Press,"expressed a similar notion:

Publishers and broadcasters of all kinds are now coming to realise that the cost of defending libel and privacy suits - and the uncertainty of result because of unclear guidelines - adds another link of self-censorship to the chain which can eventually strangle free expression through governmental intimidation rather than action.

Nonetheless, these statutes also explain ways by which publishers or broadcasters can defend themselves against libel suits. This is not to say that publishers or broadcaster will escape damages sought by readers or viewers, however. If the publication or broadcasting station has published or aired something false about a person and knows that it is false, the libel plaintiff will probably win.

PRIVACY

According to Andrew Belsey, there are three types of privacy: "(1) bodily or physical privacy"; "(2) mental or communicational privacy"; and "(3) informational privacy."The first refers to space in which one functions; the second refers to one's being left alone to think; and the third refers to personal information that is legitimately placed in files and folders within organizations and other entities.

The press is not mentioned in any of Belsey's definitions. Yet, occasionally, certain individuals may find themselves thrust into the public eye involuntarily. When this occurs, the press is usually present and will in all likelihood write about and even videotape the individuals, even if they wish otherwise.

Consent is not necessarily requested by the press in such instances. Arthur R. Miller, in "Overzealous Reporters vs. the

Right to Privacy,"wrote, Unless reporters are deterred from excessive and unwarranted curiosity, many of us may be inhibited from participating in society's affairs.

Any risk of dampening press enthusiasm for newsgathering must be measured against creating a public fear, what George Orwell called "the assumption that every sound you made was overheard, and, except in darkness, every move was scrutinized".

Nonetheless, this right is questionable when the person becomes news. For example, public officials have little claim to privacy. Similarly, movie stars, rock stars, television personalities, and such have lesser claim to privacy than average citizens.

FREE PRESS VERSUS FAIR TRIAL

Without question, the First Amendment, which guarantees a free press, seems to be at odds with the Sixth Amendment, which guarantees the accused a fair trial by an impartial jury. In other words, can the accused receive a fair trial when the press reports and comments on the crime?

Clifton Daniel, in "Fair Trial and Freedom of the Press," claimed that the press sometimes "do violence to the rights of defendants," and that the manners of news personnel "are not always impeccable." Further, "the press sometimes swarms over a news story in such a way that the story becomes warped and distorted."

Daniel stated that reporters believe reform is needed and that reporters "must be more conscientious" in their concern "for the rights of individuals". Louis Nizer made this point much stronger in "Trial by Headline."

He wrote, Frequently, those who defend the present practice of the press speak of its "right to know." There is no such right. The press has "the right to publish." No citizen owes the duty to the press to inform it about his or her personal life.

No district attorney need report the progress of an investigation. No lawyer must confide his trial plans. Nizer added, "Public trials are for the benefit of defendants, not newspapers. Attendance of the public prevents the courts from becoming instruments of persecution".

Indeed, as a result of what happened at the Bruno Hauptmann trial, the American Bar Association, in 1937, passed Canon 35, which sought to ban radio from the courtroom. (Hauptmann had been accused of kidnapping and murdering the Lindbergh child. His trial attracted more reporters than any other murder trial had up to that time. Hauptmann was found guilty and sentenced to death.) Television had become popular by 1952. As a result, it, too, was banned by Canon 35.

It should be mentioned that the press was not alone in trying Hauptmann. The attorneys as well as the police spoke freely to reporters about the case, as did the defendant. Another trial by the press instead of the jury was of Dr. Samuel Sheppard.

Like the Hauptmann case, this one had all the elements of interest. Dr. Sheppard was young and handsome, an osteopath who was accused of murdering his beautiful wife. The media played up the family's prominence, the other woman, and the other man who was supposed to have been in the house.

As in the Hauptmann case, reporters and photographers from all over the United States were present. Again, information was leaked by both the prosecution and the defence teams to members of the press, and certain experts not only discussed the evidence but added evidence in their talks with members of the press.

The jury found Dr. Sheppard guilty, and the judge sentenced him to life in prison. After ten years, in 1966, he was released. The Supreme Court ruled that the "carnival atmosphere" of the trial had deprived Dr. Sheppard of his constitutional rights.

In recent years, however, state governments and judges have allowed not only reporters but TV cameras into the courtrooms. Indeed, in the case of O. J. Simpson, the prosecution and defence teams seemed to cater to representatives of the media throughout the trial, and certain witnesses, as some legal authorities have speculated, perhaps dressed and responded to questions in a certain way as a result of knowing that they would be sitting in front of a camera.

If this is true, how much of an effect did this have on the jury's verdict? On the other hand, newsmen, to a great extent, have agreed "that there have been some spectacular abuses of news coverage of criminal cases; they will not attempt to defend such excesses".

And these excesses, it must be remembered, invite and lead to loss of freedom. In short, freedom is weakened when a breakdown in responsibility occurs. However, as Hulteng and Nelson pointed out, editors dislike the approach suggested by the American Bar Association.

Editors claim that the public needs to learn how justice operates at every stage, not just the first or last stage, particularly in high-profile cases. But newsmen have to remember that all judges have the power to cite and punish for contempt. And this includes outbursts in the courtroom and statements made orally or in print.

GOVERNMENT SECRECY

The founders who wrote the U. S. Constitution met in secrecy to discuss what should be in the document. Consequently, is it surprising that today's politicians meet in secrecy? Is it surprising that classified information is withheld from the media? The founders of this nation withheld information - perhaps important information - from the public.

Although most believed in the freedom of the press, hypocrisy filled the first assembly because the press was not present. When Washington became the first president, he established the doctrine of executive privilege, which has been relied upon by most, if not all, presidents since to thwart certain journalists.

During the Eisenhower administration, secrecy became the "in thing." The president shielded Defence Department officials from having to testify before Joseph McCarthy. Other executive departments and agencies used this tactic to conceal information. And although section 1002 of the Administrative Procedure Act holds that "all matters of official record" in the federal government must be made available for publication, it was used to conceal information because of three abstract exemptions.

As a result, the Freedom of Information Act was signed into law by President Johnson in 1966. This bill had intended to give citizens access to all public transactions, but by the time it was enacted, nine exemptions had been attached. The bill was amended in 1974 to assist the press in the information-gathering process. However, as Demac noted, numerous government agencies have taken extremely long periods of time to respond to requests and have even denied the existence of certain requested information.

Although there may be times when publishers and broadcasters should be censored, especially if suppression of the information is without question in the best interest of the nation, Thomas I. Emerson, in "The Danger of State secrecy," wrote, "secrecy in government accompanies evil in government. There is, indeed, a symbolic relationship-government wrongs are kept secret because they are evil; and evil is done because it can be kept secret". What have been the media's reactions to this secrecy? Quite negative, to say the least. Spokespersons have said that unless the information can cause harm to national security it should be given to the public so that the people may know what the government is doing. Only then can a responsible form of democracy exist. The media spokespersons have a point.

If the public is ill-informed, then the nation will have a government that is ill. As we have seen, there are laws and some court powers that do constitute government controls on the press. Yet, press freedom has not ceased to exist. As the early 1970s illustrated, the power of the press may be stronger than the power of the presidency.

DEREGULATION

The broadcast industry witnessed deregulation during

the 1980s. Although the Reagan administration has been identified with deregulation, the Carter administration actually considered deregulation.

Since as early as 1980, the Federal Communications Commission has accepted the notion that the government should allow the broadcast industry to operate in a free, marketdriven society.

Consequently, several regulations that had been applied by the Federal Communications Commission were eliminated or revised. For instance, the time devoted to commercials for advertisers had been limited to eighteen minutes per hour. The Federal Communications Commission dismissed this specific rule.

Certain regulations pertaining to programming were also discarded, as all talk broadcast stations came into existence. Even the regulation pertaining to license renewal was changed in 1981; for instance, licenses were extended from three years to five years for television and from three years to seven years for radio.

Regulations pertaining to ownership of broadcast stations were revised. Indeed, prior to August 1984, a single owner could not have more than seven AM radio stations, seven FM radio stations, and seven television stations.

The number of stations in each category that a single owner could have was increased to twelve. The only stipulation was that an owner of television stations could not have more than 25 per cent of the nation's viewers.

Dennis W. Mazzocco claimed that deregulation of the broadcast media has "contributed to a greater separation between social classes. It has also increased the political-economic division between those who are information-rich and those who are information-poor".

Mazzocco also wrote, There is less diversity of programme choices today than there was before the FCC began to deregulate the U. S. broadcast sector in the late 1970s, yet corporate profits and stock prices are at all time highs. Also true is that many more major metropolitan newspapers are interlocked via corporate connections to other segments of electronic media ownership. The result is a national and local press that has become a lapdog to government and corporate power.

MEDIA-MADE PROBLEMS: A THREAT TO FREEDOM OF THE PRESS

In the article, "First Amendment Revisionism," Ben Bagdikian warned that sins committed by the press may cause the government to revise the First Amendment. He wrote, State laws are emphasizing that the First Amendment was made for the public, not the publishers.

In the most serious legal battle to date, there is a chance that the First Amendment, as journalists have come to know it, will be altered to cover some forms of access in communications media. If that happens, the press will have only itself to blame.

In addition to what has been mentioned (i.e., reporters being harassed by judges, local, state, and federal officials, celebrities, and even private citizens), reporters and the press as an institution have lost esteem. Confidence in the press is not high.

Part of the reason is what Bagdikian termed "arrogance of power."The media - especially the people who run it have lost touch with reality. They criticize the government when they think the government is infringing on the First Amendment.

Yet, when they need a favour, such as the Newspaper Preservation Act, which exempted forty-four newspapers in twenty-two cities from antitrust action, and overturned a Supreme Court decision that would have dissolved a media enterprise in Tucson, they seemingly do not appreciate it.

Perhaps the press is filled with cynics or frustrated hopeful novelists. Or perhaps it is filled with professional business people who care little about responsible journalism. What is wrong with the media, specifically the press? Is it going to cause itself to be ruled or governed like radio and television? As mentioned, the public has little faith in the press. In fact, in some studies television news is believed by the public to be more accurate than newspaper news, whereas, the opposite should be the case.

Perhaps one of the causes to this dilemma was identified by Bagdikian when he claimed that the majority of newspapers were merely chamber of commerce boosters. In other words, they were sympathetic to the business community. Bagdikian wrote, "Most show no comparable basic interest in illuminating and reforming problems affecting the mass of readers - the poor, the lower middle class, the consumer".

At the same time, the public needs to be reminded that a controlled press or an overseen press is not good for a democratic society, especially if it is controlled or overseen by the government. However, the press needs to remember that in order to regain respect from the various factions of society it must learn the various problems of these factions, then provide appropriate information that helps solve some, if not all, of those problems.

In a democratic society, the press has more than one function. Besides informing the people, it should inform them about how and why certain problems and conflicts occur. The modern press has this responsibility. The First Amendment was written for this very purpose. So in order to remain free, the press will have to acknowledge this obligation and then act accordingly. Otherwise, the public as well as the government may demand certain revisions in legislation pertaining to the press.

Chapter 2

New Model for the Asian and the World Press

In the study of the global media, there is abundant literature about the dominance of the Western media. Much less prominent as a research subject is the dominance of Western perspectives in building media theories, such as the four theories of the press, which have been used as a universal guide to the understanding of the press systems around the world since they were created in 1956.

It is interesting to address the issue of the dominance of Western scholarship in media research in view of the ancient civilizations of the East, especially India, where several of the world's religions originated, and China, where paper and the printing press were first invented. Pi Sheng, a Chinese metalworker, invented the movable-type printing press in 1045, more than 400 years before Gutenberg did when the latter reinvented the printing press in Europe. But in some of the American media history textbooks, only the name of Gutenberg was introduced.

Since the fall of the Iron Curtain, the further opening-up of the economies in China and India, and the arrival of the Internet, the meeting of the minds of the East and West has been accelerated. More and more media researchers from both the East and the West have come to re-examine the four theories of the press as the dominant paradigm in studying world press systems. Jiafei Yin encountered major difficulties in using the theories as a guide in describing press systems in Asia because the four press theories were built primarily on Western perspectives. When theories fail to serve as an effective guide to the understanding of the subject of inquiry, it is time that new theories were developed, theories that would be based on cultural values not only from the West but also from the East.

The Asian civilization is as different from the Western civilization as any two civilizations can be. Moreover, Asia is a politically and culturally diverse continent, where reforming and developing communist countries are right next door to some of the most successful capitalist countries in the world. And no one or two religions dominate the continent.

It is hard to lump sum Asia together in any kind of description, and it is even harder to pigeonhole the vastly diverse Asian media systems into the four press categories developed by Western media scholars, who failed to include media experiences from the East in building their theories. This chapter debates the applicability of the four press theories in the Asian media context and the reliability of press freedom ratings of each country given by the Freedom House.

The chapter starts with a review of the well-established press theories and continues with an analysis of representative media systems in Asia. As Asia is a vast and diverse continent with dozens of countries, it is not feasible to analyse every media system in the region. Therefore, representative media systems were chosen in analyzing the applicability of the established press theories while more countries were included in brief discussions where common characteristics make the analysis also apply. Discussions focus on comparisons of the theories with the media systems in Asia and on identifying the difficulties in trying to match the two. The second part of the chapter proposes an alternative press model based on an analysis of Eastern and Western philosophical thinking and cultural values relevant to the media.

THE DOMINANT FOUR THEORIES OF THE PRESS

The seminal work Four Theories of the Press established the dominant paradigm in analyzing global media systems and, in particular, in assessing levels of press freedom in countries and regions throughout the world. Other theories on press systems followed, such as development journalism in developing countries, revolutionary media, and democratic-participant media. However, the newer theories were mostly complementary to the established four theories of the press.

Of the four theories, "the authoritarian system has been most pervasive both historically and geographically," according to Siebert. The goal of the media under such a system was to support and advance the policies of the government so that it could achieve its objectives. Werner J. Severin and James W. Tankard, Jr. in summarizing the major characteristics of the four theories wrote that the authoritarian concept was based on the sixteenth and seventeenth century English history and philosophy of the absolute power of the monarch.

Contrary to the authoritarian theory, libertarian theory held that man was rational and an end in himself. The happiness and the well-being of the individual was the goal of society. The social responsibility theory was an outgrowth of the libertarian theory and was first developed in the twentieth century United States by the Commission on Freedom of the Press, which emphasized social responsibility of the press.

The last of the four theories was the Soviet communist theory, which was based on Marxist ideology and value of unity - unity of the working class and unity of the Party. For the sake of unity, there should be only one right position and only one truth, the absolute truth. Under the Soviet system, the government had a division of censorship.

CRITICISM OF THE FOUR THEORIES

Dominant as the four theories have been, there is no lack of criticism of them. Critical of the social responsibility theory, John C. Merrill, who strongly argued for the independence of individual journalists in his writings, asked his students: Who should be the authority in defining what responsible journalism is? Shouldn't journalists themselves be allowed to make that judgment?

The most comprehensive criticism of the four theories came almost forty years after the theories were first published. In "Last Rights: Revisiting Four Theories of the Press," published in 1995 and written by a group of media scholars from the same school where the four theories originated, the authors found the overall theoretical framework of the four theories flawed.

The book, edited by John C. Nerone, pointed out that the four theories were not value-free despite their valuefree appearance. The theories were based on a pro-capitalist bias and were the products of capitalism and of the Cold War era. Because of such bias, the authors contended that while the four theories were critical of the Soviet communist media, they ignored the concerns of the libertarian media, especially the concentration of media ownership.

The authors argued that the theories focused only on the political control of the media, state power, but were silent on other kinds of power and restraint on the media. For example, the theories only discussed media's political freedom, not economic freedom from the market forces and ownership ties.

Another problem with the theories, the authors argued, was that it allowed only two media environments - libertarian and authoritarian - the other two being only the derivatives of the free and the controlled media environments. The book also listed "internal inconsistencies and inadequacies" among the four theories.

In a study examining the press systems in China and Japan, Betty H. Winfield et al. found that Western scholarship on press systems tended to disregard the cultures, philosophies, and traditions that distinguish Asian mass media. She said studies such as the four theories of the press keep a Western emphasis while ignoring political foundations and beliefs in Asian societies.

Shelton A. Gunaratne conducted research on West-centrism in communication theories. He believed that the four theories "ignored the dynamic diversity inherent in complex dissipative social systems" and found them "static" and "deontic".

WESTERN PRESS THEORIES VERSUS EASTERN PRESS SYSTEMS

In an attempt to research and categorize press systems in Asian countries, Jiafei Yin (2003) found major difficulties or misfits in trying to pigeonhole Asian media systems according to the four press theories, which were developed by Western media scholars and were based on Western philosophies and the analysis of Western history, politics, and culture. The following section discusses why the dominant press theories could not satisfactorily describe the realities of media in Asia.

THE "LIBERTARIAN PRESS" IN ASIA

SELF-CENSORSHIP IN THE ASIAN PRESS

The Japanese press is considered the liveliest in East Asia and was ranked the freest in Asia by the Freedom House for 2005. Reporters Without Borders gave Japan the second-highest ranking in Asia in press freedom after South Korea for its 2005 report.

Japan's press industry is the largest in the world. It has five national daily newspapers, each claiming a circulation in the millions. That compares with the top two dailies in the United States -USA Today and The Wall Street Journal - each of which has a circulation of around 2 million.

Yomiuri Shimbun, the paper with the largest circulation in the world, has a circulation of 14 million. Asahi Shimbun has a circulation of 12 million. These two Japanese national dailies are the only two newspapers in the world with a circulation surpassing 10 million. The circulations of the other three range from 2.7 million to 5.6 million.

Japanese journalists are well trained and well informed. They have to study for months to pass rigorous exams to even get hired. The exam includes a ninety-minute general intelligence test, a ninety-minute writing test, and a ninety-minute foreign language proficiency test, usually in English, Spanish, French, or Chinese.

Even if a candidate gets good scores, he or she has to pass three to four interviews. Special schools help prepare university students and graduates for the test. But Japanese journalists may find their training and skills wasted under a press club system.

To understand the nature of the Japanese press system, the economic system in Japan has to be examined first. Democracy describes Japan's political system, but freewheeling capitalism is out of the question in Japan although, theoretically speaking, Japan practices free market capitalism. The Japanese economy has thrived and become a dominant force in the global economy under state-guided capitalism.

Instead of regulating the industry, the government helps the industry to grow and compete on the global market. Government and big corporations in Japan are partners in nation building. Political freedom and rights do not translate into economic liberalism in Japan, which has much to do with the Japanese culture, or the Asian culture.

In Asian societies, especially those under the influence of Confucian thought, the strength of a country is regarded as more important than the profitability of a company, and the well-being of a family is more important than individual rights and freedom.

For a country like Japan with limited arable land and scarce resources, the survival and prosperity of the nation take priority in national life. The royal family and often the government are symbols of the nation, and they command respect.

Such a cultural tradition contradicts the Western concept of media as a watchdog and the ultimate goal of libertarian philosophies - man as an end in himself. In Japan, media keep cozy relations with the government and the big industries through the press club system, or "information cartels," which comprise press clubs, industry associations, and media conglomerates, which Freeman calls "the unholy trinity." The press clubs channel information from government offices to media organizations.

Such a club system discourages independent reporting and thoroughness in journalistic investigations and results in "uniformity of content" and "pro-establishment style of journalism". The information cartels ensure no competition among media outlets and no scoops. In Asian societies, the motto promoted is not Darwin's "survival of the fittest," but the survival of all, which may explain why in many Asian countries, such as Japan, China, and Singapore, comparative advertising is banned.

The club system works well for the Japanese press, which profits from large circulations, high advertising revenue, and exclusive information access from the government. But it is a system designed by the industry to serve media companies' economic interests, a system that has frequently led the press to support state goals. It is in this sense that the media can be understood as collaborators with the state in the management of society, Freeman said. Such a system discourages investigative reporting and places a premium on relying on official sources rather than alternative information. It interferes with the public's right to receive relevant information in a timely manner.

As a result, all the high-profile political scandals that emerged in the first half of 2002 were not uncovered by the vernacular dailies, but by the non-mainstream weeklies. Because of its less than rigorous reporting, the Japanese press fails to act as a watchdog of the government and is called a lapdog, which was blamed for failing to keep the public informed of the irregularities within the financial industry and the corruption within the government. When the Asian financial crash hit Japan in 1997, the magnitude of the crisis took the public by surprise.

An in-depth analysis of the Japanese press system makes it clear that the ideas available at the "marketplace of ideas" are rather limited. Free competition that is at the very core of the libertarian theory is stifled under the press club system, which also bars reporters from foreign and non-mainstream media outlets from attending exclusive press briefings and getting official press releases.

While government control of the press in Japan is not a major issue, control by professional associations and the media organizations themselves is still very effective and produces the same result of a less informed public. The reason why the Freedom House rated the Japanese press as the freest in Asia may be because of the fact that the Japanese government seldom takes direct actions against the press or journalists. In Japan, there is hardly such need, as the press polices itself rather diligently.

Like Japan, South Korea is a newspaper-rich country. South Koreans get their news primarily from daily newspapers. The country has ten national dailies, which are in circulation wars in the millions. In addition, there are 100 free dailies, 314 specialized dailies, 1,999 weeklies, 2,319 monthlies, and 1,245 other periodicals. All newspapers print forty-eight to fifty-six pages for advertising space. In South Korea, each household subscribes to two or three national papers and one local paper, a dream for newspaper owners in any country.

For 2005, the Freedom House rated the press in South Korea "free." And the Reporters Without Borders described the South Korean press as opposite of that of North Korea: "diverse, privately owned and critical of the government". South Korea is a relatively new democracy. After decades of fighting for democracy, South Koreans started to enjoy their political rights in 1987 when a civilian government was sworn in after a general election.

But until Kim Dae Jung, a freedom fighter and folk hero, became president in 1998, the newly found press freedom in South Korea had been contained by its press club system like Japan's, by the common economic interests of the government and big business in South Korea, including the media, and by the influence of Confucian values.

South Korean industries, like those of Japan, used to be guided and supported by the government. The press in South Korea has allied itself with the government and big businesses and is widely seen as "pro-business," "pro-government," and "conservative". Chong-Hyuk Kim, a reporter for the Joong Ang Ilbo in South Korea, told a Freedom Forum panel that South Korea's ostensibly democratic government barred publishing the size of foreign reserves and foreign debt. He said, "It has become traditional practice between government and media in South Korea not to report critical and important information.

The government insisted if that kind of information were revealed, it would be harmful to national security and the national reputation. The media accepted that kind of assertion". The result of such secrecy was the unexpected Asian financial crash in 1997, which hit the South Korean economy hard and caught its people unprepared.

A reader of the Chosun Ilbo, one of the largest papers in the country, wrote: "Korean journalism still is a superficial observer of the events and does not carry a torch for the righteous social and ethical standards in a rapidly transforming materialistic society. It still is timid and not impartial and indifferent to power politics".

The press system in South Korea had many similarities with that of Japan until Kim Dae Jung became president in 1998. Since then the South Korean press has started to develop in a new direction, and the press club system is being phased out. Press freedom in South Korea improved noticeably during the tenure of Kim, when the press became more aggressive in covering the government and more vocal in criticizing government policies. But the unprecedented press freedom in Korean history under Kirn's government was overshadowed by government's crackdown on the major papers with charges of tax evasion in 2001.

Press freedom is still fragile in South Korea, and its press system is in a transitional stage. It remains to be seen if the South Korean press is finally breaking away from self-censorship or if it still wants to maintain good relations with the government and big businesses by avoiding coverage of critical issues. Self-censorship is not only a major issue in Japan and South Korea but also a major concern in Hong Kong and Thailand. The media in Hong Kong and Thailand are in a category of their own. They are among the freest in Asia when they resort to sensationalism to survive the intense competition.

In Hong Kong, tabloids represent the mainstream press. Practice of yellow journalism, including sensationalized reporting, price wars, and stealing talent from competitors, reached its climax in 1995 and again in 1997. In both Hong Kong and Thailand, the press exercises a high degree of freedom when it is dealing with non-political topics, but starts to be cautious when news stories concern politics, the government, or the royal family.

Before Hong Kong was returned to China, many of the newspapers in the former British colony were pro-British. Since the sovereignty changed hands, more papers are now pro-Beijing. Self-censorship is considered a major concern and the main threat to an independent and free press in Hong Kong despite a great deal of aggressive reporting.

Part of the problem of press self-censorship was due to the fact that after Hong Kong was returned to China, the ownership of some of the major newspapers changed hands, including the South China Morning Post. The new press owners have investments on the Chinese mainland and do not want to offend the officials in Beijing.

BBC News introduced the media in Hong Kong as editorially dynamic, free, and diverse, but it cited increasing self-censorship and pressures on editorial policies. In Hong Kong, direct government intervention of the press is minimal. However, pressure from the central government in Beijing and new owners of the press makes many editors and reporters wary of how to handle sensitive information or topics.

A public opinion poll found that 48% of the people in Hong Kong believed the local news media practiced self-censorship. The study showed that 62% believed the local news media had qualms when criticizing the central government, while only 34% believed it had concerns in criticizing the local government. "The number of respondents who said the media practices self-censorship has significantly increased, mainly because they think the media has become apprehensive when criticizing the central government," a survey organizer said.

Newspapers in Hong Kong adopted specific strategies in the politics of self-censorship. Francis L. F. Lee and Angel M. Y. Lin argued that in transitional societies such as Hong Kong when political pressure on the press is added to a commercial media system and a professional journalistic culture, the politics of self-censorship often becomes a strategic contest between the media and political actors.

The Ming Pao daily constructed the debate as a factional rivalry in order to position itself as an arbitrator, according to Lee and Lin. In contrast, the popular Apple Daily presented the story as a sovereign people's fight against a powerful entity, which was much more critical toward the central government. "Nevertheless, it also appropriated the dominant discourse, constructed internal contradictions, and decentralized the Chinese central government to smooth out the radicalism of its criticisms".

Jasper Decker, a former staff member at the South China Morning Post, also observed less obvious characteristics of self-censorship, such as the tone and attitude in news stories concerning China. Reporting became less aggressive. Management emphasized the virtues of writing to allow readers to read between the lines. In 1997, the New York Times noted that Ming Pao had "reduced the space given to columnists critical of China and has toned down its previously aggressive reporting of China".

Other newspapers avoided devoting space to politically sensitive topics by assigning their reporters to cover other, non-controversial topics. A content analysis of 1997 editorials of major newspapers in Hong Kong found that 56.2% of the editorials addressed local issues in Hong Kong, while only 8% of the editorials discussed issues in China and 7.6% dealt with topics related to the ties between Hong Kong and China.

Self-censorship was an issue even before 1997. Jim Sciutto, a former Hong Kong journalist, claimed, "Self-censorship is nearly epidemic in Hong Kong, affecting the entire media hierarchy from publishers to beat reporters. A free Hong Kong press is already eroding."

In a 1990 survey of Hong Kong journalists, 5% admitted fear of criticizing China in their work, and 54% believed that their fellow journalists felt the same way. The anxiety was not alleviated in the following six years as a similar survey in 1996 found that one in every four journalists expressed concerns over criticizing China.

As much of the self-censorship in Hong Kong was the result of pressure from newspaper editors and owners, some local journalists and researchers argued that it was censorship, not self-censorship on the part of the reporters. Carol Lai, a former chairwoman of the Hong Kong Journalist Association, believed that the influence of editors might have impacted journalists' writing more than any threats from the government.

She believed most of the reporters wanted integrity in their reporting, tried to report accurately and objectively and seldom censored themselves. Some editors, however, watered down criticism or killed stories they deemed offensive. Media owners and editors censored their reporters in the hope of preventing interference from the central government so they could keep their papers in business.

Others might wish to expand their investment on the mainland. The Hong Kong Journalist Association noted that the South Chin Morning Post had reduced and diluted its coverage of China since Robert Kuok became an owner in 1993. "In Hong Kong, pro-Beijing forces don't fight the media, they buy it".

In order to be successful, the media in Hong Kong have learned to remain apolitical. Since the late 1960s, major newspapers in Hong Kong have become increasingly less partisan and have avoided taking less popular stand on issues, and instead, have focused more on the market and middle-class liberalism in order to increase profits.

Self-censorship in Hong Kong prompted one Hong Kong journalist to compare Hong Kong tycoons, who toned down their coverage of China, with mainland media outlets, which became more aggressive in their reporting as they sought market share. In the near future, Hong Kong may have to learn a thing or two from the mainland press when it comes to press freedom, according to Mark Simon of the Apple Daily (2002).

In Southeast Asia, the Thai press enjoys a considerable degree of freedom. Its 1997 constitution protects media freedom, freedom of expression, and access to information. Even under the media-unfriendly prime minister Thaksin Shinawatra the media were free to criticize government policies and cover cases of corruption and human rights abuses, but journalists tended to exercise self-censorship regarding the military, the monarchy, the judiciary, and other sensitive issues.

Press freedom is deep-rooted in the Thai culture. However, the tradition of self-censorship in Thailand is as long as its history of a free press. Despite the freedom they enjoyed in the 1980s, Thai editorial writers and reporters censored themselves, mindful that there were unwritten government rules regarding the coverage of the monarchy, government affairs, internal security matters, and Thailand's international image.

"Self-censorship is probably a perfect form of political control. Politicians in power don't have to risk creating public ire by openly bullying the media. Media proprietors and journalists know exactly what the 'invisible rules' are". The degree of press freedom and selfcensorship in Thailand is often dependent on the kind of government that is in power. The Thai government under Prime Minister Thaksin provided a telling example.

Since Thaksin came to power, the majority of media outlets were forced into submission. Some journalists lamented that truly independent journalists were now "a rare and endangered species" as too many members of the media were influenced by the lure of political favour, or in fear of political power. The government rewarded media outlets supportive of its policies through the allocation of advertising by telecommunications firms and state enterprises, which resulted in an increasing level of self-censorship. More sophisticated media outlets included mild criticism of the government in their coverage but avoided more serious issues or pursuing issues further.

In such a media environment, anyone in the broadcast media speaking more than "30% of the truth" could get into trouble. The media were thus forced into three categories - government partisans, government mouthpieces, and those that engage in self-censorship. Most mainstream newspapers were won over by the government either through friendly persuasions sweetened with advertising deals or through political pressure, and all television stations were pressured into practicing self-censorship in covering the government.

Using sharper words, The Nation wrote, "...the majority of those who own media outlets sense Thaksin's political invincibility and are prostituting themselves voluntarily. The broadcast media are the most obvious, acting in collusion with the government.... Nowadays, broadcasters are considered strategic partners with the government. Lump-sum financial rewards have made parts of the media into circus dogs that are ready to do summersaults."

The print media were no exception, the article said. Publishers were more willing to follow the government line to ensure their business future. Self-censorship was increasingly becoming the normal code of conduct for editors and journalists under Thaksin.

Under a climate of fear and self-censorship within the media community, the Thai media have morphed into the "custodian of the government". In one particular case, the owner of the newsmagazine, Siamrath, exercised self-censorship by canceling the distribution of 30,000 copies of an issue that contained reports critical of the government. In another case, the management of the Bangkok Post removed its editor Veera Prateepchaikul for "irritating" the prime minister by using the word "arrogance".

Concerned over the retreat of press freedom, The Nation argued, "The professional integrity of the media should never be conditional on the political power or popularity of a leader, much less his power of patronage to throw financial benefits their way". Two recent court rulings upheld the constitutional rights to freedom of expression in the country, one vindicating former iTV journalists, who were dismissed for refusing to compromise their professional integrity, and the other in favour of media-freedom advocate Supinya Klangnarong and the Thai Post, who were sued for defamation.

Also in 2006, all the free TV channels covered the anti-Thaksin activities, with the exception of only one channel. That was unprecedented under the government of Thaksin. The Freedom House can rate the Thai press as "free," such as in 2002, or "partly free" since 2003. But it is certainly a different kind of free press even though its self-censorship practices are much less systematic than Japan's.

SELF-CENSORSHIP VERSUS SOCIAL RESPONSIBILITY THEORY

There are fundamental differences between press self-censorship in Asia and the Western social responsibility press theory. First, as discussed earlier, the social responsibility theory derived from the libertarian theory, which emphasizes the freedom of the press and pluralism in the marketplace of ideas. Therefore, the basis of the social responsibility theory is still press freedom, even when the press is urged to use that freedom responsibly.

Press self-censorship in Asia, however, is based either on control by the press clubs in the case of Japan and, formerly, South Korea or on fear of government retribution in the case of Hong Kong and Thailand. In either case, freedom of the press is being severely curtailed. Second, the goal of the Hutchins report, A Free and Responsible Press, is to recommend ways in which a free press can better serve the society at large.

The report proposed five standards in improving the quality of news reporting, including the comprehensive coverage of news events to ensure its accuracy, representation of different demographic groups in society in news reports, and the provision of service to all the constituencies of society. But the primary goal of press self-censorship in Asia is for self-preservation. It is to protect the business interests of the press rather than to better serve the public. Newspapers in these Asian countries are highly profitable; thus, the management does not want to offend the government or big business.

Third, ideally speaking, if the social responsibility press theory is implemented in the newsroom, the result will be a better-informed public and a more ethical and responsible press, whereas press self-censorship in Asia can only result in uniform content, suppressed information, and a poorly informed public. If the ultimate goal of the press in these Asian societies is the pursuit of profits, it will be difficult for the press to be socially responsible or professionally ethical.

ANARCHISM IN THE ASIAN PRESS

Although Asia is rarely known for press freedom, there are some rather free press systems in the region, particularly transitional press systems such as the ones in Taiwan, the Philippines, and Indonesia, where the whole control system was torn down when martial law was ended or strongmen overthrown and where there was tremendous backlash against press control. But often the enthusiasm for newfound press freedom in these countries leaves the press bordering on a state of anarchy.

After decades of government suppression, the press in Taiwan, the Philippines, and Indonesia was enjoying unprecedented freedom and explosive growth when the rules, regulations, and bans were lifted, licenses for starting up newspapers became easier to obtain, and the enthusiasm for starting up newspapers was high. Such outpouring energy overwhelmed the governments in these societies after decades of authoritarian or military rule.

These governments had yet to establish trust and credibility among the people and construct new frameworks in regulating the press without the suspicion that democratically elected governments were reintroducing government control over the press. The booming press industry tipped the balance between supply and demand. Intensified competition combined with new press freedom drove many of the papers in these countries to "freakdom"of the press, meaning sensationalism in news coverage.

In Indonesia, now that the press is finally free, the main problem is a lack of professional standards and ethics among journalists. More and more journalists are violating the most sacred principle of the profession: tell the truth. Journalists today are accountable to no one but themselves and their proprietors because of the sweeping deregulation of the media.

The ministry of information was abolished, and gone also was the licensing system. In 1999, a new press law was passed to guarantee freedom. But excesses and abuses of press freedom have ironically prompted calls from the public for the government to restore some control of the press.

Freedom of the press is a double-sided sword, which can expose corruption and injustice but can also hurt the freedom and media if the freedom is abused. Media in Indonesia has changed its role from being a mouthpiece of the government under Suharto to being a critical watchdog today.

"Barking headlines, hard-biting editorials, sharp commentaries, satirical cartoons and investigative exposés are now common features of our media".But the media in general failed to promote the basic principles of journalism, such as accuracy and balanced reporting.

Syamsul Muarif, the state minister for information and communication, a new government agency, listed five diseases of the press: pornography, character assassination, false and provocative news, misleading advertisements, and unprofessional journalists.

Media hold up a mirror to the society they cover; in the case of Indonesia, what is reflected is pervasive corruption, which poisons the soul of journalism. Indonesia was rated as the fifth most corrupt country in the world, where corruption spread from the central government to local governments. This culture of corruption gave rise to "envelope journalism"and "bogus journalism".With "envelope journalism,"journalists receive cash from news sources to compensate for their low salaries, compromising the integrity of the press.

"Many people are willing to provide bribes for journalists to ensure that the press will cover or blow up good stories about them or stop publishing bad news about them."And this is a common practice for almost all private and state organizations. Every day no fewer than 2,000 journalists make their fortune by asking the members of the parliament for money.

The amount offered was so enticing that it attracted fake journalists to news conferences for the enveloped cash, resulting in "bogus journalists,"who reached hundreds in Jakarta alone. Some of these bogus journalists were laid-off journalists, while others had no previous connections with the media.

"Envelope journalism"brought about public complaints that news stories were inaccurate and failed to cover both sides of a story. Ulin Ni'am Yusron, chairman of the Jakarta Independent Journalists Alliance (AJI), said, "It is too much to ask them to make impartial, quality news if they are underpaid".

In Indonesia, only 30% of about 1,200 publishers in the print media were financially healthy. Therefore, not only journalists can be bought, media organizations can be bought as well. A 2005 survey published by the Alliance for Reform and Democracy in Asia found that 40% of the respondents in Indonesia did not perceive the media to be free and independent of the government and "other sources".

Respondents cited widespread bribery of journalists, the buying of air time on talk shows and other forms of advertisements by public figures, and the efforts of both political parties and big business in establishing their own media or buying into media in order to influence public opinion.

Blame was laid on the lack of professionalism and increasing competition from both the local and foreign media.

Nurbaiti contended that the immediate future did not look bright either. The outlook for 2006 was that "the Indonesian media will continue to compromise in the search for balance between profit and quality journalism".

Advocacy journalism sells papers too. During the height of the brutal communal conflict in Maluku province, the Jawa Pos media group was accused of profiting immensely from the conflict, which split up the community along ethnic and religious lines. The group's new paper launched during the middle of the conflict, the Ambon Express, was labeled a "Muslim"daily, and the group's established paper, Suara Maluku, was considered a "Christian"paper. Almost all media outlets in Maluku at that time were accused of taking sides.

The same kind of "provocative reporting"was used during the tension between Indonesia and Malaysia over the disputed Ambalat offshore oil block in the Sulawesi Sea. In their coverage, the Indonesian media failed to promote peace; instead, it contributed to the tension. The national media focused on the possibility of war rather than advocating a peaceful settlement, and the local media preferred to cover the deployment of soldiers or the recruitment of volunteers to attack Malaysia.

In the Philippines, the press claims to be the freest in Asia even though broadcasting is still subject to regulation. Sheila S. Coronel (2000) described the Philippine press as "rowdy,""vibrant,""pluralistic,"and "anarchistic."She said Filipino journalists are noisy and powerful. Media exposes have caused the resignation of officials and raised public awareness about important issues. Because of their recent history, Filipino journalists protect their freedom fiercely and are firm believers in the watchdog role of the press.

In post-Marcos days, the Philippine media were able to publish information with few restraints. But with few principles of ethics or responsibility to guide them, journalists followed their own set of rules. As a result, accuracy and truth were compromised. Many Philippine journalists believed that journalism was mostly instinctive, and that theories and principles were not much more help than as mere guidesthat there existed no rules specific enough to constitute applicable and reliable standards.

"Never has the profession been so cheapened-and cheapened yet by its own practitioners". This belief led to the general deterioration in the quality of the profession. Part of the problem was due to the mushrooming of news media outlets and the growing demand for journalists. The proliferation of news media outlets depleted the supply of qualified journalists and "opened the profession to invasion by pseudo-journalists, resulting in widespread malpractice".

The news media were criticized for irresponsible and sloppy reporting, for checkbook journalism, and for using its freedom to commercially exploit the public's taste for the sensational. Television bore the brunt of criticism. In the words of a print journalist-turned TV journalist, "Philippine TV has not reached the point of maturity, where we can say that it is really doing things in the service of Filipinos.

At this point, it is more of the service of business, making money, fighting the ratings game, and being No. 1". Journalists were eager to present to the public every possible news source without checking his or her credibility. "Anything that would raise the decibel of noise (was deemed to be) good".

A TV reporter who covered the police beat wrote an article in the Philippine Journalism Review, introducing his work. It seemed the most important story to him that day was an action-packed exclusive. The kind of exclusive he was referring to was stories like a fight in a bar between two groups of men.

He described that as his "most memorable"story - "The protagonists hurled chairs and exchanged fierce blows (one had his nose bridge badly broken; the other had his face bloodied) until police on patrol intervened. We had everything caught on tape, and my crew and I went home happy with an action-packed exclusive".

Other scoops the reporter and his crew chased included a fire that gutted a car after it crashed into a ten-wheeler, a holdup incident, carjacking in a tunnel, and a fake kidnapping case. Such stories were the focus of his news coverage and the theme of his article. Given the rampant corruption, the high profile problem of murdering journalists and other challenges the country is facing, can the freedom and the power of the media be put to better use?

The news media have also used their freedom to outdo rivals in the race to peddle newspapers and television programs. When members of the First Philippine Mount Everest Expedition scaled the world's tallest mountain, crews from both ABS-CBN and GMA-7, two TV networks, followed the team to cover the event.

Both were exclusive broadcast partners, each network sponsoring its own climbers. Both networks wanted to break the news first and have better videos. And both networks denied that they tried to dictate the pace of the ascent. The competition was viewed as a "ratings war,"or "a network war,"which the networks denied.

The race in ratings sometimes resulted in tragedy. More than seventy people died in a rush to get inside a sports stadium, where a TV extravaganza sponsored by ABS-CBN was to take place, and the network found itself the subject of news. The motivation for staging the event was again fierce competition between ABS-CBN and GMA-7.

Media ownership pattern, on the other hand, is hardly representative of the interests of different sectors of the society when anybody can buy into the media as long as he or she has money.

Media in the Philippines remain an elite enterprise, and newspapers operate in the vested interests of their owners. Media owners sometimes use their newspapers to defend and advance their businesses and political interests. And political patronage in the press is not unusual.

Similar to the situation in Indonesia, money corrupts individual journalists as bribery gets in the way of reporting the truth. "There are many journalists who allow themselves to be used as tools of the government".

One reporter wrote about a typical case where a highranking government official was trying to buy her silence with a thick envelope of cash. The reporter was investigating bribery charges against the official and his wife. The reporter was "stunned"and "humiliated"by the matter-of-fact manner in which the bribes were delivered. The case showed the prevalence of corruption in Philippine journalism.

The chase after profits and mounting libel suits against the media prompted growing criticism against the media and calls for improving professionalism. The establishment of Citizen Press Councils and calls for appointing media ombudsmen to keep down libel suits were part of the efforts by the media industry to use the power of a free press more responsibly.

In Taiwan, the press started to enjoy press freedom after martial law was lifted in 1987, and political discussions are much more open in the press since. According to the 2005 Freedom House report, Taiwan is well known for having one of the freest media environments in East Asia because of its firm commitment to judicial independence and economic freedom. Today's media in Taiwan are among the freest and most competitive in Asia.

The media in Taiwan are free and powerful. "For all its shortcomings, the press is free, bold and aggressive". Like their counterpart in the Philippines, the news media in Taiwan play a critical role in exposing government corruption, which would have remained hidden from public view without investigations by the media. Media exposés of corruption cases and scandals involving high-ranking officials resulted in devastating defeats in local elections and resignations of high officials.

However, the media in Taiwan are often criticized for abusing that power and freedom. They are often regarded as a source of social chaos and accused of stirring up disorder by making "unfounded reports"and spreading stories that were not true. Some media organizations tend to be biased or sensationalize their reports.

As Taiwan's democracy is sometimes ridiculed as "rambunctious,"its media are also considered as lacking accuracy and accountability. To win sympathy and support, the island's embattled president Chen Shui-bian trumped up his family troubles, and the media dutifully sensationalized the story as soap operas.

For circulations and ratings, the media spent too much energy on sensationalizing crime stories and the private lives of public figures. One recent example involved a police investigation of a death. For two weeks, the media provided excessive coverage of the case on a daily basis, including the daily activities of the suspect and the police's pursuit.

In another extreme case, the Scoop Weekly, a tabloid magazine, enclosed a VCD of an alleged sexual encounter of a female legislative candidate in one of its issues. The magazine defended itself by saying that the VCDs were enclosed in the magazine as "evidence"supporting the veracity of its investigative reporting.

Some reporters, in the rush to be the first to get the story out, sacrificed accuracy in their reporting rather than tried to find credible sources to check out the facts. And sometimes police complained that newsgathering and reporting got in the way of solving criminal cases. "The freedoms that were so hard to obtain, ironically, now threaten some parts of a society that considers the press the enemy because of its influence and power".

The excesses of press freedom in Taiwan, the Philippines, and Indonesia are typical of press systems in transition from being tightly controlled to almost completely free. The new democracies in Eastern Europe have encountered similar problems, such as the boom of tabloid journalism, the withering of quality press, bribery, and corruption.

The media systems in transition reflect the problems of those societies undergoing major transformations - rough politics in the fight for the power vacuum, partisan press, intense competition because of the new freedom, corruption for lack of a strong and independent judiciary system, weak financial foundation for the media, and lack of training of the journalists.

Democracy is still young in these societies; it will take time for a democratic system to mature. Because of traditions and culture, press freedom in these countries will still have its ups and downs. The newfound press freedom in Asian societies has its own distinctive social and cultural contexts.

THE "AUTHORITARIAN PRESS" IN ASIA - THE INFLUENCE OF CONFUCIANISM

The press in Singapore and Malaysia is often regarded as the prototype of authoritarian press in Asia. In both countries, the means to control the press are very similar to those used in sixteenth or seventeenth century England, including government censorship, suspension of license, legal actions against the press, and even shutdown of the offending publications.

But that is where similarities with Western authoritarianism end. The authoritarian press theory was based on the historical analysis of sixteenth and seventeenth century England while the authoritarian press in Singapore and Malaysia is shaped more by the Asian cultural tradition and the practical needs of the countries' geo-political realities.

While government authority came more from the absolute power of the monarchy in sixteenth and seventeenth century England, in Asian societies, especially in Singapore, which is under the heavy influence of Confucius's teachings, governments regard themselves both as parents and as rulers, which helps explain why even gum chewing and flushing toilets are regulated. According to the Confucian hierarchical order of political system, government is the paternalistic figure of the land.

"The ruler is the wind. People are the grass. When the wind blows, the grass is sure to bend," Confucius said. But Confucius was also a philosopher. He said, "Authority springs from morality, not force". He believed that people should accept authority, but authority must be just. Confucius asked: "When government leads by the right example, who dares to go astray?" In contrast, authoritarian theory does not address the quality of a government or the morality of the rulers.

Singapore is a society where a no-nonsense government promotes Confucian values of education, hard work and clear moral principles. The Singaporean government is one of the very few in Asia where corruption is rare. The government is as clean as the streets in Singapore, which is often considered the cleanest city in the world. The government in Singapore prides itself on its system of meritocracy and efficiency.

Different views are tolerated to a certain extent, but if the press publishes articles the government takes offense to, the government pursues the press relentlessly all the way to the court, which often has a chilling effect on the press. Confucianism extols cooperative and harmonious relations, which are what the Singaporean government hopes to cultivate both at home and abroad.

The government keeps a watchful eye on the press for any stories that address race relations, religion, or problems in neighboring countries. Such stories are banned in the Singaporean press because of the mixed racial and religious makeup of its population and its often-sensitive relations with its neighbors.

Violence and chaos caused by racial and religious differences in neighboring countries put the Singaporean government on high alert. Former Prime Minister Lee Kuan Yew said that any journalist who did not support Singapore-Malaysia relations would be sent to jail.

Malaysia has many similarities with its neighbour, Singapore, in its treatment of the press, as the two countries were once merged into one for a brief period in their history. Both governments are unequivocal promoters of "Asian values"and loud critics of Western culture.

Asian values in Malaysia include emphasis on the social role of the press, which is for development, and on morality, which in part might have resulted from the Islamic influence in the country. Confucian influences are not as heavy in Malaysia as in Singapore, where Chinese account for about 75% of the population. In Malaysia, Muslims make up about half of the population. Malaysian leaders, especially former Prime Minister Mahathir, have the government-knows-best attitude. The government has set the goal of making Malaysia a developed country by the year 2020, and it wants the press to help in that endeavor, which means highlighting government development plans, promoting racial and religious harmony by suppressing coverage of racial and religious issues, and controlling Western influences by limiting overseas TV programming to 30%.

While the Singaporean government is often criticized for trying to silence dissent and punish the press for negative coverage, the government in Malaysia has promoted positive press coverage on such topics as "Asian values"and national development.

In some aspects, Malaysian media seem to border on the communist system not only in promoting positive news coverage, but also in media ownership. Party press sets the trend in Malaysia, where political parties own major stocks in media agencies. The ruling political party UMNO owns media giants the New Straits Times and Utusan Malaysia.

The Chinese and Indian parties in the country also have acquired major stocks in media agencies that cater to their ethnic groups. The government has a direct stake in the media too by owning the national news agency, Bernama, which has the right to distribute foreign news reports. Under authoritarian rule, governments do not own the media; they punish the media when they are not happy with the coverage.

One salient feature of the authoritarian press system is government's various ways of punishing and controlling the press when the press is defiant. Even though the Malaysian government punishes occasional rebellious papers, the Malaysian press, especially the mainstream press, mostly saves the government's wrath through compliance with very restrictive press laws.

The Printing Presses and Publications Act of 1984 gives the minister of home affairs the power to revoke publishing licenses without judicial review. As a result, the Malaysian mainstream press has become so tame that its credibility has been questioned.

Zaharom Nain wrote, "... The Malaysian mainstream media - the press and broadcasting - have never aspired to be the guardians of the freedom of speech." "... The mainstream newspapers'failure to be a credible source of information is a reflection of a journalist's failure in performing her duties professionally,"a member of the National Union of Journalists said.

The inaction of the press against government suppression of press freedom came under fire too. "The credibility of Malaysian journalists has been damaged as much by dilution of professional standards and ethics as by passivity in tackling legal and administrative restrictions".

THE "COMMUNIST PRESS" IN ASIA - SWEEPING REFORMS

Today's Asia hosts the majority of the world's remaining communist countries - China, Vietnam, Laos, and North Korea. Trying to understand the press systems in these countries using the Soviet communist press theory as a guide would be misleading.

The communist press theory was based on the model of the Soviet press system, which can't satisfactorily describe the varied press systems in these remaining communist countries today, especially the Chinese press system after more than twenty years of sweeping economic liberalization and opening to the outside world.

The Freedom House rated China 7 for political rights and 7 for civil liberties, not free for 1997-98 (on a scale of one to seven with one being most free and 5.5+ being not free), the same ratings for 1972-73, which meant that for the twenty-five years in between, political rights and civil liberties in the Chinese society remained the same. For its 2005 survey on press freedom, it ranked China the 177th out of a total of 197 countries studied.

The Freedom House rating was in sharp contrast to the 1998 U.S. State Department report, which stated that Chinese citizens benefited from "(h)igher disposable income, looser economic control, greater freedom of movement, increased access to outside sources of information, greater room for individual choice, and more diversity in cultural life". Emmons wrote that, "There are those who believe that the media and freedom of speech, in general, never have been as uninhibited as they are today...". Emmons cited in his paper, "Surprisingly, the average Chinese citizen enjoys significantly more personal freedom today than ever before".

When China is undergoing economic reforms, what exactly does "media reform"mean? It meant the public's right to know according to late premier Zhao Ziyang; it meant commercializing Chinese media and building a stronger media industry according to late reform architect Deng Xiaoping; and it means the relevance of the media to the people according to current Chinese leader Hu Jintao.

Reforms bring choices, and freedom means having choices. Since the reform started, China's media outlets proliferated. Today China has around 2,000 newspapers, more than 9,000 magazines, 1,000 radio stations, and 200 TV stations broadcasting 2,900 channels. The choices and competition on the media market today stand in sharp contrast to the one voice on the media scene in the past when every city had only one Party paper. Choices, instead of one voice, symbolize the major changes Chinese media consumers have experienced.

Introducing the profit motive, which is absent from the Soviet press model, into the media sector was another reform measure that caused sweeping changes to the industry-it changed the nature of the media in China. Economic reform of the media in China began almost as early as the overall economic reform. And media commercialization becomes an important part of the development of the market economy as the government has adopted a policy of gradually cutting subsidies and encouraging commercialized financing.

Advertising, the capitalist genie, has returned to the world of communist media. To meet the new challenge, the press, including the ones directly under the control of the Party, is becoming increasingly commercialized. Even the official Xinhua news agency and the Party paper, People's Daily, are diversifying their product line to increase profits.

To be competitive on a booming media market, where the number of journalists has doubled in twenty years, media in China have to appeal to the readers, some of them by resorting to sensationalism. To speed up the reform, the government announced in June 2003 that it would end subsidies to all the newspapers in China except three papers and one journal, and all the publications in China had to sever their ties to government departments and stop mandatory subscriptions.

Those titles earning less than 50% of their revenues through voluntarily paid subscriptions had to be shut down. By November that year, a total of 1,452 Party and government newspapers had been affected, 673 of which had been suspended from publication.

The overhaul of the Chinese press system has substantially changed the economic and administrative relationships between the government and the press. From then on, the press has been financially independent of the government, even though the state remains the owner of the press. The biggest challenge facing Chinese editors today is to strike the right balance between being politically correct and economically viable.

In fact, one of the major problems hampering the development of the Chinese press today is the low ethical standards held by some local and commercial papers. Hunan TV, a challenging rival of China Central TV (CCTV), developed a huge following with a series on an orphaned woman looking for her biological parents. In its reporting, the network turned an old rape case into a love story, resulting in being sued. Some media outlets were given warnings and reporters detained for extorting large sums of money from people allegedly involved in wrongdoing.

It is no longer rare in China today that newspapers are exposed for their sensationalism, fabrications, or staged news, which are commonplace in a free press environment but seldom occur under a tightly controlled communist media system. Orthodox communist papers are serious and "clean."

The Soviet press model mostly prescribes a promotional role for the press - the press should be an agitator, an organizer, and propagandist for the socialist cause, but never a watchdog. In the Chinese press today, there is no lack of exposés or negative news, which is a taboo in the rigid communist media model, as bad news is perceived as demoralizing.

Given the rampant corruption among government officials in China, some high-level government officials encouraged the press to play the watchdog role by engaging in more investigations. Zhang Baoming, head of the State Administration for Production Safety, called on the media for more active participation in the investigation of major industrial accidents, almost every one of which, he said, was connected with corruption.

Caijing, a financial magazine, made a name for itself for its investigative reporting of the financial sector. Who would have imagined that the communist press would engage in investigative reporting? Former Chinese Premier Zhu Rongji tried to promote the watchdog role of the media.

Commenting on a popular talk show on China Central Television, "Focal Point"(Jiaodian Fangtan), which routinely exposes official corruption and mismanagement, Zhu praised the programme as "a mirror and watchdog of the government and a supervisor of the government through public opinion". Wu Guanzheng, secretary of the Central Commission for Disciplinary Inspection, also urged the media to play the watchdog role in the national campaign against corruption. He said media publicity was vital to the campaign, and the authorities should listen to "the voice of the media."

The Zhejiang provincial government encouraged the news media to provide tips directly to its inspection department as the government found it effective to follow and prosecute corruption cases exposed in the media. The government even offered rewards of up to 20,000 yuan ($2,500) if the tips were verified and led to prosecution. In contrast, the municipal government of Nanjing was widely criticized for stipulating that all corruption exposés be signed off by the person exposed in the story.

In Qijiang County, Chongqing municipality, hidden cameras were installed to monitor the performance of government officials. The Southern Metropolis Daily and the Beijing News both carried editorials, arguing that the watchdog role of the media would be much more powerful and effective than the hidden cameras, as it is a bottom-up rather than a top-down approach.

In many cases, the news media are playing such a vigorous watchdog role that a "Witness Protection Law"is being proposed as investigative reporting invites reprisals. Some news sources were detained, jailed, or sent to labour camps. In one case, an editor was beaten to death by Taizhou city police for an embarrassing exposé.

Attacks against journalists have increased in China in recent years as reporters have become more aggressive in reporting sensitive social issues. At least 100 journalists were physically attacked in 2003. In 2002, the central government was investigating provincial government officials in Jiangxi and Zhejiang provinces for punishing journalists who exposed problems in their jurisdictions.

The Soviet communist media did not carry exposés. In China, exposés of high-ranking officials, though allowed, still have to be approved by the government however. One other important feature of the communist press system is the state ownership of the media. The majority of the media outlets in China today are still owned by the state.

However, foreign investment is entering the Chinese media sector, and such investment as mandated by the rules of the World Trade Organization is increasing with the deepening of press reforms. Interest in China among international media groups surged in 2005 after the Chinese government issued rules allowing foreign investment in joint-venture television, radio, and film production companies. News Corporation, Viacom, and Sony Pictures were among the big names involved in joint ventures with Chinese media companies.

The current policy stipulates that investors are denied decision-making power in the media outlets'editorial content. But in practice, the situation is getting murky. The editorial staff of the China International Business, a monthly economic review, gets its salaries from Ringier AG of Switzerland. Such business arrangements are not rare. Many foreign publishers sign deals in media advertising or consulting but actually help produce content.

Under the Soviet press system, there was tight control of information and very limited access to government information, resulting in more propaganda than information in the news media. In China today despite government control, access to information has gained substantial progress in recent years.

In 2000, the government of Anhui Province took the unprecedented step of issuing a regulation banning its officials from refusing interviews to the press. Other provinces and cities followed suit. Such regulations were unimaginable before the reforms or under the Soviet media model. The central government now has also installed a spokesman system to meet the needs of the press, both national and international.

In Shanghai, a reporter, based on a city ordinance mandating the disclosure of public information, sued the city planning department for repeatedly declining interviews. This was the first such case in China where a reporter sued a government department for violating his rights to reporting.

The reporter complained that city government departments often denied interviews to him. The city ordinance required city departments to disclose information concerning the economy, city management, and public services. Such ordinance was listed as top priority in the legislative plan of the State Council.

It would make disclosure as the principle and non-disclosure as the exception rather than the other way around as in the past. China is opening up. It has opened up its market to the world, including the media market, even though it is only the entertainment media for now. It is not difficult today to find popular foreign consumer magazines on the newsstands in China.

International Data Group, a Boston publisher, alone has invested $20 million in China, publishing twenty-eight titles and planning another four. These operations are either in the form of joint ventures or through licensing the titles and content for publication in China.

China is also working on an international media centre with a total floor space of 130,000 square meters, which will serve as an office building for more than 100 foreign media organizations in Beijing. And in 2001, Reuters's Qing Niao website, a site for trade information and e-business, made a low-key entry into China.

The Soviet communist media model was a closed system. But China has opened up, and it wants to reintegrate itself into the world community. The one medium that provides a public forum for the ordinary Chinese and connects the Chinese people directly with the rest of the world is the Internet, which claims about 137 million users in China by the end of 2006, the second largest in the world after the United States.

China has witnessed the fastest growth of Internet use among countries whose annual per-capita is less than $2,000, and the number of net users is expected to increase by at least 15% annually before 2010. The Internet is breaking through the silence of traditional media by posting stories rejected by official newspapers.

With its power of reaching millions of people at the same time, the Internet has directly helped in effecting legislative changes in the country by exposing police brutality, which brought about public outrage on an unprecedented scale and caught the attention of legislators and the government.

The Internet, with its public forums where people can discuss topics shunned by the traditional media, is producing a better informed, more vocal public and a more open society. Inadvertently, it has ushered in a public discourse that has been absent for almost half a century.

It also enabled direct communication between ordinary citizens and government officials. The acceptance of the Internet in China itself is one important indicator of the passing of the rigid communist media system in China, as Internet, a revolutionary medium, defies total control. Some media researchers argue that as long as there is government control, the media in China should be categorized as communist media.

It is true that there is still government control of the media in China - there are news topics on which diversity of opinion is not allowed, there are websites that are blocked, and there are newspaper editors that have been fired. However, since the start of the reforms, the changes that are occurring in China have substantially reduced government controls.

These changes are happening because of the intention of the government to open up, the new financial independence of the press, the proliferation of media outlets, and the availability of the Internet. Sometimes the sheer size of the country poses a challenge to effective control. For example, when the government could not effectively implement a ban on satellite dishes in 1994, it changed its policy by licensing them instead.

A year later the government also specified permissible programs and viewing hours. Foreign affairs used to be an area off limits for public discussions in the media. The advent of the Internet with its convenient online forums has made it a hot topic for public debate. Government control of the press is a universal phenomenon. The issue is the degree of control.

In the age of the Internet, total control is out of the question. And in the case of China, that control is being relaxed and challenged from all sides. More recent examples include the suspension and the return of the supplement of a major newspaper in Beijing and the debate over a section of a draft law on managing disasters and accidents.

The weekly "Freezing Point"published by the popular China Youth Daily, which stands out from other newspapers in China for its aggressive reporting and biting commentary, was shut down in late January 2006, and its editors removed to its research department because some government officials were not happy with one article.

The case was widely publicized by the media worldwide. The supplement resumed publication one month later following public outcry against such heavy-handedness against the press, including staff letters protesting the actions and an open letter to top Party officials signed by thirteen prominent scholars and former officials who were contributors to the supplement.

The writers of the open letter included Zhu Houze, a former Central Propaganda Department official; Hu Jiwei, a former editor-in-chief of the People's Daily, and He Weifang, a law professor from Peking University, who said, "The purpose (of the letter) is to change the current incorrect policies on freedom of speech"(f 3), The letter said although not all signatories approved of the article, they all supported Freezing Point's right to publish it.

They quoted Chinese leader Hu Jintao as saying no organization in China has special legal privileges. The letter said that the newspaper suspension was neither legal nor sensible and it violated citizens 'basic rights to speech and freedom of information, which are their constitutional rights.

Another controversy arose over a draft law on emergency management, which included industrial accidents, natural disasters, and health and public security crises. Part of the draft law addressed the news coverage of emergency situations by the media, stipulating that media outlets could face fines between 50,000 yuan (U.S.$6,250) and 100,000 yuan (U.S.$12,500) if they reported the emergency situations without authorization or released fraudulent reports and if such reports led to serious consequences.

The law was drafted following the aftermath of the outbreak of SARS, when health department officials hid the facts from the public, resulting in rampant rumors in the press and in the streets. Government officials said the purpose of the law was to ensure timely release of accurate information by local officials.

Opposition to the draft law was loud and clear. A legislator, He Keng, said journalism had its own rules and argued that the watchdog role of the media was not strong enough in China. The New Express, a commercial newspaper published by the Yangcheng Evening News, carried an editorial arguing that the law would diminish the watchdog role of the media, that there was no guarantee that the information released by government departments was accurate and that some "natural disasters"were man-made.

In a column in the outspoken Southern Metropolis Daily, Changping pointed out that in the case of coal mine disasters, often local officials and mine owners colluded with each other in covering up the facts of accidents as both profited from the mines. In such situations, how could the media wait for the local government to release accurate information? Changping argued.

One often ignored issue is the self-censorship in the newsrooms in China, which sometimes applies tighter control than the government does for the interests of the media organization or the management. For a lack of laws and regulations, the new media are trying to police themselves.

Nineteen websites jointly issued a set of self-disciplinary rules against bloggers'personal attacks, fabricated stories, plagiarism, and pornographic and violent content. Hosts of the sites said they were ready to delete such materials once they appear on their sites. Min Dahong, a journalism professor said that many big websites in the world have explicit written rules on deleting or editing users'messages that they regard as abusive, defamatory, offensive, obscene, or in violation of a specific law.

Ultimately how much freedom or control the Chinese media will experience is not only up to the government; it is also up to the editors and reporters of the media, especially those leading media organizations in Beijing, as to how far they will push. So far the most vigorous push comes mainly from local media outside of Beijing.

Following China's example, Vietnam started its own economic reforms in 1986 and "remains wedded to the Chinese model of reform". Its press system is also undergoing similar changes. The liberal economic reforms eroded the pervasive authority of the Party. As a result, "Vietnam is no longer as tightly controlled as it used to be although it does remain an authoritarian one-party system". Facing a rise in corruption like China, the government encouraged the press to expose corruption, made new laws to facilitate news gathering, and warned against officials trying to obstruct journalists.

Even though strict censorship still exists in Vietnam today, meaningful independent journalism is possible on certain occasions. There are instances where journalists successfully challenged the police and the court in violating reporters'rights in newsgathering and forced the police and the court to back down.

"In terms of freedom, the press here in Vietnam has been getting better and more aggressive". One editor at Lao Dong (Labour), Nguyen Due Tuan, said, "There is no question we have more freedom today.... Now, reporters like to see how far they can push and still get their stories published".

Similar to the situation in China, editors in Vietnam now have more discretion in deciding the content of their publications. The press in Vietnam is surprisingly lively in terms of the types of newspapers and magazines. Since the reforms, both the quantity and quality of the press have improved.

The press today is becoming more information oriented than ideology dependent, as the importance of information is generally recognized in a more market-oriented economy. The Internet entered Vietnam in 1997. By the end of 2006, the number of Internet users had reached 14.5 million.

Despite government announcement that access to the Internet would be unrestricted, the Freedom House reported that in 2004 the Vietnamese government suppressed dissent on the Internet with new guidelines of government control and censorship, including a permanent monitoring system aimed at the country's privately run Internet cafes.

Despite the reforms, the majority of the media outlets in Vietnam are still state-owned. But the government has permitted some form of private ownership of periodicals, a bolder step than China's. The condition for ownership is that the publication should be a joint undertaking between the owners and the relevant state agency. An example is the

Vietnam Investment Review, the first foreign-owned, Western-style periodical in the country. The government also abolished direct subsidies to the press even though some form of state funding is still continuing.

As a result, the press is forced to become more commercialized, and the survival of the press is subject to market forces, which seems to dictate a success formula of tabloid journalism. Some papers publish uncommon crime stories gathered from police records, all in the name of exposing social problems. In the pursuit of profits, newspapers in Vietnam start to face criticisms about their low ethical standards. Some journalists in Vietnam now claim that they are having more debates on "responsibilities and morals of journalists"than on press freedom.

Early in the reform, the sensationalism and the increasingly aggressive investigative reporting alarmed the Party leaders, who worried that the state was losing control of information flow and wanted to rein in this threatening trend. The government began clamping down on the press in 1989 and tightened control of the media by establishing a new press department aimed at monitoring and controlling press coverage about security matters, issuing new rules regarding passing information to foreign news organizations, amending the 1990 press law, requiring compensation if news coverage leads to losses to the business interests of organizations or individuals.

The government also reminded the press to champion the fight against corruption and other social evils instead of seeking profits alone, but questioning Party rule remains expressly prohibited. The Vietnamese leaders are still ambivalent about the degree of control and the liberal reforms, which help with the country's economic development but threaten the power and control of the Party. North Korea may be the only communist country in Asia left with a press that could still fit the Soviet media model. There has been very little change in the country despite the fact that other remaining communist countries in Asia are undergoing major reforms to open up and revive their economies. Perhaps because of the poor performance of its economy, the widespread and chronic famine, and tremendous external pressure to change, the government is exercising strict control of information flow across its borders.

As a result, information about the country is scarce even with CNN's 2006 documentary, which was shot inside the country with a hidden cell-phone camera. North Korea is the most censored country in the world. Its people experience the world's deepest information void, and the country has no independent journalists.

The main role ascribed to the press is that of spreading the viewpoint of the government. All newspapers and broadcasting stations are under direct government control, and all news is positive. According to the 2003 annual report by Reporters Without Borders, all the news media in the country focused on the personality cult of Kim Jong Il.

The report said three subjects dominated the coverage in the print media: the personality of Kim Jong II, praise of the army, and criticism of the country's foes, especially South Korea, the United States, and Japan. In a story, the official Korean Central News Agency reported that Kim Jong Il was so beloved that after a deadly munitions train explosion in a populated area, people ran into buildings to save the ubiquitous portraits of the "Dear Leader" before they rescued their own family members.

Nothing was mentioned in the news media about the malnutrition among children and urban populations or the failure of the government's "self-reliance"policy. In the leading Party paper, the Rodong Shinmun, commentaries carry greater weight than news stories, and reporters do not compete for scoops among themselves, who are given instructions from the Central Party Committee's propaganda and agitation department on what to cover and in how many pages. Anyone disobeying the instructions is severely punished. Reporters may be jailed for a commentary that deviates from the Party line. Harassment, psychological pressure, intimidation, and round-the-clock surveillance are routine. The North Korean newspapers do not carry any advertisements except a handful of government notices. For the mass media in North Korea, there is neither private ownership nor market competition. North Korea's revised 1998 constitution guarantees citizens'rights of freedom of speech, of the press, of assembly, demonstration, and association.

But the government prohibits the exercise of these rights in practice. There are strict controls to prevent access to any kind of news coming from abroad. Radios sold in North Korea can receive only domestic programming. Radios obtained from abroad must be altered to work in a similar manner. The national news agency has Internet sites hosted in Japan. Direct access to the web is limited to the privileged few ("North Korea,"2003). And to prevent Western influence, very few journalists in North Korea receive training in the West.

It is also hard for the foreign media to do reporting inside the country as they are all portrayed by the regime as liars seeking to destabilize the government. Foreign journalists visiting North Korea have to be on guided tours.

However, in 2006, the Associated Press became the first Western news organization to have a permanent bureau in the country. AP Television News's full-time office in Pyongyang operates in association with the country's state-run broadcaster and is staffed mainly by local reporters. With the increase in international trade, even North Koreans have started to have greater contact with foreigners, which might result in greater access to information from the outside world.

The press in North Korea seems to be the prototype of the communist press, but it does not represent the trend where the press in other communist countries is heading. It is misleading to put the press systems in China, Vietnam, and North Korea in the same category. To do so, media researchers have to disregard the sweeping changes in the Chinese and Vietnamese press.

THE "DEVELOPMENT MEDIA"IN ASIA

Neglected by the authors of the four press theories were media in the poorer countries of the world-development media. The press in South Asia may best be described by the concept of development journalism, a concept developed later to supplement the four theories, as the development of communities and giving voice to the underprivileged are major goals of many of the local media in the region.

The development press is popular in the region perhaps because South Asia is the least economically developed region on the continent. More than half of the world's underweight children lived in India, Bangladesh, and Pakistan, said a recent UNICEF report on the global progress on children's issues.

In India, approximately 47% of the under-five population was underweight. The report found that South Asia was the only region that showed a gender bias with regard to child nourishment, with girls more likely to be underweight than boys. The issue of undernourishment points to the problems of poverty, lack of education, and inequality in the region.

In India, communication not only means the transfer of information, but also includes the participation in the society and in the community. The Indian brand of development journalism "focuses on the needs of the poor, the deprived, and the marginalized and emphasizes their effective participation in developmental planning". It motivates the participation of the people and advocates for their interests instead of the views of the policy makers and the planners. And it promotes social justice for all.

Journalists in the country believe that the media should not only carry stories about health campaigns like the one against AIDS but also discuss issues that are important for a civil society because only the mass media can reach the vast rural population and give them a voice in debates affecting their lives.

The mass media can also play a crucial role in social progress, as any transitional society will encounter new attitudes, a new mindset, and a new value system.

Development journalism enthusiasts in India conducted workshops for social activists to train them to write stories about development issues and workshops for local editors and journalists to familiarize them with realities and issues in local communities. Commercial newspapers also play a role in development journalism.

The Jharkhand-based Prabhat Khabar had been doing development journalism by giving people information on science, information technology, economics, and the comparative financial progress of different states. The paper also conducted "readers'courts,"where readers could interact with journalists and discuss ways of improving the quality of the paper, much like the role of the focus groups in civic or public journalism in the United States.

Radio plays a special role in development journalism in South Asia because of its easy and wide reach in the vast rural areas, where literacy rate is still relatively low. The Indian communications NGO (non-government organization) had been highlighting the importance of community radio in India for over half a decade and called for the extension of community broadcasting.

In India, awards are given to mentors of development journalism for encouraging and nurturing journalists to investigate and write on development issues and for supporting journalism initiatives towards "a common social good". Journalists and media researchers in India and Pakistan criticized some of the mainstream media for their elitist approach, focusing on the prominent while ignoring the plight of the underprivileged in rural communities by following Western news values.

The degree of press freedom in South Asia, however, varies considerably from country to country. Once the largest colony in the world, India is the largest democracy in the world today. Only under Prime Minister Indira Gandhi was an attempt made to curtail press freedom by declaring a political emergency to suspend civil rights.

The government of Narasimha Rao tried to prevent exposés of government corruption under the pretext of protection of privacy. Despite such government attempts at control, the press in India has largely remained private, free, and vibrant. Cushrow R. Irani, editor-in-chief and managing director of The Statesman, said that India's press today is as free as it chooses to be. N. P. Chekkutty, editor of Media Focus, wrote, "The Indian media works in an atmosphere of freedom. We are the purveyors of free thoughts and opinions. We do reflect the freedom of expression the Constitution guarantees to our citizens, and we, therefore, are the epitome of a free, liberal society".

With the freedom it enjoys, the press in India often plays its watchdog role seriously. "Newspapers in India are completely free, as free as the newspapers in the United States, as they are privately owned and free of censorship". It is the newspapers that have exposed corruption in India, though some journalists are attacked for their investigative reporting. The Indian press has always been vigilant about protecting its freedom and aggressive in reporting.

Free as it may be as the press in the United States, the Indian press clearly differs from the Western libertarian press system in the perception of its mission. For its social role, the Indian press may be closer to the civic or public journalism in America, which also prescribes an advocacy role for the press. However, in India development journalism represents the aspirations of many journalists, while in America the ethical implications of civic and public journalism are still being debated.

In India, press freedom is guaranteed by the Constitution and the independent court system, which is very similar to the situation in neighboring Pakistan, formerly a part of India before its independence. Behind India, which has a relatively low literacy rate of 65%, Pakistan's literacy rate is even lower at 38%, which limits the growth of its press industry.

There are about 1,330 newspapers in print in Pakistan, but only 1% of the population buys a newspaper (Isa, 2001, p. 137). The press in Pakistan is independent of the government and mostly privately owned.

Major public issues are debated in the press, which has become an instrument for change. In Pakistan no law governs the registration of publications. In recent years, Pakistan has been moving toward greater press freedom, and its press is among the most outspoken in South Asia. In both India and

Pakistan when the government tries to crack down on critical press coverage of the government, the courts often strike down government charges in support of press freedom.

There are exceptions to the constitutional guarantees of the freedom of speech and of the press in Pakistan, the most important of which is the "reasonable restrictions imposed by law in the interest of the glory of Islam". The Constitution prohibits the ridicule of Islam, of the armed forces, or of the judiciary.

Development journalism is perhaps less developed in Pakistan than in India. Circulation of newspapers in the rural areas of the country is one of the lowest in the world because of the urban orientation of the papers and the cost of subscription in addition to a low literacy rate. The rural market is largely untapped.

The dramatic increase in the number of publications in recent years is not supported with trained staff. Many journalists, especially rural ones, lack the basic skills to cover the complex issues important to their communities. However, electoral politics has increased the importance of rural centres in the emerging democracy of Pakistan.

Supporting development journalism, the Pakistan Press Foundation (PPF) was established to help raise the standards of journalism, particularly of the vernacular and regional press, and to promote greater awareness of social and development issues through the media. In 1999, PPF restarted the rural journalists'skills development project.

By 2002 hundreds of Pakistani rural journalists have attended the workshops. The emphasis of the workshops is on improving basic skills of newsgathering and news writing, as participants are given exercises using actual issues, such as violence against women, environmental issues, child labour, bonded labour, and crime rates.

The end of monopoly of the electronic media in Pakistan provides new hopes of reaching a rural audience as radio is acknowledged to be a more suitable and affordable means of providing local communities with a voice of their own. It is more interactive and more suitable for community development. In less than six years, between 2000 and 2006, the broadcast sector completely changed the monolithic landscape that existed for about fifty-three years.

But the proliferation of radio stations has created the co-existence of robust liberty and open lawlessness, and commercial interests dominate the airwaves while development journalism still needs time to take hold. Research on the topic, however, is several steps ahead of the media industry.

Development journalism is regarded as an Asian model of journalism, stemming from the dissatisfaction with the Western news values that do not serve the cause of national development. Western news values of timeliness, prominence, proximity, conflict, and the bizarre exclude the ordinary people in the news unless they are involved in accidents, violence, or catastrophes.

Development journalism, on the other hand, should focus on the educational function of the news, stories about social needs, self-help projects, and obstacles to development. In the exploration of the development journalism model by Asian media researchers, the watchdog role of the media was emphasized, and the media were urged to remain vigilant against government involvement.

In Sri Lanka, three newspaper groups dominate the island's newspaper scene - the ANCL, the Upali Newspapers Ltd. and the Wijeya Newspapers Ltd. The ANCL has been under government control since 1973, while the other two are privately owned but have close family connections to political parties. In the broadcasting sector, Sri Lanka was perhaps the first British colony to introduce radio broadcasting a few years after its inauguration in Europe in 1920s. The country liberalized its radio and TV sectors ahead of the rest of Asia.

It permitted the establishment of more commercial radio stations than any other country in the region and put the state-controlled Sri Lanka Broadcasting Corporation under considerable competitive pressure. It also allowed private radio stations to broadcast news and current affairs, unlike some of its neighboring countries.

Efforts at setting up community radio have never stopped in Sri Lanka. Universities in Sri Lanka and UNESCO played host to regional workshops on community radio for participants from South Asian countries. The goal of such workshops was to make community radio a reality in South Asia and encourage- cooperation among community radio advocates in the region. Radio still is a popular medium in South Asia, particularly in rural areas. In Sri Lanka telephone boxes, where a radio station button is installed, allow listeners to contact a station without paying a fee. The system makes it easier for listeners to participate in the programs and solve problems in the communities.

The mass media in Sri Lanka also play a role in environmental education. Most people in both urban and rural areas use different media outlets as their primary source of environmental education, especially the print media. Television is the next major source of information for the urban population, while radio for the rural population. The media cover environmental issues in the form of news, editorials, investigative stories, entertainment, and educational programs.

Development journalism in the country can have a bigger potential if the government allows even greater participation by the public in media discussions, which is often limited when there is an increase in guerrilla warfare in the country.

It is evident from the above discussions that the degree of press freedom under the development concept varies from country to country, and that is where the controversy with the concept lies. While one scholar describes it as "the pursuit of cultural and informational autonomy"and "support for democracy"among other goals, another scholar criticizes it as "a rationale for autocratic press control"and "guided press".

Where do all the discussions about the press systems in Asia leave us theoretically? When theories encounter major difficulties in serving as a guide to the understanding of the realities they are supposed to describe, new paradigms are needed. So are the criteria of the Freedom House for assessing global press freedom and civil liberties when their rankings fail to reflect changing realities. Obviously, more factors should be taken into consideration than the current criteria.

The Last Rights concluded that the four theories were a "durable"but now "questionable"map and that a "more adequate"map is needed. The book presented inspiring criticism of the four press theories but stopped short of proposing a new paradigm.

CONSTRUCTING ALTERNATIVE PRESS THEORIES AND MODELS

Both Eastern and Western media researchers have tried to redress the deficiencies of the four-theory model by creating their own models. Three more theoretical concepts-development journalism, democratic-participant media, and the revolutionary media-were developed to accommodate the progress and changes in press systems and to supplement the dominant paradigm's four press categories.

Of the new theoretical concepts, development journalism has caused more controversies because the degree of press freedom varies greatly from society to society, and the very concept may imply a role for the government. The controversy also seems to stem from the fact that the deciding factor in creating the four press theories was the presence or absence of press freedom, which was defined mainly in terms of government control.

Based on such a criterion, how can one type of press system allow vastly different degrees of press freedom in different societies? When a new concept cannot be fit into the established paradigm, it becomes "controversial."Progressive, insightful, and creative as these new theories are, they are mostly supplementary to the established four press theories.

More ambitious efforts were made by Ralph Lowenstein, J. Henry Altschull, John C. Merrill, and Shelton A. Gunaratne, who constructed alternative models reclassifying press systems. Ralph Lowenstein developed a "progressive typology,"according to which, "press systems evolved from authoritarian to libertarian, to social libertarian or social centralist, and then to a big futuristic question mark".

This typology seems to have the same tendency as the established four theories of basing its discussions mainly on the development paths of Western press systems, which makes it less relevant to the evolution of press systems elsewhere in the world. J. Henry Altschull proposed three basic media models - market, Marxist, and developing. To make the concepts value free, Altschull described them as market, communitarian, and advancing. In trying to reclassify media systems, Altschull brought in the element of culture and belief systems.

He explained that the market system emphasized the "individual"while the communitarian system focused on the "communal life"or the "collective."Altschull also analysed the role of the media - preserving status quo under both market and communitarian models and advocating change under the advancing model. He explained that there were variations within each model, giving the classification much flexibility.

With the exception of the advancing model describing press systems in the South, Altschull's models were also based mainly on the analysis of Western media systems even though he classified his models also as East, West, and South, where East refers to Marxism and the former Soviet communist bloc in Eastern Europe rather than to Asia.

The only Eastern society mentioned in the analysis was Japan. Altschull explained that despite the variations within the market model, the basic belief systems - hostility to a communitarian belief system - remain intact. "Discord notwithstanding, the broad sweep of the first movement of the symphony is heard throughout the industrialized capitalist world, in Japan as in Denmark and Canada".

Despite Western influence, the Japanese society, steeped in Asian culture and Confucian traditions, has no such hostility.

As discussed earlier in this chapter, the press club system in Japan dictates communal behaviour within the industry by discouraging competition and scoops and encouraging collective reporting. A mixture of the East and the West, Japan proves to be a difficult case to be classified.

John C. Merrill's circular model shows that individualistic press systems gravitate toward libertarianism and more collectivistic systems are at the authoritarian end. Merrill said, "... the basic model is a simple spectrum, with authoritarianism at one end and libertarianism at the other. All press systems fall somewhere along this continuum".

Merrill's model resembles Altschull's models without the "advancing"or "South"element. Men-ill's model has the merit of built-in flexibility. The classification of a press system depends on in which direction the system gravitates. But it is still difficult to place Japan on Merrill's model. The Japanese press is mostly free from government control, but it is not individualistic. The press club system emphasizes collective action, but it cannot be described as authoritarian.

The models proposed by Altschull and Merrill represented major improvements over the four-theory model - AltschulPs model moved away from the exclusive emphasis on government control, and Men-ill's model had the merit of built-in flexibility to accommodate different types of press systems and changes within those systems.

Despite Men-ill's inclusion of the communitarian factor, the two models still seem to largely rely on Western philosophies, scholarship, and examples of Western media performances. Jiafei Yin (2003) called for the construction of a new model, which would be based on a broader foundation of both Western and Eastern philosophies and cultural influences, but did not produce an actual model.

Shelton A. Gunaratne brought in both Eastern and Western philosophical, religious, and cultural traditions in building his model-The Dao of the Press. There are two parts to Gunaratne's model: one part is the libertarian-authoritarian (L-A) continuum with varying shades of social responsibility across the continuum, and the other part is a centre-semiperiphery-periphery world system with individuals and groups, nation-states, and the world system at different levels.

And all the three levels "autopoietically adjust the degree of free expression"along the L-A continuum. Gunaratne's model emphasizes both Eastern and Western cultural values in the definitions and interpretations of the term "social responsibility,"giving the model much needed flexibility in accommodating different shades of social responsibility found in world cultures.

Merrill also addressed the relativity of the concept of responsibility among societies and even within a society. Similar to many of the previous press theories and models, Gunaratne's L-A continuum also focuses on the libertarian-authoritarian dichotomy, reflecting Western emphasis on freedom and liberty.

With the rich heritage of Asian philosophies and cultures, can a new model reflect diverse global cultural values and describe and explain press systems around the world without bias either from the West or the East?

After all, different cultures prioritize values differently. Therefore, press theories that are supposed to address global press systems should have a wider base to reflect a broader, more balanced global view. With adequate attention to factors such as world history, global cultures, and economic pressure, the problems inherent in the four established theories because of the authors'Western bias and their sole focus on governmental influences can be addressed.

For a new paradigm of press theories, the optimal balance between specificity and universality should also be considered. The four theories of the press have the beauty and elegance of a very simple but clear structure - four categories under a dichotomy, which aimed to describe and explain press systems in the whole world.

Conveniently general as they are, the four or five theories have difficulties in providing a reliable guide to the global press systems. The universality of the theories is limited. However, if categories are too specific and accurate in describing particular press systems, there may be too many categories for the model to be an effective guide.

One other important factor that needs to be paid attention to in building a more reliable press model is that the model should be dynamic so that it can accommodate the changes in the press systems around the world. Obviously, press systems in the new democracies in Eastern Europe are very different from the press systems in the West even though they all operate under democratic systems now.

The press systems in the new democracies in Asia, such as Indonesia, Cambodia, the Philippines, Taiwan, and South Korea, vary from those in Eastern Europe despite the fact that they are all new democracies and share some similarities. And the press system in China today cannot be compared with the Chinese press system two decades ago, or the press system in North Korea. It would defeat the purpose of having models if every time any changes occur, new models have to be created.

A DICHOTOMY OF VALUES, EAST AND WEST

A new paradigm of press theories requires new ways of thinking in order to broaden the foundation. In this section, an examination is conducted of the dominant Eastern and Western cultural values, which are by no means exclusive to either the East or the West but rather reflect the quintessence of each.

To summarize Asian, or more particularly the Confucian, culture, leading Confucian scholar Tu Wei-ming said: "Industrial East Asia, under the influence of Confucian culture, seems to have developed a different kind of modern civilization, less adversarial, less individualistic, and less self-interested. One sees there the coexistence of market economy and government leadership, democratic parity with meritocracy and individual initiatives with group orientation."

THE INDIVIDUAL VERSUS THE STATE AND FAMILY (THE GROUP)

Western libertarian philosophy values the independence and rights of each individual. John Stuart Mill's On Liberty spelled out classic liberal individualism-it "set out the limits to the legitimate interference of collective opinion with individual independence". Mill wrote that the only warranted interference with the liberty of an individual is for mankind's self-protection, that is, to prevent harm to others, and that no power should be exercised over an individual for his own good. "Over himself, over his own body and mind, the individual is sovereign."

The Confucian thought, however, focuses on the state and the family. Confucius believed that only when the state and families are strong can the well-being of individuals be guaranteed. In the equation of the state, family, and individuals in Confucian societies, individuals are often encouraged and expected to sacrifice their own rights and interests for the sake of the state and family if contradictions should arise, which is in sharp contrast to Mill's belief that the individual is sovereign.

In Confucian societies, the state is sovereign. In Western culture, individualism is extolled, but in Eastern culture, people are taught to think about "us." In the West, ideal societies are composed of free individuals while in Confucian societies the individual "is not viewed as an isolated individual but as a centre of relationships".

The Chinese tradition has largely been influenced by a Confucian-based relational and social definition of person instead of by any concept of discrete individuality. "Under the sway of this relational understanding of human being, the mutuality and interdependence of personal, familial, societal, and political realization in the classical Chinese model can and has been generally conceded."

FREEDOM AND RIGHTS VERSUS RESPONSIBILITY

John Locke, an early libertarian, believes that freedom is essential to the full development of a human being. Merrill summarized Locke's philosophy as "Each person has a natural right to be free and not to be subjected to the will of another." Freedom, for Locke, is a "natural" right.

"Besides being bound by natural law, humans possess natural rights, in particular the right to life, self-defence, and freedom. They have also duties; in particular, the duty not to give away their rights". The Enlightenment in eighteenth century Europe led to the rise of classical liberalism and capitalism. It also led to the French and American revolutions, which uprooted the power of religion and the aristocracy in France and heavily influenced the most distinguished leaders of the American Revolution-Jefferson, Washington, Franklin, and Paine.

"The language of natural law, of inherent freedoms, of self-determination, which seeped so deeply into the American grain, was the language of the Enlightenment..". "Give me liberty or give me death." Patrick Henry's rallying call meant that there was no compromise over liberty-to be free is the precondition to live.

In the East, the emphasis is on being responsible and loyal rather than on being free. Western libertarian philosophers' focus of attention falls on the welfare of the individual, so it is only logical that these philosophers advocate that these individuals should be equal and free to pursue what they want. Confucian thought lays emphasis on the group; hence, there is the concern of being responsible and loyal to the group. In his research, Tu pointed out the Asian focus on the ethic of service and obligation.

INDIVIDUAL FREEDOM AND HAPPINESS VERSUS PUBLIC GOOD AND RESPONSIBILITY

Mill, a defender of personal and political liberty, said in his On Liberty: "The only freedom which deserves the name, is that of pursuing our own good in our own way, so long as we do not attempt to deprive others of theirs, or impede their efforts to obtain it".

Mill's "sovereign self" echoed the U.S. Bill of Rights and the Declaration of Independence in upholding individual freedom and rights and the pursuit of happiness, not individual or collective responsibility.

So when President Kennedy demanded, "Ask not what your country can do for you; ask what you can do for your country," it was refreshing to the American youth as their civic education focused mostly on the value of equality, freedom, and rights embedded in the Constitution when they grew up. Confucius teachings emphasize a strong commitment to the world and encourage sacrifice of self-interest to be ethical. The Confucian concept of the ethical links up directly with the public good. And Confucius believes "self-realization is fundamentally a social undertaking, therefore, 'selfish' concerns are to be rejected as an impediment to one's own growth and self-realization".

LEGAL VERSUS MORAL

In Western democratic societies, the legal system is very well developed as the law embodies the ideal that everyone is equal before the law. And citizens have a strong sense of the law, which sets the boundary of people's behaviour, including what parents legally can or cannot do in disciplining their children. In Asian societies, especially more traditional and less developed societies such as China, the legal system is much less well developed.

With the opening up of the country's economy, China's legislative body, the National People's Congress, has been busy making laws as conflicts in the past were resolved mostly through mediation based on judgments of who was right and who was wrong.

And a major part of Confucius's teachings comprises moral guidelines, which is why he was also considered a moralist. Confucius firmly believes that children are the responsibility of their parents and that aging parents are the responsibility of their grown-up children whether it is legally required or not. As a result, Chinese press occasionally exposes cases of mistreating aging parents by their grown-up children even though it is a private matter.

Likewise, Confucius believes that it is parents' fault if a child goes astray. Even today some immigrant Asian parents are surprised by the child abuse laws of the United States, where children are encouraged to call the police if they are spanked by their parents. Such laws would shock Confucius. Confucius's teachings also place emphasis on being just and public minded. It would be unimaginable to Confucius that one country could have billionaires the same time it had a trillion dollars of national debt.

According to the moral teachings of Confucius, those who pursue only personal interests (li) are the "little men" (xiaoren), people of no character; only those who think about what is appropriate and beneficial to all concerned (yi) are the "gentlemen" (junzi), people of noble character.

TO BE FREE TO EXPLORE VERSUS TO KNOW RIGHT FROM WRONG

Western libertarians advocate for a free marketplace of ideas, where the public should be left free to explore and discover the truth on their own. In his pamphlet, Areopagitica, John Milton argues that truth would emerge victorious over falsehood should the two be locked in a grapple.

John Milton also wrote about the importance of diversity of opinions and perspectives. In Asian societies influenced by Confucian thinking, especially in the case of China after almost 5,000 years of civilization, truth seems to be self-evident. In such cases, the focus is on teaching the people what is right and what is wrong rather than the freedom to explore what is right and what is wrong.

The real challenge becomes the task of convincing the people, or in an ideal Confucian way, for people to convince themselves, to always make the right choice. Confucian scholar Tu Wei-ming phrased the contrast as "the right to think" versus "right thinking."

In Western democracies, the emphasis is on the process-if decisions are made with public input. In Confucian societies, the emphasis is on the result-if the right decision is made. The process often is deemed less relevant.

DEMOCRACY VERSUS MERITOCRACY

The U.S. Declaration of Independence states unequivocally at the very beginning, "all men are created equal." The conviction in the equality among men forms the basis of Western democratic governments-government of the people, by the people, and for the people. Such libertarian thinking has deep roots in the history of Western philosophy. In Two Treatises of Civil Government, Locke maintains that before there were any states to make statutes, men were aware of a natural law, which taught that all men were equal and independent.

"These men, with no earthly superior above them, are in a state of liberty, but not a state of licence."In his book, A Theory of Justice, John Rawls (1971) promotes the adoption of a "veil of ignorance," which would ideally eliminate all the personal identifiers of each individual-male or female, black or white, rich or poor, intelligent or not-and return everyone to his or her original position of being equal with everyone else.

"Rawls believes that justice will come forth from a discussion by rational and equal people concerned with their own interests but without anyone being advantaged or disadvantaged". Western societies are democratic and horizontal, emphasizing public participation in the government, while Confucian societies are hierarchical and vertical, believing in meritocracy instead of democracy.

For more than a thousand years in the history of China, only top scholars after rigorous national exams became government officials. In Singapore today, the brightest young people are selected for education in world's top universities supported with government funding so they will become the next generation of worthy leaders. "Statecraft is an integral part of Confucian learning". The ideal Confucian officials are people with "inner sagehood and outer kingliness."

Equality in human relations is a foreign concept in Confucian thinking as he decreed three sets of subservient relationships: subjects should obey their kings, sons should obey their fathers, and wives should obey their husbands. Confucius was not a democrat as some Confucian scholars tend to believe.

CIVIL LIBERTIES VERSUS SOCIAL ORDER AND STABILITY

The concept of human rights was developed during the Enlightenment. The Bill of Rights as amendments to the U.S. Constitution marked a milestone in mankind's fight for civil liberties. Western democratic societies keep a watchful eye on the government to prevent it from encroaching upon those rights. The most recent example was the heated U.S. Congressional debate on the Bush administration's domestic spying programme.

In contrast, a salient feature of Confucian thinking in government is the primacy of political order. In China, the traditional assumption has been that personal order and the order of a society entail each other. Thus, in Confucian societies, governments expect respect and obedience to keep social order.

Social stability often takes precedence over civil liberties and is regarded as vital to the strength of a country and the welfare of its people. The Confucian order was built on traditional values and norms. Confucius's unwavering focus on social order and stability might have been the result of the endless wars China was embroiled in during his lifetime.

Thousands of years later, some Asian leaders could not agree more with the ancient Chinese philosopher. Fighting back criticism about too much control in his country, Lee Kuan Yew, first and former prime minister of Singapore who led the city-state for thirty-one years, said, "Without order and stability, nothing can be achieved". Lee was responsible for turning Singapore from a fishing village at the end of the Second World War into one of the cleanest and richest countries in the world today.

COMPETITION VERSUS HARMONY

Capitalism thrives on free competition on the market, which is supposed to drive economic growth even though such growth may be achieved at a social cost. Competition presupposes freedom and equality, but competition spawns conflicts as well-disputes between management and labour, hostile business takeovers, smearing political campaigns, fights in sports arenas, and even the constant race to be the most popular teen in high school.

As a result of competition, people are labeled as winners and losers. And the rule of competition decides that there are often more losers than winners, resulting in many unhappy people.

In some Asian societies such as China and Singapore, and even in some European countries such as Germany, comparative advertising is banned. In Japan and South Korea, state-guided capitalism softens real competition. "Harmony is at the core of the Chinese culture". Preferred methods of resolving conflicts are building consensus and making compromise rather than many voices competing.

"A pertinent contrast can be developed between the western liberal commitment to many voices and the traditional Chinese concern for a communitarian consensus as a social good". One values pluralism; the other harmony. The "promotion of harmony and goodwill among individuals and their families and community in the context of the five constants: ran, yi, li, zhi, and xin (humanity, righteousness, decorum, wisdom, and trust) is a social responsibility from the Confucian point of view".

However, the ancient Chinese sage would be flabbergasted to witness the transformations China is going through today. Since China ushered in the market economy and private enterprise, competition is becoming a new way of life, bringing relentless assault on traditional values and leaving the conservatives lamenting the decline in moral standards.

ADVERSARIAL WATCHDOG

Press in the West takes pride in being a watchdog of the government. The uncovering of the Watergate scandal has inspired young journalists to follow the footsteps of Bob Woodward and Carl Bernstein. Dan Rather's dogged pursuit of the truth in Bush's service in the National Guard cost his career. To deal with an inquiring press, government officials hide behind press secretaries.

In traditional societies, people tend to be in deference to their governments. In Confucian societies, the government is supposed to take care of the people, and the people are expected to respect the government. "Confucianism holds that man is born for uprightness, and that people's goodwill is essential for good government in the context of an intellectual democracy headed by a benevolent ruler".

Chinese "benevolent despotism" fascinated Western thinkers. In Confucian societies, the press becomes a tool for nation building. Even in Japan and South Korea, both democratic societies, press tends to keep cozy relationships with the government and is, thus, reduced to a lapdog.

The dichotomy of dominant Western and Eastern values does not imply that there are no overlapping areas between Western and Eastern cultures. There are Western philosophers such as Plato and Rousseau who put emphasis on the state and the collective rather than the individual and preferred rule by the elite, which is very close to the Confucian ideal of government.

In The Social Contract, Rousseau promotes public good and common interest instead of interests of individuals. In the East, there are also philosophical schools such as Taoism that focuses on individuality and extols the virtue of being free, free from the constraints of governments and institutions for the full and free development of the potential of each individual.

But these philosophical schools in the East or the West have not become the dominant influence in their respective cultures. By and large, contemporary Western societies extol freedom and individuality, while Asian societies emphasize interests of the collective and the concept of responsibility regardless of political systems.

Some critics may contend that few Asian societies today including China can be described as Confucian societies because of the influence from the West. Indeed, modernization has inevitably had an impact on Asian societies, especially the young, who are much more accepting of what is Western.

Tu Wei-ming said: "The Westernization of Confucian Asia, including Japan, the two Koreas, mainland China, Hong Kong, Taiwan, Singapore, and Vietnam, may have forever altered its spiritual landscape. But its indigenous resources, including Mahayana Buddhism, Daoism, Shintoism,

Shamanism, and other folk traditions, have the resiliency to resurface and make their presence known in the new syntheses."

Confucianism is neither a political system nor a religion; it is a way of thinking and a way of life. It is deep-rooted in the cultures of Confucian societies, and it is reflected in the decisions people make in their everyday lives, including the value of family ties, education, and hard work. A recent media farce in China provides a glimpse of the undisputable respect Confucius still enjoys in China today.

A Peking University professor was quoted in the media as saying that Zhang Ziyi, an internationally known Chinese actress, who was featured on the cover of an issue of Newsweek in 2005 and at the Oscar award ceremony in 2006, was greater than Confucius.

The statement, perceived as an insult to the Chinese culture, sparked a public outcry on the Internet condemning the professor. Bombarded with interview requests from the media, the professor had to post an article on his blog, claiming that he was misquoted by the media for sensationalism.

He explained that Confucius represented China's elite culture, while Zhang Ziyi represented its pop culture. The professor hoped that with the actress's international appeal, she could attract more worldwide interest in Confucianism.

An examination of dominant Eastern and Western values helps provide a more balanced foundation for building a new press model. A New Model: The Two-Dimensional Freedom Responsibility Coordinate System

THE SYSTEM

Based on earlier press models and on an analysis of the salient values of the Western and Eastern cultures, a new press model is proposed here, which is a two-dimensional coordinate grid with the horizontal axis denoting the degree of freedom in a press system and the vertical axis indicating how responsible a press system is. The system illustrates that a free press can be responsible or irresponsible, and that a press that is not free can also be responsible or irresponsible. Merrill also believes in the possible existence of responsible authoritarian systems and responsible libertarian systems.

THE TWO-DIMENSIONAL MODEL

The major difference between what is proposed here and most of the theories and models before it is that this proposed model has departed from the traditional one-dimensional models, which focus mainly on the degree of freedom in a press system, reflecting Western philosophical emphasis on the concept of freedom.

The proposed two-dimensional model, instead, has broadened the foundation of theory building to include a key Asian cultural emphasis on the concept of responsibility. The Asian emphasis on the concept of responsibility is not only a result of Confucian moral influence, but also a result of the socio-economic realities of Asia, where development journalism originated and is still being pursued and where guerrilla warfare or religious and ethnic rivalries can flare up as a result of provocative news articles.

And even in Hong Kong, where dominant discussions tend to focus on the survival of press freedom, Chief Executive Donald Tsang encouraged journalists to think about what was important to society rather than what was popular to readers at the 2005 News Awards ceremony.

Confucius's teachings mesh well with the aspirations of development journalists in Asia, who see the role of the press as agents for social change. Through their work, they want to improve the quality of life of their people. Pakistani media researcher Owais Aslam Ali (undated) analysed the major differences between Western news values and Asian news values, which he summarized as elitist press versus press for national development.

He pointed out the futility of Western news values in "the monumental uphill struggle" of the Third World toward economic progress. Given the diverse economic and social realities of the countries of the world, it is not difficult to see why different philosophies of journalism and news values exist around the world. Some Western libertarian thinkers also addressed the issue of responsibility, rationality, or limits in exercising freedom.

Locke gave impetus to the concept of "responsible individualism," predicated on a love of reason and the importance of natural law. According to Locke, individuals live in a social context and need order, not anarchy, for their own well-being.

"Therefore, reason serves as an automatic limitation on freedom. In order to guide themselves in living an orderly and moral life, which is the essence of humanity, rational people voluntarily give up much freedom". Even though well known for his libertarian ideas in his pamphlet On Liberty, Mill held an elitist view on entitlement to freedom. "Mill felt that his freedom principle was appropriate only in societies of relatively high educational standards in which people could rationally exercise freedom".

In the field of journalism, debates on press responsibility and accountability have never stopped, such as the work of the Hutchins' Commission, which gave rise to the social responsibility press theory, and the ongoing experimentation with civic or public journalism in the United States. If there is public concern over press responsibility, the concern should be addressed in building a new theoretical model.

The newly added dimension of press responsibility adds balance to existing press models by bringing in cultural values important not only to the West but also to the East, presents a fuller description of a press system, and helps address an important public concern over press responsibility and accountability.

DEFINING AND MEASURING PRESS RESPONSIBILITY

The immediate question that arises is the definition of responsibility as what is considered responsible in one culture may be viewed as irresponsible in another culture. The notion of responsibility is always culture-specific. Similar to the argument that all concepts of responsibility are relative, the concept of "a free press" is also relative, as there is no absolute freedom of the press in this world, not even in the United States.

Addressing press freedom worldwide, Merrill said, "... in fact, there are no free-press nations". Because of the challenges in setting the standards of a responsible press that can be universally accepted and in deciding who should have the authority in setting the standards, and because of media's aversion to the concept of "a responsible press" imposed from the outside as illustrated by the fate of the Hutchins' report and by the "survey methodology" section of the 2005 Freedom House report that practically equates press responsibility with government control, discussions about press responsibility often hit a dead end.

They do not have to be. Ali (undated) emphasized the watchdog role of the media in development journalism, warned against the discussions on Asian values in journalism being hijacked by government officials as justification for the control of the media, and urged Asian journalists, "who have been struggling to reduce government involvement in the media," to create a form of journalism relevant to the needs of their societies. Only then will the concept of Asian values have credibility, Ali wrote.

UNIVERSAL VALUES IN JOURNALISM

A starting point in exploring the standards of a responsible press can be the search for universal values in journalism, and the Hutchins' report can serve as a helpful reference, such as being accurate and providing balance and diversity of opinion in news coverage, acting as a watchdog of the government, businesses and all other powerful social institutions, addressing issues of public concern, covering all sectors of the society instead of just the prominent, and avoiding invasion of privacy and sensationalism.

If the list continues to include the elimination of hate speech, which is banned in Germany, and pornography, which is banned in the Muslim world, most of the Asian countries, and perhaps some African and South American countries as well, the exploration for universal standards of a responsible press will soon become controversial. And questions such as what is balanced to one may not seem to be balanced to another remain.

CURRENT COMMUNITY STANDARDS

To deal with such tricky issues in setting the standards of a responsible press, the standards used for deciding what is obscene can be borrowed-current community standards. If the majority of readers believe their press is responsible, then they have a responsible press. Vice versa, if the majority of readers believe their press is irresponsible, then they have an irresponsible press. As the concept of responsibility is highly cultural-specific, the best solution is to let the local population decide instead of imposing standards from the outside.

INDEX OF PRESS RESPONSIBILITY-A COMBINATION OF UNIVERSAL VALUES AND LOCAL STANDARDS

Based on accepted universal values in journalism, which may include truth, accuracy, and balance, and results of public opinion surveys on press responsibility, an index of press responsibility can be compiled for each country to help media researchers and students better analyse the characteristics of a particular press system. If survey results distort reality such as in a controlled society, where a survey of honest public opinion is not feasible, universal values in journalism can serve as primary checkpoints.

In the meantime, despite the fact that they sometimes serve as a helpful reference, the criteria of the Freedom House in determining the ratings of press freedom in each country should be revised to add balance to the current standards, which do not take into account media content. The current methodology examines the legal, political, and economic environment of the media, but not the results of those environments-media content.

The survey questions are predominantly negative. Data are not collected through systematic or scientific method but through arbitrary answers by a small group of hand-picked interviewees, including "correspondents overseas, staff and consultant travel, international visitors," and "specialists in geographic and geopolitical areas." Such data collection methods raise serious questions about both the reliability and validity of the results.

THE FOUR CORNERS AND FOUR QUADRANTS

If a pair of dotted diagonal lines are superimposed on the coordinate grid, four corners of the grid will appear, representing four extreme types of press systems-free and responsible, free but not responsible, not free but responsible, and not free and not responsible. As the four corners indicate maximum or minimum degrees of freedom and responsibility, very few press systems fall exactly on those four corners; most of the press systems will fall somewhere within the four quadrants.

FREE AND RESPONSIBLE

While it may be hard to find a perfect example of a free and socially responsible press, some media endeavors are definitely directed toward that goal, such as public broadcasting in Britain and the United States, the civic and public journalism in the United States, and community and development journalism in India and Pakistan. Even though these types of journalism do not represent the mainstream media in their respective societies, they are the free press's attempts to be responsible and relevant to its readers.

The press in this group is mostly free and chooses to avoid sensationalism and play a positive role in society on its own. With or without public funding, it provides mostly quality information and often a public servicefighting crime in neighborhoods, boosting voter turnout, and educating and empowering the poor rural population.

Depending on events of the day, its content can be a mixture of negative and positive stories. In well-developed and free media markets, the press can afford to choose to be responsible because such a press would be assured of market support if there is public demand for a free and responsible press. Even in underdeveloped societies such as those in South Asia, press responsibility in the form of development journalism can exist because of support from the vast rural audience. For the press to be free and responsible, the market has to demand it and has to be well developed enough to finance it.

FREE AND NOT RESPONSIBLE

It is not very difficult to find free but irresponsible press around the world, press that chases profits or power under the name of press freedom.

Under such press systems, the press is free to pursue whatever story sells on the market with little concern for the consequences of such reporting. In the race to be the first on the market, accuracy in reporting and ethical standards are often compromised.

If criticized for their low professional standards and lack of accountability, journalists in such media environment often invoke the defence of freedom of the press. Such press systems tend to exist in intensely competitive media markets, such as new democracies in Taiwan, Indonesia, the Philippines, and some East European countries, where media outlets mushroom and bring immense pressure on the media market and where new regulations are still taking shape.

Even in China where the press is becoming increasingly commercialized, tabloids, sensationalized news, or even made-up news stories are not hard to find. Such press systems may also exist in well-developed, saturated and consolidated media markets where it is very challenging to expand market share such as Hong Kong and Thailand.

Because of the profit-oriented nature of such press systems, media companies are regarded as moneymakers, regulated by market demand only. Circulations and ratings become the only measure of success.

Whatever sells is repeated in the media, resulting in over-coverage of some topics and events, such as celebrity journalism and press conferences, and the undercoverage of other less glamorous topics and events, such as poverty. Under such systems, the media spend far too much time covering and far too little time uncovering.

As they become pure businesses, such media are financed mostly with advertising dollars and subscriptions. Another form of press irresponsibility is the partisan press or political patronage of the press, in which case some press allows itself to be used as political tools especially when the democratic system is still young.

With a political power vacuum as a result of the dismantling of control mechanisms, political families, parties, or organizations often rush to take control of the media and use the media to advance their particular agendas, often employing such tactics as personal attacks or smear campaigns. Such a press tends to exist in free but less developed media markets as political patronage provides much needed financial support for the media.

Under such press systems, media content is often negative, full of political attacks in partisan press, or sex and violence in tabloids instead of stories about progress, which is often a long and less dramatic process. Tabloids and partisan press are typical products of such a press system.

RESPONSIBLE BUT NOT FREE

The very term seems to be an oxymoron. Critics may ask how a press can be classified as responsible if it is not free. The answer can depend on the definition of responsibility according to local community standards.

Such press systems tend to exist in more traditional societies where the emphasis is on the group rather than the individual and where cultural traditions or religions have a major impact on public life. Press in this group tends to stress the importance and interests of the country, society, community, and families rather than freedom and rights of individuals.

It tends to follow moral or religious principles and societal goals in news coverage rather than follow market demand because to publish what is perceived to be responsible is more important than to publish what sells. The emphasis is on publishing what is right versus the right to publish, which is the difference between what is ethical and what is legal.

The goals of such a press may vary from country to country, including social order and stability, economic development, or reinforcement of religious values. The press in this category tends to support these societal goals under government or public pressure, or both.

For example, in Saudi Arabia and much of the Islamic world, newspapers devote sections to the teachings or discussions of Islam while criticism of Islam is forbidden. And in most of the Islamic press, the content is very clean, free of pornography. Elsewhere in the world, many of the developing countries in Asia, Africa, and South America see national development as the top priority and expect the media to serve as a tool for nation building.

In Singapore, because of the fear of ethnic and religious riots and the importance of its relations with its neighbors, the press cannot report on issues concerning race, religion, or its neighbors to maintain order and stability.

If the majority of the people in these societies support those goals, then the press is responsible. However, in some cases, especially when a country is involved in a war, current community standards may prove unreliable when the public is caught up in a patriotic frenzy. When that happens, it would depart from the universal values in journalism, such as accuracy and balance.

Because it has special roles to play in society, press in this group may obtain financial support from the government, public or social institutions, or the church even though a major part of its income may still come from the market.

NOT FREE AND NOT RESPONSIBLE

The press in this group does not enjoy much freedom of operation, and the controls applied unilaterally by the government are most likely not supported by the people. The most typical examples are perhaps the press in North Korea and Turkmenistan, where there is very little information but plenty of glorifications of the state leaders in the press. Hardships endured by the people can hardly be found in the news media.

The press in this group is also prohibited from criticizing the government or exposing corruption. The press in this group does not have the freedom to make its own editorial decisions, and public opinion is suppressed. After a review of the different types of press systems, where should the Japanese press be plotted on the coordinate grid?

It should perhaps be placed somewhere close to the origin of the coordinate grid as being partly free and partly responsible. It is free from government control but not free from industry control. And if the press refrains from uncovering high-level scandals in the government or big corporations, it cannot be described as socially responsible.

But until the Japanese people start to reject their press, which is opposite to the fact that Japanese newspapers enjoy the highest circulations in the world, the press in Japan cannot be described as irresponsible either. A responsibility index as discussed earlier plus a more accurate press freedom rating can help determine the position of the Japanese press on the grid and the positions of the press in other countries.

A Dynamic Model

The proposed two-dimensional Freedom-Responsibility coordinate system attempts to provide a more balanced press model in explaining press systems around the world, measuring not only the degree of press freedom but also the level of press responsibility. The validity of the new model will be determined by how many press systems in the world it can satisfactorily describe and explain. But societies are constantly changing, and so are their press systems. One of the advantages of the new model is that it can accommodate such changes in the system.

For example, the American press seems to be trying to be more responsible and relevant to its readers while having some of its freedom curtailed because of the War on Terror.

Comparing with the press elsewhere in the world, the American press is best known for being free but not necessarily for being responsible.

The low credibility of the news media in repeated public opinion polls shows public dissatisfaction with media performance. Civic and public journalism seems to be pushing the American press toward more press responsibility when the press tries to be more relevant to its readers and more conscious of the role it can play in society, such as helping crime-fighting and boosting voter turnout.

And in the age of war on terror, the Bush administration is tightening up press access to information, citing national security concerns. It also launched an investigation into the leaking of the National security Agency's domestic spying programme to discourage such disclosure of information.

During the war in Iraq, the government controlled reporters' access on the battlefield with a system of embedded reporters. And the concentration of ownership also reduces the independence and freedom the press once had.

The press in China seems to be moving slowly in the opposite direction-freer but messier even though sometimes more relevant to its readers. The press in China used to follow only Party lines. Now it also has to follow market demand by addressing public concerns.

Some local papers target rural poverty by providing tips on how to grow better crops or how to generate cash by engaging in non-farming businesses. Competition, unheard of before the economic reforms, has given rise to diversity in the media. The Internet has provided a channel for news stories turned down by the traditional media. These changes are clearly pushing the Chinese press toward more freedom and responsibility.

However, competition also drives down the quality of news coverage and the ethical standards of journalists as sensationalism and bribery are prevalent. The Chinese press is in a state of flux as different factors are pulling it in different directions with deepening economic reforms. The most important factor, however, is still government policies. The press in Russia presents perhaps the most intriguing case for study as the degree of press freedom and responsibility shifted dramatically with the changing political climate of the country. Described as the prototype communist media, the press in the former Soviet Union was a political tool, following Lenin's ideal of press's functioning as collective agitator, propagandist, and organizer.

After the fall of communism, the press in Russia changed overnight from not free to completely free. Then under the presidency of Putin, press freedom in Russia was once again being curtailed. With a new president coming into the Kremlin, the status of press freedom in Russia is yet to be determined.

The proposed new Freedom-Responsibility model is dynamic not only because it can accommodate the changes within particular press systems, but also because it can reflect changes in the structure of the model. In the debate on press freedom and press responsibility in the West, the concept of press freedom often trumps the concept of press responsibility.

The same is true on the global scene as free news media in the West dominate the global information flow. The call for the New World Information and Communication Order from developing countries was drowned out in the West's battle cry for the free flow of information.

And the Freedom House measures press freedom, not press responsibility. Given the dominant position of press freedom in the coordinate system, the press freedom axis represents the yang arm of the coordinate system while the press responsibility axis stands for the yin arm of the system. The yang and yin axes complement each other, forming a balanced system.

However, the pendulum of history never stops swinging. Laozi, an ancient Chinese philosopher, sees reversal as the way the natural order operates: "everything that has gone far in one direction will move in the opposite direction, and to be in a low or weak position is to be in a state in which one will thrive". That is the law of the dialectics. If the abuse of press freedom becomes a global issue and the world's press is forced to be more responsible because of public pressure, there can be a paradigm change within the coordinate system with the concept of press responsibility becoming the dominant feature of the model and thus, the yang axis of the system, and the concept of press freedom becoming the yin axis of the system. But that may take a long time to occur even though such changes will never stop.

Confucius advocated the "middle path" and Aristotle promoted the "golden mean," each avoiding the extremes at either end. The same principle applies to press performance-there is neither absolute press freedom nor absolute press responsibility. The desirable middle path would be the optimal combination of press freedom with press responsibility, a blend of the West and the East.

The two-dimensional system proposed in this chapter is an attempt at exploring a more balanced model in studying press systems around the world. The major challenge in the application of the model would be the measurement of press responsibility in a press system. So far no effort is ever made in that regard, given the expected controversies it is bound to draw.

If media observers and researchers can agree that development journalism and press responsibility do not automatically translate into government control of the press, measuring press responsibility does not have to be a forbidden task. The compilation of a global press responsibility index can provide a helpful guide in studying the characteristics of a press system.

A good starting point can be the identification of universal values in journalism as discussed earlier. The more universal values societies can agree upon, the more reliable the index can be. "Current community standards" in the form of public opinion surveys offer a way of accommodating values specific to local culture.

Debates on universal values in journalism can be messy, but the results can be crystallizing and enlightening. With more research, media researchers from the East and the West may find more common ground than they expect. One weakness of the model is perhaps that Western and Confucian philosophies and values tend to dominate the discussions even though there are so many other religious and philosophical influences in the world. Therefore, this study is only exploratory in nature. It can be enriched and improved with perspectives from more cultures or serve as a starting point for future research.

In future research, alternative concepts or dichotomies can be explored in building new models, such as an observer-interventionist/activist dichotomy, or commercial-ideological dichotomy. The point of departure will depend on the angle of analysis and on the perspectives and approaches of researchers.

Chapter 3

Freedom of Speech and Information Privacy

Privacy is a popular word, and government attempts to "protect our privacy"are easy to endorse. Government attempts to let us "control ... information about ourselves"sound equally good: Who wouldn't want extra control? And what fair-minded person could oppose requirements of "fair information practices"?

The difficulty is that the right to information privacy--my right to control your communication of personally identifiable information about me--is a right to have the government stops you from speaking about me. We already have a code of "fair information practices,"and it is the First Amendment, which generally bars the government from controlling the communication of information (either by direct regulation or through the authorization of private lawsuits), whether the communication is "fair"or not. While privacy protection secured by contract is constitutionally sound, broader information privacy rules are not easily defensible under existing free speech law.

Of course, the Supreme Court and even lower courts can create new First Amendment exceptions or broaden existing ones; and if the courts did this for information privacy speech restrictions, can't say that I'd be terribly upset about the new exception for its own sake. Speech restrictions aimed at protecting individual privacy just don't get my blood boiling. Maybe they should, but they don't. Perhaps this is because, from a selfish perspective, I'd like the ability to stop others from talking about me, and while I wouldn't like their stopping me from talking about them, the trade-off might be worth it.

Nonetheless, I'm deeply worded about the possible downstream effects of any such new exception. Most of the justifications given for information privacy speech restraints are directly applicable to other speech controls that have already been proposed. If these justifications are accepted in the attractive case of information privacy speech restrictions, such a decision will be a powerful precedent for those other restraints and for still more that might be proposed in the future.

Thus, for instance, some argue that information privacy laws are defensible because they protect an intellectual property right in one's personal information. Such arguments don't fit well into the intellectual property exceptions to the First Amendment, which generally don't entitle anyone to restrict the communication of facts.

And if we are to consider extending the existing exceptions, we should also consider that an intellectual property rights rationale is already being used as an argument for other speech restrictions: the proposed database protection law, the attempts to expand the right of publicity, and more. Before wholeheartedly endorsing the principle that calling certain information "intellectual property"lets the government restrict speech communicating that information, we should think about the consequences of such an endorsement.

Similar problems confront the arguments that information privacy speech restrictions are constitutional because they restrain only commercial speech, restrain only speech that is not on matters of public concern, are narrowly tailored to a compelling government interest in protecting people's dignity, emotional tranquility, or safety, are needed to protect a countervailing civil right, or pass muster under a "context-sensitive balancing."

First, for these arguments to succeed, existing First Amendment precedents would have to be substantially stretched. Second, the stretching may make the doctrine loose enough to give new support to many other restrictions. Bans on sexually themed speech might become justified under a "no public concern"rationale. Campus speech codes might be justified under a "countervailing civil right"rationale or a "narrowly tailored to a compelling government interest"rationale.

Restrictions on online discussion about economic matters or on consumer complaints might be justified under a broadened commercial speech rationale. Restrictions on online distribution of information about encryption or drugs might be justified under a crime prevention rationale. And who knows what might be allowed under "context-sensitive balancing,"which has in practice long been a tool for judges to justify a wide range of speech restrictions?

In making these arguments, I will try to identify concrete, specific ways--doctrinal, political, and psychological--in which upholding certain kinds of information privacy speech restrictions could affect the protection of other speech. I will try to avoid making general slippery slope arguments of the "today this speech restriction, tomorrow the Inquisition"variety; the recognition of one free speech exception certainly does not mean the end of free speech generally, or else all would have been lost long ago.

But slippery slope concerns are still quite sensible, especially when accepting a proposed speech restriction entails accepting a principle that is broader than the particular proposal and that can logically cover many other kinds of restraints. Our legal system is based on precedent.

Our political life is in large measure influenced by arguments by analogy. And many people's normative views of free speech are affected by what courts say: If the legal system accepts the propriety of laws mandating "fair information practices,"people may becomes more sympathetic to legal mandates of, for instance, fair news reporting practices or fair political debate practices.

This chapter is an attempt to consider, as concretely as possible, the possible unintended consequences of various justifications for information privacy speech restrictions. I ultimately conclude that these consequences are sufficiently troubling that I must reluctantly oppose such information privacy rules. But I hope the chapter will also be useful to those who are committed to supporting information privacy speech restrictions, but would like to design their arguments in a way that will minimize the risks that I identify; and even to those who welcome the possibility that information privacy speech restrictions may become a precedent for other restrictions, because they believe the Court has generally gone too far in protecting, say, nonpolitical speech or speech that injures the dignity of others. Thinking ahead about the possible unintended implications of a proposal--even, and perhaps especially, if it seems viscerally appealing--is always worthwhile.

CONTRACT

PERMISSIBLE SCOPE

To begin with, one sort of limited information privacy law—contract law applied to promises not to reveal information—is eminently defensible under existing free speech doctrine. The Supreme Court explicitly held in Cohen v. Cowles Media that contracts not to speak are enforceable with no First Amendment problems. Enforcing people's own bargains, the Court concluded (I think correctly), doesn't violate those people's rights, even if they change their minds after the bargain is struck.

Some have criticized this conclusion on the grounds that it slights the interests of the prospective listeners, and this criticism has some force. Still, I think that ultimately the free speech right must turn on the rights of the speakers, and that it's proper to let speakers contract away their rights—and certainly this is the view that the Cohen v. Cowles Media Court took. Insisting that people honour their bargains is a constitutionally permissible "code of fair practices," whether information practices or otherwise.

And such protection ought not be limited to express contracts, but should also cover implied contracts (though, as will be discussed below, there are limits to this theory). In many contexts, people reasonably expect—because of custom, course of dealing with the other party, or all the other factors that are relevant to finding an implied contract—that part of what their contracting partner is promising is confidentiality.

This explains much of why it's proper for the government to impose confidentiality requirements on lawyers, doctors, psychotherapists, and others: When these professionals say "I'll be your advisor," they are implicitly promising that they'll be confidential advisors, at least so long as they do not explicitly disclaim any such implicit promise.

Laws that explicitly infer such contracts from transactions in which there's no social convention of confidentiality are somewhat more troublesome, especially if they require relatively formal disclaimers. Imagine, for instance, a law providing that all questions by reporters will be interpreted as implicitly promising not to quote the source by name in a published article, unless the source consents in writing after being given full disclosure of the true purpose for which the quote is to be used.

Or consider a law providing that people who buy a product implicitly promise to give the seller equal space to respond to any negative article they publish about the product, unless the seller consents in writing after being given full disclosure of the true purpose for which the product is being bought.

Though journalists could avoid the restriction by getting the requisite explicit consent, the request for the consent may deter many of the sources and especially many of the sellers; and this in turn may deter journalists from publishing hostile reviews or stories that include quotes which show the sources in a bad light.

These concerns may justify treating the Cohen v. Cowles Media principle as applicable only to those implied contracts where confidentiality really is part of most people's everyday expectations. This would mean the implicit contract theory could uphold laws that by default prevent lawyers, doctors, psychiatrists, sellers of medical supplies, and possibly sellers of videos and books from communicating information about their customers; but it wouldn't uphold laws that by default prevent reporters (who are notorious for communicating embarrassing things, not keeping them confidential) from revealing what was said to them, prevent consumers from reviewing products, or prevent sellers of groceries or shoes from communicating who bought what from them. I doubt that most of us expect that someone selling us our food is implicitly promising to keep quiet about what they sold us.

On the other hand, I'm not sure that such a narrow application of Cohen v. Cowles Media is proper or ultimately workable.

It's often hard to determine exactly what most people expect. When someone buys a video, especially a video whose title he wouldn't want associated with his name, he probably assumes that the video store won't publicize the purchase, at least in part because a video store that does publicize such purchases would lose a lot of business. But is he assuming that the video store is promising not to publicize such a purchase? He probably isn't even thinking about this.

If he is assuming such a promise, is he assuming that the video store is promising not to communicate information about such a purchase at all, or only promising not to pass it along to the public or his neighbors, while reserving the right to communicate it to others in the same business? Again, most buyers probably have not even thought about the matter. One advantage of statutory default rules is precisely that they clarify people's obligations instead of leaving courts to guess what people likely assumed.

So I tentatively think that a legislature may indeed enact a law stating that certain legislatively identified transactions should be interpreted as implicitly containing a promise of confidentiality, unless such a promise is explicitly and prominently disclaimed by the offeror, and the contract together with the disclaimer is accepted by the offeree. True, this might justify laws that treat reporters as implicitly promising that they won't reveal or even quote their sources, which troubles me.

But so long as the implicit promise is genuinely disclaimable, I'm not too troubled. Even if this might eventually lead to the reporter hypothetical, I don't think too much would be lost; and what is gained from allowing statutorily defined default nondisclosure rules is the clear enforceability of promises that often are reasonably inferred by one of the contracting parties, and that can be important parts of the bargain.

Furthermore, though Cohen v. Cowles Media involved traditional enforcement of a promise through a civil suit, there should be no constitutional problem with the government enforcing such promises through administrative actions, or using special laws imposing presumed or even punitive damages for breaches of such promises.

I suspect that even with purely contractual remedies, the threat of class action suits could be a powerful deterrent to breaches of information privacy contracts by e-commerce sites, especially since the suits would create a scandal: In the highly competitive Internet world, a company could lose millions in business if people hear that it's breaking its confidentiality promises. But I think it would be constitutional for the government to try to increase contractual compliance either by providing an extra incentive for aggrieved parties to sue or by bringing a complaint itself, Though breach of contract has traditionally been seen as a purely private wrong, to be remedied through a private lawsuit, it's similar enough—especially when it's willful—to fraud or false advertising that there's nothing startling about a government agency such as the Federal Trade Commission prosecuting some such breaches itself.

The great free speech advantage of the contract model is that it does not endorse any right to "stop people from speaking about me." Rather, it endorses a right to "stop people from violating their promises to me."

One such promise may be a promise not to say things, and perhaps there may even be special defaults related to such promises or special remedies for breaches of such promises. But in any event, the government is simply enforcing obligations that the would-be speaker has himself assumed.

And such enforcement, in my view, poses little risk of setting a broad precedent for many further restrictions, precisely because it is founded only on the consent of the would-be speaker, and thus cannot justify the many other restraints-such as the Communications Decency Act, database protection legislation, and so on—to which the speaker has not consented.

LIMITATIONS

Contract law protection, though, is distinctly limited, in two ways. First, it only lets people restrict speech by parties with whom they have a speech-restricting contract, express or implied. If I make a deal with a newspaper reporter under which he promises not to identify me as a source, I can enforce the deal against the reporter and the reporter's employer, whom the reporter can bind as an agent. But if a reporter at another news outlet learns this information, then that outlet can publish it without fear of a breach of contract lawsuit.

Likewise, there are no First Amendment problems with an employer suing an employee for breach of an express or implied nondisclosure agreement, but if the employee leaks the information to a newspaper, the employer can't sue that newspaper, at least under the Cohen v. Cowles Media theory. The newspaper simply hasn't agreed to anything that would waive its First Amendment rights, which is the premise on which Cohen v. Cowles Media rests. The disclosure tort would similarly not be justifiable under a contract theory.

Second, Cohen v. Cowles Media cannot validate speech-restrictive terms that the government compels a party to include in a contract; the case at most validates government-specified defaults that apply unless the offeror makes clear that these terms aren't part of the offered deal.

Thus, while the government may say "Cyberspace sales contracts shall carry an implied warranty that the seller promises not to reveal the buyer's personal information," it may not add "and this implicit warranty may not be waived, even by a prominent statement that is explicitly agreed to by a customer clicking on an `I understand, and agree to the contract in spite of this' button."

This flows directly from the rationale on which Cohen v. Cowles Media rests: "The parties themselves... determine the scope of their legal obligations, and any restrictions which may be placed on the publication of truthful information are self-imposed." A merchant's express promise of confidentiality is "self-imposed"; so, one can say, is an implicit promise, when the merchant had the opportunity to say "by the way, I am not waiving my rights to speak about this transaction and am thus not promising confidentiality" but didn't do so.

But when someone is legally barred from communicating, even if he explicitly told his contracting partner that he was making no such promise, then such an obligation is hardly "self-imposed" or determined by mutual agreement. Thus, I certainly do not claim that a contractual approach to information privacy, even with a large dollop of implied contract, is a panacea for information privacy advocates. As Paul Schwartz and others have pointed out, there is much that information privacy advocates may want but that contract will not provide. I claim only that contractual solutions are a constitutional alternative and may be the only constitutional alternative, not that they are always a particularly satisfactory alternative.

GOVERNMENT CONTRACTS

Cohen v. Cowles Media does not decide to what extent the government, acting as contractor, may require people to sign speech-restrictive contracts as a condition of getting data from the government itself. This question raises thorny issues of unconstitutional conditions and often of the government's right to restrict access to government records that have historically been in the public domain (such as court records).

Unfortunately, the Supreme Court case that some thought would help resolve this matter was decided on procedural grounds, and the dicta in the many opinions in that case shed little light on exactly where the Court would have come down had it confronted the question on the merits. I deal with this issue by setting it aside.

CONTRACTS WITH CHILDREN

Finally, this discussion of contracts presupposes that both parties are legally capable of entering into the contract and of accepting a disclaimer of any implied warranty of confidentiality. If a cyber-consumer is a child, then such an acceptance might not be valid. This is also a difficult issue, but one that is outside the scope of this Chapter.

PROPERTY

INTELLECTUAL PROPERTY RULES AS SPEECH RESTRICTIONS

Partly because of the limitations of the contract theory, many information privacy advocates argue that people should be assigned a property right in personal information about themselves. Such a property approach would bind everyone, and not just those who are in contractual privity with the person being talked about.

Database operators would have to stop communicating information about people unless people give permission, even though the database operators have never promised, expressly or implicitly, to keep silent. Likewise, people could stop newspapers from publishing stories about them, even if the information was gleaned through interviews with third parties or was taken (with no contractual constraints) from public records.

Calling a speech restriction a "property right," though, doesn't make it any less a speech restriction, and it doesn't make it constitutionally permissible. Broad, pre-New York Times v. Sullivan libel laws can be characterized as protecting a property right in reputation; in fact, some states consider reputation a property interest.

The right to be free from interference with business relations, including interference by speech urging a boycott as in NAACP v. Claiborne Hardware, is often seen as a property right. A recent attempt at banning flag burning rested on the argument that the flag is the intellectual property of the United States, and that flag desecration thus violated property rights.

Restrictions on speech that uses cultural symbols in ways that the cultures find offensive might likewise be reframed as property rights in those symbols. A ban on all unauthorized biographies, whether of former child prodigies, movie stars, or politicians, can be seen as securing a property interest in the details of those people's lives.

Similarly, an early right of publicity case took the view that people who aren't public figures have the exclusive right to block all photos and portraits of themselves, with no exceptions for news stories.

Each of these "property rights," though, would remain a speech restriction. A property right is, among other things, the right to exclude others; an intellectual property right in information is the right to exclude others from communicating the information—a right to stop others from speaking.

Like libel law, intellectual property law is enforced almost entirely through private litigation, but like libel law, it's still a government-imposed restriction on speech. Some such restrictions may be permissible because there's some substantive reason why it's proper for the government to restrict such speech, but not because they are intellectual property fights.

The question isn't (as some suggest) "who should own the property right to personal information?" Rather, it's whether personal information should be treated as property at all—whether some "owner" should be able to block others from communicating this information, or whether everyone should be free to speak about it.

EXISTING RESTRICTIONS AS SUPPOSED PRECEDENTS

The Court has, of course, upheld some intellectual property rights against First Amendment challenge, acknowledging that they are speech restrictions but holding that those restrictions were constitutional.

In all these precedents, though, the Court has stressed a key point: The restrictions did not give the intellectual property owners the power to suppress facts. And this power to suppress facts is exactly the power that information privacy speech restrictions would grant.

Copyright Law

Harper & Row v. Nation Enterprises, which held that copyright law is constitutional, is the best example of this. Under copyright law, I may not publish a book that includes more than a modicum of creative expression from your book, even though my book is neither obscene nor libelous nor commercial advertising; such a restriction, Harper & Row held, is indeed a speech restriction, but a permissible one.

But the main reason Harper & Row gave for this conclusion is that copyright law does not give anyone a right to restrict others from communicating facts or ideas. "[C]opyright's idea/expression dichotomy strike[s] a definitional balance between the First Amendment and the Copyright Act by permitting fee communication off acts while still protecting an author's expression." "No author may copyright his ideas or the facts he narrates.

"Copiers "possess an unfettered right to use any factual information revealed in [the original]," though they may not copy creative expression.

There ought not be "abuse of the copyright owner's monopoly as an instrument to suppress facts." "In view of the First Amendment protections already embodied in the Copyright Act's distinction between copyrightable expression and uncopyrightable facts and ideas," copyright law is constitutional.

Under the copyright exception to free speech protection, then, speech that borrows creative expression is restrictable, but speech that borrows only facts remains free. This limitation on the copyright exception is both theoretically and practically significant.

Theoretically, this limitation is what leaves speakers ample alternative channels for communicating their message—speakers still possess "an unfettered right to use any factual information" that they please. Practically, people do indeed take advantage of this limitation.

If a historian spent years of effort uncovering some remarkable, hitherto unknown facts, you may freely use those facts, as historians indeed do (though ethical rather than legal concerns may dictate that the users give credit to the original discoverer).

Exactly where to draw the line between idea and expression is sometimes uncertain, but there are fewer uncertainties about the line between fact and expression; people who don't care about using the original author's rhetorical flourishes can definitely communicate facts that they've learned from others' work.

Trademark Law

Likewise with trademark law. Though trademark law restricts certain uses of trademarks in advertising a product or on the cover of the product, it does not prohibit speech that communicates facts or opinions about the product, even if the speech uses the product's name.

You are free to write a book about the Coca-Cola Company—a book that will be commercially sold, but that is itself not commercial speech because it's not commercial advertising—or a book describing the nutritional qualities of various soft drinks, or even a novel in which the main character constantly drinks Diet Cokes.

Likewise, if you're distributing or selling product reviews or a table mapping product names to cost and quality, you don't need permission from the trademark owner. Even in ads, factually accurate statements about the relationship of your products to others' products are permitted, either because they are in context not misleading or because they fall under the rubric of "nominative fair use."

The new federal trademark dilution statute, which has not yet been considered by the Court, also follows this principle; it is limited to commercial advertising, and even there provides a fair use defence.

Even the Gay Olympics case, which involved an unusually broad quasi-trademark law that gave the U.S. Olympic Committee the exclusive right to use the word "Olympic" for advertising and promotional purposes, stressed this point: "By prohibiting the use of one word for particular purposes, neither Congress nor the USOC has prohibited the [plaintiff] from conveying its message."

The case did not involve any congressional attempt to let the USOC stop people from discussing the Olympics, conveying facts about the Olympics, writing fiction about the Olympics, and so on. Even given this limitation, the law considered in the Gay Olympics case has been criticized as going too far, and I generally agree with these criticisms. But even if the law improperly gave the USOC too much power, it didn't give it the power to stop the communication of facts.

Right of Publicity Law

The same is true of Zacchini v. Scripps-Howard Broadcasting Co., in which the Supreme Court endorsed a narrow subset of the right of publicity: a right to block others from retransmitting one's entire performance. Zacchini concluded that a TV station's rebroadcast of Hugo Zacchini's entire human cannonball act was restrictable for the same reasons that copyright infringement was restrictable; and, as it would eventually do as to copyright, the Court stressed that the law did not restrict the communication of facts.

The case would have been "very different," the Court said, if "respondent had merely reported that petitioner was performing at the fair and described or commented on his act, with or without showing his picture on television"; liability was permissible because it was based not just on for-profit "reporting of events" but on "broadcast[ins] or publish[ing] an entire act for which the performer ordinarily gets paid."

The Supreme Court has never confronted the broader right to restrict speech that uses one's name or likeness;

Zacchini explicitly stressed that it wasn't deciding anything about this right, and though some courts and commentators have omitted this critical limitation and have cited Zacchini as generally "hold[ing] that the right of publicity is constitutional," such a characterization is mistaken. But even to the extent that lower courts have recognized such a right, they too have adopted limiting principles that keep the right from restraining the communication of facts.

To begin with, though the right of publicity is sometimes described as a right to stop others from using one's name, likeness, and other attributes of identity "in commerce" or "for trade purposes," courts and legislatures have long recognized that use of name or likeness "in news reporting, commentary, entertainment, or in works of fiction or nonfiction" must be excluded.

These uses are sold in commerce and in trade, but they are nonetheless protected from right of publicity claims, in large part because of free speech concerns. The right is not allowed to stop the communication of facts about a celebrity, even if it is allowed to block advertising or merchandising that merely tries to associate the advertiser or the consumer with a celebrity.

Moreover, even the use of name or likeness in an advertisement that is incidental to the permitted uses—for instance, a billboard advertising an unauthorized biography, which will necessarily use the subject's name and probably likeness—is likewise excluded from the right of publicity, though it's clearly "in commerce" and "for trade purposes." This again relates directly to the need to prevent the suppression of facts.

Letting Elizabeth Taylor block the unauthorized use of her name in ads for clothing would rarely substantially interfere with the manufacturer's ability to convey the facts about the clothing. Letting her block the use of her name in ads for an unauthorized biography, however, would mean that the biographer couldn't communicate to potential buyers the critical fact that the book is about Taylor. The right of publicity may have gotten too big, but even it basically respects the principle that there ought to be no "abuse of the [intellectual property] owner's monopoly as an instrument to suppress facts"; supporters of property rights in facts thus can't get much analogical support out of it. For whatever it's worth, the few cases that have considered right of publicity claims based on the sale of databases containing personal information have rejected such claims.

Misappropriation and Trade Secret Law

The above discussion has covered all the intellectual property speech restrictions that the Court has upheld against a First Amendment challenge. There are two other quasi-intellectual-property rules that may purport to confer limited property rights in facts, but the Court has never considered whether these speech restrictions are constitutional.

The first such rule is the right to be free from "unfair"misappropriation of hot news (and possibly of other information). This right was recognized by the Court in 1918 in International News Service v. Associated Press as a matter of pre-Erie federal common law, but has been mostly rejected since then, most prominently by the Restatement (Third) of Unfair Competition.

Perhaps because this tort has largely (though not entirely) withered, the Court has never decided whether it passes muster under the First Amendment. Certainly the 1918 decision recognizing the tort didn't confront a First Amendment defence, and in any event First Amendment protections have been dramatically strengthened since then. I believe that if the Court does confront this question, it should conclude that such a right to stop others from communicating hot news is indeed an unconstitutional content-based restriction on fully protected speech.

The second such quasi-property right is secured by trade secret law. Trade secret protection generally flows from a contract, express or implied, between the trade secret owner and the defendant who is threatening to use or expose the secret; in such a case, Cohen v. Cowles Media strongly suggests that the defendant can be held to the bargain.

Occasionally, trade secret claims may be based on illegal acquisition (for instance, through a trespass) by the defendant; certainly such acquisition can be punished without First Amendment difficulties. The serious First Amendment problems arise when a trade secret owner seeks to restrict the speech of those who are not in contractual privity with it, for instance when a company whose employees leaked secret information to a newspaper wants to enjoin the newspaper from publishing the information.

The newspaper has never promised anyone not to speak about this, so Cohen v. Cowles Media doesn't apply; the speech restriction can be justified only on the theory that the leaker's initial violation of his confidentiality promise bars otherwise innocent third parties from reporting on the leaked information.

The same issue arises in other confidential information contexts, for instance when a newspaper publishes information illegally leaked by a government employee, or illegally taped by someone who then passed along the tape recording.

The Supreme Court has never decided whether such speech restrictions are constitutional, and lower courts are divided on the subject. I think those courts that come out against such speech restrictions have it right: Speech by people who have never promised to remain quiet about something may not be suppressed simply because someone else wrongfully revealed the information to them.

Newspapers must be able to publish leaked information (at least absent some overwhelming national security concerns), even if the leaker breached a contract or even broke the law; a contrary rule would dramatically undermine newspapers'ability to report. Intercepting confidential communications is properly outlawed, but a newspaper need not stay silent about such communications if they come into the newspaper's hands.

People shouldn't be legally forbidden from telling their friends the truth about someone's medical condition (for instance, that the friend's prospective lover is suffering from a contagious disease) even if the information originally came from a source who had no right to reveal it (such as the prospective lover's doctor).

Thus, there are no existing First Amendment exceptions that justify restrictions on communication of hot news and restrictions on the publication of illegally leaked facts. One could, of course, argue that the Court should create such new exceptions, but one can't argue that these exceptions already provide support for information privacy speech restrictions. Rather, it is Supreme Court recognition of a property-rights-based First Amendment exception for information privacy speech restrictions that would substantially strengthen the calls for a hot news exception and an illegally leaked facts exception.

There are other limitations on many of these intellectual property rights that make any analogies to information privacy speech restrictions quite doubtful: For instance, copyright law and the Zacchini right are in large measure justified as necessary incentives for authors to create new works; likewise, most of trademark law and most of right of publicity law apply only to commercial advertising.

But the core principle at the heart of all these restrictions is that they create a fairly narrow right that may affect the form of people's speech but ought not prevent people from communicating facts. Any putative right in one's personal information can thus be adopted by analogy only if one is willing to relax this limitation, a limitation that is critical to protecting free speech.

UPHOLDING INFORMATION PRIVACY SPEECH RESTRICTIONS UNDER A PROPERTY THEORY

Avoiding "free-riding" and Unjust Enrichment

Some argue for property fights in personal information on functional grounds: Those who communicate personal information about others are engaging in a sort of free riding, enriching themselves without compensating the people whose existence makes their enrichment possible; and property rights, the argument goes, are the way to avoid this free riding. As one article argued, in 1988 three leading credit bureaus made almost $1 billion put together from selling credit information, but "ow much did these credit bureaus pay consumers for the information about them that they sold? Zero."This, though, cannot be the justification for restricting speech, unless we are willing to dramatically redefine free speech law.

Newspapers and radio and TV news programs, after all, make billions from stories that are made possible only by the existence of their subjects. The essence of news is precisely the reporting of things done or discovered by others; the essence of the news business is profiting from reporting on things done or discovered by others.

But news organizations generally don't pay a penny to the subjects of their stories--in fact, it is seen as unethical for news organs, though not entertainment organs, to pay subjects. Likewise, unauthorized biographers and historians make money from publishing information about others, information that only exists because those people exist.

Comedians who tell jokes about people make a living from those they mock. In a sense, all these speakers are free-riding: They are taking advantage of something that relates to someone else and that exists only because of that other person's existence, and they aren't paying that person for it (though they are usually investing a good deal of time, money, and effort in the project-this free-riding is certainly not mere literal copying). But our legal system correctly allows a great deal of free-riding.

It has never been a principle of tort law that all free-riding is illegal, or that all such enrichment is unjust. In the words of the Restatement (Third) of Unfair Competition, [T]he principle of unjust enrichment does not demand restitution of every gain derived from the efforts of others.

A small shop, for example, may freely benefit from the customers attracted by a nearby department store, local manufacturer may benefit from increased demand attributable to the promotional efforts of a national manufacturer of similar goods, and a newspaper may benefit from reporting on local athletic teams. Similarly, the law has long recognized the right of a competitor to copy the successful products and methods of others absent an infringement of patent, copyright, or trademark rights.

And it has certainly not been a principle of free speech law that speech may be restricted simply to assure the subject of the speech a piece of the profits. What intellectual property law has generally tried to prevent is not free-riding as such, but free-riding of a particular kind: the use not just of something that relates to another, but the use of the product of another's substantial labour, and even that only in limited cases.

Such a use runs the risk of dramatically diminishing the incentive to engage in such labour, which is what makes the defendant's enrichment socially harmful rather than merely unjust in some abstract moral sense. This concern is at the heart of copyright law, of the right to prevent the unauthorized transmission of an entire act, and to a large extent of trade secret law. But this concern does not apply to personal information about people, where the incentive arguments don't really apply.

Again, I stress that my critique here only relates to the intellectual property justification for information privacy speech restrictions; perhaps there are some other justifications that can support such speech restraints. But the fact that information distributors are profiting while the subjects of the information does not itself provide such support.

Internalizing Costs and Maximizing Aggregate utility

Another functional argument often made on behalf of a property rights theory of information privacy speech restrictions is that the property rights model is the best way to require speakers to "internalize the cost"of their speech "by paying those whose data is used."Such internalizing, the theory goes, would maximize aggregate social utility: By "recogniz[ing the] diversity"of people's desires for information privacy, the property rule could make sure that information about each person is communicated only if the benefit to the speaker exceeds the felt cost to the subject.

The principle of free speech law, though, is that speakers do not have to internalize all the felt costs that flow from the communicative impact of their speech. The NAACP didn't have to internalize the tangible economic (not just emotional) cost that its boycott imposed on the Claiborne County merchants. Movie producers don't have to internalize the tangible cost that their movies impose on victims of viewers who commit copycat crimes. Cohen, Johnson, and Hustler didn't have to internalize the emotional distress cost that their speech inflicted on passersby or on its subject.

Again, if there's an independent reason why this speech should be treated differently from other speech, for instance because it falls within some new free speech exception, then the law may require that its costs be internalized. But the desire to maximize aggregate social utility doesn't itself justify a new exception; on the contrary, it's only the new exception that would legitimize speech restraints aimed at maximizing aggregate social utility.

THE POTENTIAL CONSEQUENCES

I have explained why I think that merely calling information privacy speech restrictions "property rights" doesn't advance the First Amendment inquiry, why such speech restrictions aren't justifiable under any existing intellectual property exceptions, and why such monopolies in facts, not just expression, are theoretically troubling.

Of course, despite all this, the Court is always free to carve out a new First Amendment exception or broaden an existing one; my goal now is to explain why I think this would be a bad idea.

Speech that reveals private information is not the only speech that some want to restrict under the property rights model. As many leading commentators have recently argued, we are now in the midst of a broad movement that uses intellectual property rhetoric to broaden people's rights to restrict others' speech. The proposed database protection legislation would give database owners a form of property right in collections of information.

Some recent cases have revived the misappropriation tort, recognizing a property right in news. Many recent cases have broadened trademark owners' rights to restrict parodies and other transformative uses (though fortunately some courts seem to be resisting this trend). Copyright terms are being lengthened and some argue that fair use is being unduly contracted.

The right of publicity is growing to include any advertising, merchandising, and even interior decor that reminds people of a celebrity, even if it doesn't use the celebrity's name or likeness. Many have criticized this creeping propertization of speech, often on First Amendment grounds. They have decried the tendency of many courts to merely label speech restrictions "property rules" as if such a re-labeling could eliminate the First Amendment objections.

They have pointed out that cases upholding the propriety of some speech restrictions—such as the core of copyright law, traditional trademark law aimed at preventing consumer confusion, or the right to control the rebroadcast of one's entire act—don't necessarily validate all new restrictions that one might call "copyright," "trademark," or "fight of publicity" (much less "intellectual property" generally).

But if the arguments that "it's not a speech restriction, it's an intellectual property rule" or "the Supreme Court has upheld property fights in information, so property rights in information are constitutional" are accepted for information privacy speech restrictions, they will be considerably strengthened as to the other restrictions, too.

If, for instance, courts hold that information privacy speech restrictions are proper because they merely "internalize th[e] cost" of their speech "by paying those whose data is used," it will be easy to argue the same as to other "data" that someone may say is his. Likewise, if courts hold that such speech restrictions are permissible because the restrictions encourage "a process of voluntary exchange, [that,] like the free market generally, would assure that 'human satisfaction as measured by aggregate consumer willingness to pay... is maximized,'" the same argument could apply to broad new rights in all sorts of information.

Of course, courts already can, if they really want to, uphold new intellectual property rules by analogy to the existing old ones; but the creation of yet another kind of intellectual property speech restriction—and one that promises to be quite popular—will strengthen the argument.

Ask yourself: Would the courts be less likely to accept the notion of property in personal information if trademark and right of publicity had never existed, and the only intellectual property speech restriction were copyright? Probably yes; there are too many distinctions between personal information and copyrightable expression for this one analogy to be that helpful.

But as other potential analogies are added, the argument becomes easier—one can say "this proposal is sound because it's like precedent A in one respect, like precedent B in another respect, and like precedent C in a third respect," so even if the proposal is unlike any particular precedent, it can be seen by observers as similar to their aggregate. If this is so, then the case for new intellectual property speech restraints would be further strengthened by the recognition of yet one more kind of such speech restriction to which people can analogize.

Moreover, a new exception for a property right in personal information would be the first (but I fear not the last) First Amendment authorization for a property right in pure facts. Right now the database protection proposals are being confronted with the objection that the law does not generally recognize intellectual property rights that restrict communication of facts.

The analogy to copyright law actually works against those proposals, because they seek to protect exactly what the Court in Foist Publications, Inc. v. Rural Telephone Service Co. said copyright doesn't protect, and they seek to do exactly what the Court in Harper & Row said would violate the First Amendment—use an "[intellectual property] monopoly as an instrument to suppress facts."

But if information privacy speech restrictions are upheld, they would provide an excellent new analogy for the database protection bill supporters. The same is true for the asserted right to property in hot news, which is today subject to powerful free speech attack, but which would be strengthened if the courts accept another property right in facts.

Now perhaps my parade of horribles isn't so horrible; maybe we should have more property rights in facts, which is to say restrictions or speech that communicates facts. Or if I am right to be skeptical of such new property rights, perhaps supporters of property rights in personal information can come up with a narrow justification for those particular rights that will provide little precedential support for the other proposals.

Nonetheless, people who are worried about the general trend towards propertization of information should look very carefully at even those proposals that might at first seem benign and even just; such proposals could have effects far beyond the context in which they are first suggested.

COMMERCIAL SPEECH

There's an independent reason why this speech should be treated differently from other speech, for instance because it falls within some new free speech exception, then the law may require that its costs be internalized. But the desire to maximize aggregate social utility doesn't itself justify a new exception; on the contrary, it's only the new exception that would legitimize speech restraints aimed at maximizing aggregate social utility.

THE POTENTIAL CONSEQUENCES

It was already explained why I think that merely calling information privacy speech restrictions "property rights" doesn't advance the First Amendment inquiry, why such speech restrictions aren't justifiable under any existing intellectual property exceptions, and why such monopolies in facts, not just expression, are theoretically troubling. Of course, despite all this, the Court is always free to carve out a new First Amendment exception or broaden an existing one; my goal now is to explain why I think this would be a bad idea. Consider a recent example of the government trying to regulate cyberspace speech about economic matters on the grounds that it's "commercial speech."

In Taucher v. Born, several operators of commodities-themed Web sites successfully sued to set aside a prior restraint system which bars people from distributing for profit any unlicensed speech that relates "to the value of or the advisability of commodity trading" or that contains "analyses or reports" about commodities.

And the license that speakers must get to be allowed to speak isn't just a modest tax; the Commodities Futures Trading Commission can refuse a license if it finds "good cause" to do so, and speaking without a license is illegal. Nor is this speech restriction limited to individualized, person-to-person professional advice: The regulation is broad enough to cover people who "never engage in individual consultations with their customers" and who "under no circumstances make trades for their customers."

The law essentially restricts the Web equivalent of books and newspapers about commodity training—it's as if the government claimed the right to refuse the Wall Street Journal a license to publish articles about the market.

As it happens, the law specifically excludes publishers who publish such data "incidental[ly]" as part of a broader news enterprise of "general and regular dissemination," so the Journal can sleep easy—and the CFTC can sleep easy without the risk of incurring the ire of established, powerful news organs. But under the logic of the law, newspapers and book publishers could also be subject to a prior restraint system, just as the small commodities-focused electronic publishers were subject to it until the court's ruling.

The CFTC argued that speech about commodities is mere "commercial speech," but the court correctly rejected this: "The plaintiffs' publications in this case do not propose any commercial transaction between the plaintiffs and their customers." If, however, the commercial speech doctrine had been extended to cover the sale of speech about a business's clients, the court's decision might well have been different.

After all, the Web business journalist who writes about commodities is likewise selling information that's primarily of economic concern, and that has little to do with broad political debates. If that's enough to deny free speech protection to communications about customers, it may be enough to deny such protection to communications about commodities.

Consider another example: disgruntled homebuyers putting up signs criticizing the developer that sold them their homes, or consumers leafleting outside a business that they claim sold them defective goods, often hoping that the business will give them a refund or at least will do a better job in the future. In cyberspace, the analogy would be consumers putting up a corn site or circulating messages to a long list of acquaintances or to a Usenet newsgroup.

In my view, the First Amendment fully protects such speech that is aimed at creating public pressure on someone to do what you think is right, even in economic contexts—that, after all, is what much advocacy is about. The fact that the speech exposes alleged problems with a product and aims at redressing an economic harm should not strip it of protection.

Again, for many people problems with their homes and redress for shoddy wares are more important than problems with politicians and redress for shoddy policies, and far more important than art, entertainment, or many other kinds of fully protected speech.

If the consumer's speech is an intentional lie (or perhaps in some circumstances if it's merely negligently false), the business can sue for libel; false statements of fact, whether on economic matters or not, lack constitutional protection. But the law shouldn't impose extra restrictions on the speech just because the speech deals with economic issues.

It shouldn't, for instance, punish true speech on the grounds that it interferes with a business's prospective economic advantage. It shouldn't impose prior restraints such as preliminary injunctions on the speech, even if the court tentatively concludes that the speech is probably false.

And even if the speech is found to be in error, the law shouldn't impose liability unless some fault on the speaker's part is shown. Though some such speech restrictions may be permissible as to commercial speech, they're not permissible as to noncommercial speech; and under current doctrine, consumer criticisms aren't commercial speech because they don't propose a commercial transaction between the speaker and the listener.

Again, though, a broadening of the commercial speech doctrine would jeopardize speech of this sort. If communicating information about a person's bad credit record is mere "commercial speech," then communicating information about a business's bad service record should be, too. Both, after all, involve speech on economic matters.

Both involve speech that's primarily of economic interest to listeners. Both are motivated by the speaker's economic interest—either a desire to get money from the buyer of the information, or a desire to get redress from the business. Either both are commercial speech or neither is.

In a free and competitive economy, people naturally want to talk about economic matters. Often their motives for such speech are largely economic: They want to learn how to make more money. They want to persuade people that some course of action is economically better. They want to alert people to what they think are others' dishonest business practices.

Giving the government an ill-defined but potentially very broad power to restrict such speech—not just speech that proposes a commercial transaction between speaker and listener and thus directly implicates the risk of fraud—risks exposing a great deal of speech to government policing.

SPEECH MATTERS OF PRIVATE CONCERN

THE ARGUMENT

One feature of virtually all information privacy proposals (except those built on a contract model) is their distinction between speech on matters of public concern and speech on matters of private concern. Even people who argue that newspapers should be forbidden from publishing a private person's long-ago criminal history or a politician's sexual orientation would probably agree that they have a right to publish the politician's criminal history, no matter how old. Warren and Brandeis would have called this a "matter which is of public or general interest"; others call it "political speech" or "speech on matters of public concern" or "newsworthy" material.

Speech that fits within these labels, they would argue, is constitutionally protected, while speech that is merely of private concern is not protected, at least against information privacy speech restrictions. But this approach, I will argue, is theoretically unsound; it is precedentially largely unsupported; in the few circumstances in which it has been endorsed, it has proven unworkable; and, if adopted, it would strengthen the arguments for many other (in my view improper) speech restrictions.

THEORETICAL OBJECTIONS

Under the First Amendment, it's generally not the government's job to decide what subjects speakers and listeners should concern themselves with. A private concern exception essentially says "you have no right to speak about topics that courts think are not of legitimate concern to you and your listeners," a view that's inconsistent with this understanding.

A clear example of the danger of such government power comes in a disclosure tort case, Diaz v. Oakland Tribune. Diaz, the first woman student body president at a community college, was a transsexual, and the Oakland Tribune published this fact. Diaz sued, and the court of appeals held that her lawsuit could go forward; if a jury found that Diaz's transsexuality wasn't newsworthy, she could prevail.

As usually happens in these cases, the court didn't define newsworthiness but left it to the jury, subject only to the instruction that "[i]n determining whether the subject article is newsworthy you may consider [the] social value of the fact published, the depth of the article, [its] intrusion into ostensibly private affairs, and the extent to which the plaintiff voluntarily acceded to a position of public notoriety."

But the court did stress that a jury could find that the speech wasn't newsworthy: "[W]e find little if any connection between the information disclosed and Diaz's fitness for office. The fact that she is a transsexual does not adversely reflect on her honesty or judgment."

Now I agree with the court's factual conclusion; people's gender identity strikes me as irrelevant to their fitness for office. But other voters take a different view. Transsexuality, in their opinion, may say various things about politicians (even student body politicians): It may say that they lack attachment to traditional values, that they are morally corrupt, or even just that they have undergone an unnatural procedure and therefore are somehow tainted by it.

These views may be wrong and even immoral, but surely it is not for government agents—whether judges or jurors—to dictate the relevant criteria for people's political choices, and to use the coercive force of law to keep others from informing them of things that they may consider relevant to those choices. I may disagree with what you base your vote on, but I must defend your right to base your vote on it, and the right of others to tell you about it.

This is the clearest example of a court using the public concern test to usurp what should be a listener's and speaker's choice, but other public disclosure cases raise similar problems. Consider, for instance, the criminal history cases, in which some courts held that it was illegal for newspapers to print information about "long past" criminal activity by people who are now supposedly rehabilitated and are leading allegedly blameless lives.

The leading such case is Briscoe v. Reader's Digest Association, in which Reader's Digest was held liable for revealing that Briscoe had eleven years earlier been convicted of armed robbery (a robbery that involved his fighting "a gun battle with the local police").

The court acknowledged that the speech, while not related to any particular political controversy, was newsworthy; the public is properly concerned with crime, how it happens, how it's fought, and how it can be avoided. Moreover, revealing the identity of someone "currently charged with the commission of a crime" is itself newsworthy, because "it may legitimately put others on notice that the named individual is suspected of having committed a crime," thus presumably warning them that they may want to be cautious in their dealings with him.

But revealing Briscoe's identity eleven years after his crime, the court said, served no "public purpose" and was not "of legitimate public interest"; there was no "reason whatsoever" for it. The plaintiff was "rehabilitated" and had "paid his debt to society." "[W]e, as right-thinking members of society, should permit him to continue in the path of rectitude rather than throw him back into a life of shame or crime" by revealing his past.

"Ideally, [Briscoe's] neighbors should recognize his present worth and forget his past life of shame. But men are not so divine as to forgive the past trespasses of others, and plaintiff therefore endeavored to reveal as little as possible of his past life." And to assist Briscoe in what the court apparently thought was a worthy effort at concealment, the law may bar people from saying things that would interfere with Briscoe's plans.

Judges are of course entitled to have their own views about which things "right-thinking members of society" should "recognize" and which they should forget; but it seems to me that under the First Amendment members of society have a constitutional right to think things through in their own ways.

And some people do take a view that differs from that of the Briscoe judges: While criminals can change their character, this view asserts, they often don't. Someone who was willing to fight a gun battle with the police eleven years ago may be more willing than the average person to do something bad today, even if he has led a blameless life since then (something that no court can assure us of, since it may be that he has continued acting violently on occasion, but just hasn't yet been caught).

Under this ideology, it's perfectly proper to keep this possibility in mind in one's dealings with the supposedly "reformed" felon. While the government may want to give him a second chance by releasing him from prison, restoring his right to vote and possess firearms, and even erasing its publicly accessible records related to the conviction, his friends, acquaintances, and business associates are entitled to adopt a different attitude.

Most presumably wouldn't treat him as a total pariah, but they might use extra caution in dealing with him, especially when it comes to trusting their business welfare or even their physical safety (or that of their children) to his care. And, as Richard Epstein has pointed out, they might use extra caution in dealing with him precisely because he has for the last eleven years hidden this history and denied them the chance to judge him for themselves based on the whole truth about his past.

Those who think such concealment is wrong will see it as direct evidence of present bad character (since the concealment was continuing) and not just of past bad character. Revealing Briscoe's name, under this view, may have little to do with broad political debates, but it is still of intense and eminently legitimate public concern to one piece of the public: people who know Briscoe, the very same group whose ignorance Briscoe seemed most concerned about preserving.

These members of the public would use this information to make the decision, which is probably more important to them than whom they would vote for next November, about whether they could trust Briscoe in their daily dealings. This isn't speech on political matters, but rather on what I might call "daily life matters."

Under the First Amendment, which protects movies, art, jokes, and reviews of stereo systems, such speech on daily life matters is at least equally worthy. At least as much as those kinds of protected speech, daily life matter speech—communication related to "the real, everyday experience of ordinary people"—indirectly but deeply affects the way we view the world, deal with others, evaluate their moral claims on us, and even vote; and its effect is probably greater than that of most of the paintings we see or the editorials we read. Consider how much our view of crime and punishment, secrecy and publicity, and many other topics would be indirectly influenced-towards greater liberalism, conservatism, or something else—by the knowledge that some of our seemingly law-abiding neighbors have been concealing a criminal past.

In any event, which viewpoint about our neighbors' past crimes is "right-thinking" and which is "wrong-thinking" is the subject of a longstanding moral debate. Surely it is not up to the government to conclude that the latter view is so wrong, that Briscoe's conviction was so "[il]legitimate" a subject for consideration, that the government can suppress speech that undermines its highly controversial policy of forgive-and-forget. I can certainly see why all of us might want to suppress "information about [our] remote and forgotten past[s]" in order "to change... others' definitions of [ourselves]." But in a free speech regime, others' definitions of me should primarily be molded by their own judgments, rather than by my using legal coercion to keep them in the dark.

The same goes for databases of personal information as much as for news stories about such information. Many such databases—for instance, credit history databases or criminal record databases—are used by people to help them decide whom it is safe to deal with and who is likely to cheat them.

Other databases, which contain less incriminating information, such as a person's shopping patterns, may be less necessary for self-protection; but of course for the same reason the data stored in them will also generally be much less embarrassing to their subjects, which makes the supposed harm to the subjects of the communication of such data much smaller. And in any event, even this data is of direct daily life interest to its recipients, since it helps them find out with whom they should do business.

In some instances, it may be quite unlikely that certain speech would be useful to the listeners either for political purposes or for daily life purposes; this largely has to do with information that shows people in ridiculous, embarrassing, or demeaning contexts without revealing any useful new information about them.

Everybody knows that I go to the bathroom; printing a picture of me on the toilet would embarrass me not because it reveals something new about me, but because it shows me in a pose that by cultural convention is seen as ridiculous or undignified.

This may explain cases such as Daily Times Democrat v. Graham, so where a newspaper was held liable for printing a picture of a woman whose dress was accidentally blown up over her waist, and it may partly explain why most people would gladly restrict the nonconsensual publication of photographs of people naked or having sex with their spouses.

These pictures aren't embarrassing because of the facts they reveal (except in rare cases where they show embarrassing deformities); everyone knows that we're all naked underneath our clothes, and that spouses generally have sex. Rather, they are embarrassing because these poses are conventionally seen as lacking in dignity.

Whatever else sex may be, it isn't dignified, and while we may have little concern about our dignity while engaging in the act privately, this lack of concern may stem precisely from the fact that we know other people aren't watching.

But while there may be a narrow zone of fairly uncontroversially nonpublic-concern topics, the danger is that the vague, subjective "public concern," "newsworthiness," or "legitimate public interest" test will flow far beyond this zone; and as Briscoe and Diaz, among others, show, this danger has materialized.

This risk may be enough to abandon the test altogether, and it is certainly enough to demand that the test be rephrased as something much clearer and narrower before it is accepted.

We can all think of examples of entertainment that has no connection to public issues, but Winters v. New York was right to conclude that entertainment should be protected despite this, because "[t]he line between the informing and the entertaining is too elusive for the protection of [the] basic right [of free speech]."

If the word "fuck" were forcibly expurgated from public debate, discussion would likely not be substantially impoverished, but Cohen v. California was right to conclude that the word should be protected despite this, because otherwise "no readily ascertainable general principle [would] exist[] for stopping short of" far broader restrictions.

If vitriolic, relatively nonsubstantive parodies such as the one in Hustler v. Falwell were banned, "public discourse would probably suffer little or no harm," but the Court correctly refused to uphold such a ban, since it could find no "principled standard to separate" them from speech that had to be protected.

Likewise, the notion that otherwise protected speech should be restrictable when it doesn't relate to matters of public concern strikes me as so potentially broad and so vague that it deserves to be abandoned, even if it would yield the right results in a narrow subset of the eases in which it would be applied.

DOCTRINE

That, then, is why I think the public concern test is theoretically unsound. The doctrinal discussion is easier: Though the Court has often said in dictum that political speech or public-issue speech is on the "highest rung" of constitutional protection, it has never held that there's any general exception for speech on matters of "private concern."

Political speech, scientific speech, art, entertainment, consumer product reviews, and speech on matters of private concern are thus all doctrinally entitled to the same level of high constitutional protection, restrictable only through laws that pass strict scrutiny. The two situations where the Court has adopted a public concern/ private concern distinction are narrow exceptions to this general principle. The first such exception, established in Connick v. Myers, is that the government acting as employer may freely restrict speech on matters of private concern by its employees.

The government's power as employer to fire its employees for what they say has always been far greater than its power to fine or imprison private citizens for what they say, and the Connick Court explicitly stressed that private-concern speech remains protected against the government acting as sovereign.

The restriction on such speech by government employees was justified only by the special role of the government acting as employer, in which the government's interest in efficient day-to-day operation would make it infeasible to let people sue the government over every discharge that was based on any sort of speech.

The second exception, established in Dun & Bradstreet v. Greenmoss Builders, is that plaintiffs in libel cases involving false statements on matters of purely private concern may be awarded punitive and presumed damages without a showing of actual malice. This, though, also came in a context where the government has special power to restrain speech: restrictions on false statements of fact.

Such statements, the Court has held, have "no constitutional value"; any protection they get stems from the need to prevent the undue chilling of true statements, which are indeed constitutionally protected, Dun & Bradstreet thus says little about the propriety of applying the "private concern" test to speech that, unlike false statements of fact, is presumptively constitutionally valuable.

And Dun & Bradstreet's reasoning confirms that the lower protection given to private-concern speech flows precisely from the speech being false and thus presumptively unprotected. The economic interests of the speaker and its audience, the Court argued, warrant no special protection when "the speech is wholly false."

Likewise, the "chilling" effect on constitutionally protected true statements would be minimal because accurate credit reports are "hardy and unlikely to be deterred," are "more objectively verifiable," and are in any case likely to have been heavily verified by successful credit agencies. Neither verifiability nor the market pressure for accuracy is relevant outside the context of restrictions on false statements of fact.

THE TWO "PUBLIC CONCERN" DOCTRINES

In practice, neither of these doctrines has been a success story for the public concern test. As many critics have pointed out, the government employee private concern doctrine has proven both vague to the point of indeterminacy and extremely broad. Much speech that would clearly fit within a normal reading of the words "public concern" has been found to be of purely private concern and therefore unprotected, with seemingly little justification other than the desire to make life easier for government employers confronted with troublemaking employees.

Connick itself found that speech among District Attorney's office employees about "the confidence and trust that [employees] possess in various supervisors, the level of office morale, and the need for a grievance committee" was "not of public concern," hardly a commonsense reading of the term "public concern."

And in trying to flesh the test out further, the Court could only say that it was supposed to turn on the "content, form, and context" of the speech, an approach that virtually guarantees that the inquiry will be both unpredictable and little related to the phrase "public concern."

Later cases have likewise found, for instance, that speech criticizing the way a dean runs a public university department, alleging race discrimination by a public employer, and criticizing the way the FBI decides whom to lay off was not "of public concern," though other cases reached opposite results on seemingly similar facts.

Whether or not the government should have the power to dismiss employees for such speech, surely the government ought not have the power to censor such speech by citizens at large on the grounds that it's supposedly of insufficient "public concern."

Under Dun & Bradstreet, the concept of "speech of purely private concern" has ended up similarly vague, and has sometimes covered speech that clearly seems to be of public concern under any normal definition of the term: for instance, speech discussing the competence of psychologists to whom children are sent by government-run schools, the business practices of car dealers, and alleged misconduct by the owner of a gymnastics school.

Again, perhaps it's permissible to allow presumed and punitive damages for false statements on such topics, but surely it would be unconstitutional to restrict true statements on these matters on the grounds that they aren't of "public concern." The experience of the public concern test in these two areas thus suggests that the theoretical criticisms of the public concern/ private concern distinction are sound: There's a substantial practical risk of the courts finding too much speech to be of "private concern," and while some facially vague and broad tests have the merit of being tied to an existing body of clarifying and narrowing caselaw, that's hardly the case here.

Maybe for want of anything better, the public/ private concern distinction may remain sensible as to the genuinely hard and necessarily vague government employee speech cases, but its track record hardly seems to encourage expanding it elsewhere.

POTENTIAL CONSEQUENCES

Direct Analogies

All this discussion is not just academic or just applicable to information privacy speech restrictions. The argument that certain speech should be more restrictable because it's not "political speech," not "high-value speech," or not of "legitimate public interest" is routinely marshaled in favour of a broad range of speech restraints. The classic example is sexually themed speech. A recurring argument in favour of restrictions on such speech, from pornography to art to sexual humour, is that such speech has little to do with self-government, politics, or any of the important, legitimate topics of public debate.

What, the argument goes, is lost if such speech is restrained, especially if the restraint serves noble goals such as preserving morality, preventing antisocial attitudes, and shielding children against improper influences? Not political debate, not scientific discourse, just people saying and listening to things that they have no really good reason to say and listen to.

The more courts endorse some speech restrictions on the grounds that the First Amendment doesn't protect speech that's "not of legitimate public interest," the stronger this pro-restriction argument will be in other cases.

Right now, the two areas where the courts have accepted a "public concern" test are at least cabinable as involving areas outside the core of First Amendment protection: restrictions imposed by the government acting as employer, where the government has always had a relatively free hand, and restrictions on false statements of fact, which already constitute a First Amendment exception.

Analogies between, say, the Communications Decency Act and those restrictions can be rebutted by pointing out that the CDA involves the government acting as sovereign, restricting otherwise constitutionally protected speech.

Say, though, that courts accept a private concern justification for restrictions on speech that reveals personal information, which are restrictions on otherwise constitutionally protected speech imposed by the government acting as sovereign. Supporters of restrictions on sexually themed speech would then acquire several useful related arguments.

First, they would be able to argue that there is already a general "no public concern" exception to free speech protection. Second, they could point to the information privacy speech restrictions as a specific precedent in favour of similar restrictions on sexually themed speech: Both, after all, involve restrictions on otherwise valuable speech imposed by the government acting as sovereign, and sexually themed speech, they'd argue, is no more important than are politicians' sexual identities or neighbors' criminal pasts.

If courts accept the argument that personally identified data is unprotected because (1) it is not communicated "for its expressive content at all," (2) it is only "a tool for processing people, not a vehicle for injecting communication into the `marketplace of ideas,'" and (3) "in the ways that matter, [it isn't] really `speech' at all," some will quickly argue that sexually themed speech (1) is not communicated for its expressive content at all, (2) is only a tool for sexually arousing people, not a vehicle for injecting communication into the marketplace of ideas, and (3) in the ways that matter, isn't really speech at all.

What's more, information privacy speech restrictions are likely to prove quite popular; what better way to support your argument for restrictions on other "no public concern" speech than by analogizing not just to technical, little-known restrictions but to a widely liked and viscerally appealing one? Third, the precedential value of the government employee speech cases and libel cases would itself be strengthened.

Right now these cases can be limited on the grounds that they don't involve the government as sovereign restricting otherwise valuable speech, but once those cases are accepted as an analogy for information privacy speech restrictions, such a limitation will be lost. Those who want to protect sexually themed speech will try to distinguish it from speech that reveals private information.

The definition of sexually themed speech, they'll argue, is either so vague or so broad that it includes matters that are of clearly legitimate public interest—discussions of sexually transmitted diseases, political statements about sexual matters that rely on graphic sexual imagery for their force, or moral or scientific statements about certain sexual subjects that are best made frankly and not throu gh sanitized euphemism. But the same, of course, is true of speech that communicates others' personal information, which often can be either of public interest or of daily life interest. If this argument is rejected for private information speech, it will also be easier to reject for sexually themed speech.

Likewise, opponents of restrictions on sexually themed speech will argue that the government has no business deciding which topics are "legitimate"and which aren't--that the First Amendment leaves this decision to speakers and listeners, not government officials. But again, if this argument is rejected for speech that reveals private information, and the government does get to decide that people really have no business talking about certain topics, the argument will also be much easier to reject for sexually themed speech.

Any new "no public concern"exception will help support other restrictions, too. Restrictions on profanity and on flag burning have been urged on the grounds that the speech is not really necessary for the communication of important ideas; campus speech codes have often been defended on the same grounds.

Though people have the right to express offensive or bigoted ideas, the argument goes, profanity, flag burning, and slurs don't really add anything much to such expression; the idea can still be expressed just as well without this valueless component. Bans on such speech, the argument might go, "would not damage the communication of a message,"just as some argue that information privacy speech restrictions are constitutional because "[r]estraints on the circulation of personal information would not damage the communication of a message."

If courts accept the notion that publishing people's names in news stories can be restricted because the "need of the people to be informed of matters of general or public interest"could be "served as well without identifying""the people concerned"they will also be likely to uphold other government attempts to excise offensive and supposedly valueless components of other speech.

Similarly, businesses criticized by disgruntled consumers have already argued that such consumer criticism doesn't relate to speech on matters of genuinely "public concern,"and should therefore be restrictable even if it's true or if it's mere opinion.

Allowing tort liability under the disclosure tort for speech on supposedly "private matters"(such as a person's criminal history or failure to pay his debts) would provide strong support for allowing tort liability under the intentional interference tort for speech on "private matters"(such as a business's unfair practices or breaches of warranty).

Indirect Influence

So far, I've discussed the purely doctrinal ways that accepting a "speech on matters of private concern"theory as to information privacy speech restrictions could support other proposed speech restrictions. Let me now suggest three other less direct but still significant ways in which this can happen.

First, "privacy"is a word with many meanings, and with such words both judges and laypeople often shift from one meaning to the other even in cases where the meanings have little in common. Consider how often privacy arguments commingle the Griswold/Roe constitutional right of decisional privacy, the Fourth Amendment right to privacy from physical government intrusion, and the four distinct privacy torts, even though these doctrines are at best distant cousins.

Or consider how often Zacchini v. Scripps-Howard Broadcasting Co. is cited for the proposition that a broad right of publicity is constitutional, even though the case itself upheld only a narrow and unusual subset of the right of publicity--the right to block the rebroadcast of an entire act--on grounds that are specific to this narrow right and with the specific statement that it wasn't deciding the constitutionality of the broader right of publicity.

Our legal system (and perhaps human nature) operates by analogy, and analogies that rely on multiple meanings of the same word are unusually powerful. Because of this, once restrictions on people's speech are accepted in the name of "privacy,"people will likely use them to argue for other restrictions on "privacy"grounds, even when the matter involves a very different sort of "privacy."

For instance, many people have already urged restrictions on sexually themed speech on the grounds that it invades people's "privacy"by being accessible in their homes (and thus in a way intruding on their seclusion), by being accessible to their children (and thus interfering with their "privacy"right to familial autonomy), or by lowering the moral tone of society in a way that affects people's most private relationships.

Second, a strong free speech principle necessarily requires the protection of speech that many sincerely believe is evil and dangerous. One way of mustering support for this principle, both among courts and among the public, is to stress that all sorts of groups are in this boat: If people are upset that the speech they hate is protected, they should take comfort in the fact that speech that they may like and that other people hate is protected, too.

The converse of this, though, is that people's willingness to accept protection of the speech they hate decreases as they see new exceptions carved out for restrictions on other speech which they may see as much less harmful.

We see this reaction already: Why should the harm that racist advocacy imposes on its victims remain unremedied, some supporters of campus speech codes ask, when harms to copyright owners, to libel victims, and the like have been found to justify punishment?

One article even makes the same argument in favour of information privacy speech restrictions themselves: "If the powerful may exert property rights or invoke contractual obligations to prevent or limit speech"(alluding to the existing free speech exceptions for contract law, trademark law, and contract law), "so too may others"asserting informational privacy rights.

But the longer the list of permissible restrictions, the stronger these arguments for further restrictions will be. Imagine that the Court upholds information privacy speech restraints. Why should the harm to my child and my family stemming from the child's exposure to online indecency remain unprevented, some may then argue, when the indignity that someone feels from having his shopping habits communicated by one business to another justifies a speech restriction? Both, after all, involve nonpolitical speech.

Neither involves threats of violence, or false statements of fact, or any other traditionally accepted reason why the speech should be treated differently. If your favourite restriction is accepted on "private concern"grounds, some will ask, why not mine? If some people may exert a growing list of rights to prevent or limit speech, after all, so too may others.

Finally, and relatedly, free speech is not always an intuitively appealing or intuitively delineated principle. Many people's commitment to protection of speech is neither ideologically very deep nor at the forefront of their thoughts. In this situation, the law as it is profoundly influences people's evaluation of the law as it should be (what some call "the normative power of the actual")--just recall how often you've heard people argue "well of course this restriction should be permissible, look how many similar restrictions there are."

As more restrictions of a particular genre are in fact allowed, many people will become more used to the notion that such restrictions are normatively proper, and will become more sympathetic to other restrictions of that genre. In Madison's words, once the power to enact certain restrictions "strengthen[s] itself by exercise, and entangle[s] the question in precedents,"it becomes far more likely to generate other, still broader restrictions. This is why a "prudent jealousy"of government restraints on constitutional rights, even when the restraints are urged in a seemingly good cause, is indeed "the first duty of citizens."

The law of course already allows quite a few speech restrictions, including restrictions justified on a "not of public concern"theory. But the Court has been careful to draw even those restrictions narrowly: The plurality opinions in Young v. American Mini Theatres and FCC v. Pacifica Foundation, for instance, upheld certain restraints on supposedly not very important speech such as pornography or profanity, but at the same time stressed that the restraints only regulated the time and place where the speech is communicated.

The restrictions on speech that reveals personal information would impose much broader bans than those approved in Young and Pacifica. And more importantly, the precedential influence that I describe is never all or nothing. Arguing by analogy to one restriction is hard, both because that restriction looks like an unusual exception and because few proposed restrictions will be closely analogous to it.

Arguing by analogy to two restrictions is easier, by analogy to several restrictions easier still. Political tacticians know this, which is why they are often willing to proceed step by step, building a body of political precedent that will make further steps easier and easier. Legal tacticians know this too; consider the NAACP's successful campaign to erode "separate but equal"one step at a time. Those who want to defend legal principles from erosion should also keep it in mind.

COMPELLING INTEREST

The last argument for many proposed information privacy speech restrictions is that the government interest behind the restriction is just so great. Speech that reveals personal information about others, the argument goes, violates their basic human rights, strips them of their dignity, causes serious emotional distress, interferes with their relations with family, friends, acquaintances, and business associates, and puts them at risk of crime.

Moreover, such speech itself undermines other rights of constitutional stature, such as the right to privacy or free speech itself. The government must be able to step in and prevent this, even at the cost of creating a new free speech exception.

COUNTERVAILING CONSTITUTIONAL RIGHTS

Let me begin by discussing the "constitutional tension" argument, which comes in two flavors:

1. Because the Constitution has been interpreted as protecting privacy (possibly including information privacy), attempts to restrict speech in the name of

protecting information privacy involve a "tension" between two constitutional values.

2. Information privacy speech restrictions "promote some of the same values protected by the First Amendment," because "[g]ranting people privacy, recognizing that despite their entering into the public debate on an issue... they remain a private person to some degree, encourages people to come forward and engage in the debate." I have elsewhere argued at length against this sort of analysis, but for now let me make two observations about it.

First, the speech vs. privacy and speech vs. speech tensions are not tensions between constitutional fights on both sides. The Constitution presumptively prohibits government restrictions on speech and perhaps some government revelation of personal information, but it says nothing about interference with speech or revelation of personal information by nongovernmental speakers.

If, for instance, a private group organizes a boycott of a newspaper to pressure it into dropping a columnist whose work the group finds offensive, the group is not thereby violating the columnist's First Amendment rights; he has a constitutional right to speak free from government restraint, but not free from private censure or private pressure.

Likewise, information privacy speech restrictions involve a tension between a constitutionally secured right to speak free of government restriction and a proposed statutory or common-law right to speak free of private revelation of private information. The fact that the proposed statutory or common-law right is in one way analogous to a constitutional right does not give it constitutional stature.

Second, as the boycott example shows, changing First Amendment doctrine to let free speech rights be trumped by other "constitutional values" derived by analogy from constitutional rights would permit a broad range of speech restrictions. Lots of speech has the effect, and often the purpose, of discouraging people from exercising their speech rights in certain ways. Political bullies try to silence their opponents not only by revealing embarrassing private information about them, but also by calling them nasty (but nonlibelous) names, citing their interracial marriages as evidence that they are traitors to their race, attacking them with bitter and unfair parodies, or saying things aimed at undermining their business affairs.

Depending on the era, the risk of having your arguments called "Communist," "un-American," "racist," or "sexist" (even if your arguments really don't fall into those categories) has discouraged many people from expressing viewpoints that might draw such rhetoric—and I suspect that the rhetoric was often used precisely to deter people from expressing certain viewpoints.

Who among us hasn't at times decided to stay quiet in order to avoid having to deal with our opponents' vituperation? Consider a telling example from an article arguing that information privacy speech restrictions serve free speech values: "[S]tudies indicate that the threat of continued exposure to adverse public opinion curtails an individual's willingness not only to voice dissenting or nonconformist opinions but also curtails the willingness to entertain such positions privately."

Exactly right—the threat of adverse public opinion, whether it flows from the revelation of embarrassing personal information about the speaker, demagoguery about the supposed heinousness of his views, pure insults, or for that matter reasoned counterargument, does deter speech. The logic of the argument I quoted, if accepted, would thus justify restriction on all these kinds of speech.

And yet our right to use speech to pressure others into not speaking is a fundamental aspect of the First Amendment; recall that a recurring (and correct) argument of those who fight against advocacy of evil ideas—even advocacy that is concededly constitutionally protected against government suppression—is that such speech should be deterred by social ostracism and condemnation.

Likewise, accepting the other constitutional tension argument, which urges that speech be restricted when it undermines the unwritten constitutional "value" of privacy, would provide strong support for restrictions on speech that vehemently criticizes a religion and thereby discourages people from publicly adhering to it (and thus supposedly undermines the explicitly constitutionally described values of religious freedom), speech that urges people to treat others unequally (and thus undermines equality), speech that tries to pressure people into not exercising their property or contractual fights (and thus undermines private property rights or the obligation of contracts), and so on.

A rule that constitutional fights to protection from the government may be turned into justification for government restrictions on speech by private actors would have a broad effect indeed.

DIGNITY, EMOTIONAL DISTRESS, AND CIVIL RIGHTS

Other arguments for information privacy speech restrictions claim that the speech injures people's dignity or emotionally distresses them. This injury is sometimes also characterized as an interference with people's basic "civil right" not to have others know or say certain things about them. Some of the more extreme claims put this in rather extravagant terms: "[A] rampant press feeding on the stuff of private life would destroy individual dignity and integrity and emasculate individual freedom and independence."

"The man who is compelled to live every minute of his life among others and whose every need, thought, desire, fancy or gratification is subject to public scrutiny, has been deprived of his individuality and human dignity. Such an individual merges with the mass. His opinions, being public, tend never to be different.... Such a being, although sentient, is fungible he is not an individual."

Without privacy, "intimate relationships simply could not exist." "Privacy is an essential part of the complex social practice by means of which the social group recognizes—and communicates to the individual—that his existence is his own. And this is a precondition of personhood." It's not entirely clear what exactly these claims mean. If the assertion is simply that complete lack of privacy—a situation where people are indeed compelled to live "every minute" among others and where their "every... thought" is indeed subject to public scrutiny—would dramatically affect freedom and intimacy, that might be true.

It would be grim indeed to live in a hypothetical environment where there is no private property, where the government constantly listens to and watches every conversation, where some thought-reading device reaches into people's heads (the only way in which literally "every... thought" would be subject to scrutiny), and where there are no market pressures, contracts, or social conventions that prevent monitoring or revelation of private information.

But of course this grim vision tells us little about any supposed need for extracontractual prohibitions on nongovernmental speech that reveals personal information. Even if all such speech restrictions were unconstitutional, we'd still have a world where much of our privacy can be protected by legal rules that restrain private trespass, wiretapping, and electronic eavesdropping; by constitutional restraints on government searches; by statutory restraints on government collection and revelation of personal information; by contractual obligations on the part of people to whom we must reveal data; by market pressure on many businesses not to reveal data about their customers; by technological self-protection that can hide our identity in many online transactions; and by social norms.

Some might still think that this world permits undue intrusions on privacy, but it hardly seems to risk the actual destruction of dignity, integrity, freedom, and independence, or the impossibility (not just difficulty, but impossibility) of intimacy and even personhood. Claims about what would happen if privacy were totally destroyed tell us nothing about which particular privacy rules (and especially which restrictions on others' constitutional rights) are indispensable.

To give an analogy, one might plausibly argue that a society where "every minute of [one's] life"—at home, in public, reading a newspaper, or watching television—one is constantly confronted with nongovernmental proselytizing of a particular religion and with warnings of hellfire and damnation if one doesn't conform would rob people of dignity, integrity, freedom, individuality, and intimacy.

But such an argument provides no support for the government banning non-governmental proselytizing in the society we have today. On the other hand, if the claim is that the ability of private parties to communicate personal information about others by itself "destroy[s] individual dignity and integrity and emasculate[s] individual freedom and independence," "deprive[s people] of [their] individuality," makes it impossible for "intimate relationships [to] exist," or denies that a person's "existence is his own," such a claim is simply false.

Today, private parties do have very broad rights to communicate personal information about us, but because of the other protections described above, our dignity, freedom, individuality, and capacity for intimacy still seem largely intact. I suppose it's theoretically conceivable that at some unknown future time information technology might get so powerful that these values will indeed be threatened with "destruction" by such speech; but free speech—whether it's speech that reveals personal information, speech that communicates socially harmful ideas, or speech that allegedly coarsens public discourse—ought not be restricted today merely on the grounds that some decades hence such speech might possibly "destroy individual dignity."

Once the hyperbole is set aside, there remain some more modest claims. Speech that reveals private information about people may not destroy individuality or dignity, but some argue that it does diminish their dignity, that it can severely distress them, that it fails to properly respect them, and that it interferes with a basic civil right not to have people communicate such information.

But is it constitutional for the government to suppress certain kinds of speech in order to protect dignity, prevent disrespectful behaviour, prevent emotional distress, or to protect a supposed civil right not to be talked about? Under current constitutional doctrine, the answer seems to be no.

Though the Supreme Court has sometimes left open the door to the possibility of restricting truthful speech simply on those grounds, the general trend of the cases cuts against this: Even offensive, outrageous, disrespectful, and dignity-assaulting speech is constitutionally protected. And there is good reason for this approach. All of us can imagine some speech that is so offensive and at the same time so valueless that we would feel no logs if it were restricted, but the trouble is that each of us has a somewhat different vision of which speech should qualify.

The more courts conclude that avoidance of disrespect or emotional distress is a "compelling interest" that justifies restricting the speech we find worthless, the more likely they will be to accept the same arguments for restricting the speech we value. Just consider how many proposed new exceptions have been urged on the grounds that they protect "basic human rights" or people's "dignity."

Proposed bans on "hate speech," on university campuses or elsewhere, have been defended on exactly these grounds, and their supporters have likewise argued that such speech causes serious emotional distress, interferes with the target groups' social and business opportunities, and lacks constitutional value to boot.

The same has been said for sexually themed speech, which many people argue strips all women of their dignity, interferes with the personal and business relationships of women who have to deal with men who watch such speech, and is irrelevant to matters of public concern.

Jerry Falwell quite plausibly argued that Hustler's criticisms of him were extremely undignified, disrespectful, and distressing, and interfered with a legally recognized right to freedom from intentional infliction of severe emotional distress. Proposed flag burning bans are defended on the grounds that such speech insults the dignity of veterans and of all Americans, is unnecessarily disrespectful, lacks substantial constitutional value, and inflicts severe emotional distress on those whose relatives died defending the nation for which the flag stands. Parents claim a civil right to not have their kids exposed to certain kinds of speech.

If the government can declare it to be my "civil right" to prohibit others from saying the truth about me behind my back, then the arguments for these proposed restrictions and for many others would be considerably strengthened. The government could similarly declare it a civil right to have others not say insulting things about me (and my kind) in print or in broadcasts, where I may directly see or hear such speech; other countries have indeed done this.

Similarly, say that true statements—statements about past crimes, current sexual orientation, credit history, and the like—can be restricted because of the danger that they will change people's attitudes about their subject.

Why wouldn't sociological or political claims that the government considers false or misleading (group libel or seditious libel) or statements of opinion (general bigoted or antigovernment advocacy) be likewise restrictable, on the grounds that they may change people's attitudes about a group, and that there's a "compelling governmental interest" in preventing such changed attitudes?

The same applies to sexually themed speech. Many people are offended by the very knowledge that men are reading and watching things that lead them to see women as sexual objects. Many women rightly suspect that many men think of them in crude sexual terms, and perhaps may make sexually themed remarks about them behind their backs (which some see as an "invasion of privacy").

It's plausible that much sexually themed speech fosters such attitudes, and that sexually themed speech may influence its consumers' personal and business relationships with women. If the government has a compelling interest in preventing people from thinking highly offensive thoughts and saying highly offensive things about us behind our backs in the information privacy context, why not in the sexually themed speech context? Proponents of information privacy speech restrictions might argue that such restrictions are different because speech that reveals private information about someone is of no legitimate public concern, or is not necessary to public debate.

But many equally think that there's no legitimate reason for people to spread harmful opinions (and misleading sociological claims) about groups, to burn flags, to gratuitously insult public figures, or to display nude pictures to each other.

Likewise, many argue that even if racist opinions are a legitimate subject of public debate, personal insults, racial slurs, profanities, sexually themed art, and explicit discussion of sexual subjects are not necessary to such debate, since it's possible to express one's views without such speech.

On the other side of the comparison, as Part V argued, a good deal of speech that reveals information about people, including speech that some describe as being of merely "private concern," is actually of eminently legitimate interest.

Some of it is directly relevant to the formation of general social and political opinions; most of it is of interest to people deciding how to behave in their daily lives, whether daily business or daily personal lives—whom to approach to do business, whom to trust with their money, and the like.

True, this speech isn't a candidates' debate, or an editorial regarding a ballot measure; allowing restrictions on this speech will only minimally jeopardize such intensely political advocacy. But the speech I describe is at least as relevant to people's lives as is much speech that is today constitutionally protected, be it art, product reviews, or humour; restricting it on "compelling interest" grounds will indeed set a precedent for restricting those other kinds of speech, too.

Beyond the purely legal precedent, though, I am especially worried about the normative power of the notion that the government has a compelling interest in creating "codes of fair information practices" restricting true statements made by nongovernmental speakers. The protection of free speech generally rests on an assumption that it's not for the government to decide which speech is "fair" and which isn't; the unfairnesses, excesses, and bad taste of speakers are something that current First Amendment principles generally require us to tolerate.

Once people grow to accept and even like government restrictions on one kind of supposedly "unfair" communication of facts, it may become much easier for people to accept "codes of fair reporting," "codes of fair debate," "codes of fair filmmaking," "codes of fair political criticism," and the like.

It is conceivable that as to some kinds of speech, for instance the revelation of the names of rape victims or the unauthorized distribution of pictures of a person naked or having sex, courts will find that the speech is so valueless and so distressing that there is indeed a compelling interest in restricting it.

Though I empathize with the reasons for such restrictions, I reluctantly oppose them, precisely because of the dangers and earlier in this section—"lack of legitimate public concern" and "severe emotional distress," while intuitively appealing standards, are so vague and potentially so broad that accepting them may jeopardize a good deal of speech that ought to be protected.

But while these narrow restrictions would merely increase the risk that more speech might be restricted in the future, other proposed restrictions cheerfully embrace this possibility. Broad readings of the disclosure tort would, as Part V argues, restrict speech about elected officials that many voters would (rightly or wrongly) find quite relevant, or restrict speech about people's past crimes, which many of the people's neighbors may find important.

Likewise, many of the proposals to restrict communication of consumer transactional data would apply far beyond a narrow core of highly private information, and would cover all transactional information, such as the car, house, food, or clothes one buys.

I don't deny that many people may find such speech vaguely ominous and would rather that it not take place, and I acknowledge that some people get extremely upset about it. But knowing that some business somewhere knows what car you drive is just not in the same league as, say, knowing that all your neighbors (and thousands of strangers) have heard that you were raped.

If such relatively modest offense or annoyance is enough to justify speech restrictions, then the compelling interest bar has fallen quite low. And watering down the threshold for when an interest becomes "compelling" will of course have an impact far beyond information privacy speech restrictions.

Finally, on the purely doctrinal level, Florida Star v. B.J.F. made clear that information privacy speech restrictions are unconstitutional if they are underinclusive with respect to the interest in information privacy. One of the reasons Florida Star gave for striking down the statutory ban on publishing the names of rape victims is that such a ban applied only to the media and not to the victim's acquaintances or neighbors. "[T]he communication of such information to persons who live near, or work with, the victim may have consequences as devastating as the exposure of her name to large numbers of strangers," the Court pointed out; and this "facial underinclusiveness... raises serious doubts about whether Florida is, in fact, serving, with this statute, the significant interests which appellee invokes in support of affirmance."

This argument casts into doubt most states' disclosure torts, which also apply only to broad dissemination and not communication to a small group of acquaintances, as well as bans on merchants (and not others) communicating clients' personal data.

KEEPING THE INTERNET ATTRACTIVE TO CONSUMERS

Some have argued that privacy restrictions are needed to keep Internet access attractive to consumers: Consumers are so concerned that online sites will collect and reveal information about them, the argument goes, that they are being deterred from engaging in e-commerce, and thus e-commerce in particular and the economy in general is suffering. It seems to me, though, that fostering economic growth and increasing Internet use, while laudable goals, can hardly be "compelling government interests" justifying content-based bans on certain kinds of speech, at least if the "compelling" threshold is to have any meaning.

And the potential consequences of accepting this sort of justification for restricting speech are both clear and dire: The same rationale, after all, would easily justify bans on TV broadcasts that warn of cyberspace privacy risks, since such speech even more directly frightens consumers away from e-commerce and other Internet use.

Furthermore, if this is really such a great concern—which is far from clear, given the explosive growth of e-commerce even in the absence of non-contractual information privacy speech restrictions—it stands to reason that many Internet businesses would invest a lot of effort into preventing such consumer alienation: They'll promise not to communicate consumer information, set up enforcement mechanisms aimed at giving consumers confidence that such promises will be kept, distribute software that helps protect people's privacy through technological means, and so on.

I'm not sure whether these tools would work quite as well as a total ban on speech about customers, but I suspect they would eventually go a long way towards assuaging consumer fears, precisely because online businesses would (by hypothesis) have such an economic stake in reassuring consumers. And the availability of these tools further undercuts the case for restricting First Amendment rights in order to protect e-commerce.

PREVENTING MISCONDUCT AND CRIME

Discrimination

Speech that reveals some kinds of information about people may make it easier for the listeners to act illegally or supposedly unfairly towards those people. One commonly given example is the risk that certain health-related information might fall into the hands of your health insurance company. "Say that the insurance company learns that you eat a lot of pizza and steak, and therefore concludes that you'll probably have higher cholesterol and a higher risk of heart disease," the argument goes; "it might then raise your rates."

Another example is the risk that information about people's past crimes, alcoholism, or drug abuse will become known to employers, who will then refuse to hire these people. I can certainly see why people might be offended by their insurance company "snooping" on them this way. I can also see why it might be in the unhealthy eaters' financial interest (and I should mention that I love meat and cheese) not to be identified as such, so they can be subsidized by the healthy eaters with whom they pool their risk.

Similarly, closet smokers would prefer, if possible, that life insurance companies not be able to identify them as smokers. But the question is not just whether the communication of this information is offensive or financially costly to its subjects, but rather whether the government may suppress such communication.

If discrimination in insurance based on the insureds' eating habits is legal, as it is with respect to smoking habits, then it's hard to see how the risk of such lawful discrimination can justify restricting speech. True, one's buying habits are not a perfect proxy for one's eating habits (maybe the buyer is a healthy eater who is buying the pizza entirely for his roommate), but insurance is all about using imperfect but lawful predictors.

Being above twenty-five and being a good student don't perfectly predict whether someone will drive safely; smoking and being older don't perfectly predict whether someone will die soon; but virtually nothing perfectly predicts anything else. Likewise, many employers might consider a person's criminal record, alcoholism, or drug abuse relevant to whether they should entrust their property, their clients' well-being, or a $100 million oil tanker to that person.

But even if the government outlaws discrimination based on insureds' eating habits, or discrimination based on a person's alcoholism, drug use, or criminal past, the basic First Amendment rule is that while the government may restrict conduct, it generally can't restrict speech simply because some people may at some time be moved by the speech to act illegally. The law has plenty of tools to fight such discrimination directly.

They are not perfect tools, but under the First Amendment the government may not try to compensate for their imperfection by suppressing speech. The government may not suppress advocacy of discrimination based on race, criminal history, alcoholism, drug use, or pizza consumption, even though such advocacy may lead some people to actually engage in such discrimination.

Likewise, the government may not suppress speech about particular people's criminal history, alcoholism, drug use, or pizza consumption, even though such speech may lead some people to engage in the discrimination.

Fraud and Violent Crime

In a few cases, revealing certain information about people may make it easier for others to defraud them or even to commit violent crimes against them. Thus, LEXIS/NEXIS was faulted for putting people's social security numbers in a searchable online database; market pressure promptly led it to change its policy. Likewise, the authors of the anti-abortion Nuremberg Files Web site were found civilly liable for, among other things, putting online the names, addresses, and other personal and family information about abortion providers.

A few disclosure tort cases have also punished the publication of the identity of witnesses who were vulnerable to attack by the criminals. Under what circumstances the government may restrict speech that facilitates the commission of crime is a difficult and so far largely uninvestigated question. It arises in many cases which have nothing to do with revelation of personal information, because personal information is just one of many kinds of information that can make it easier for people to commit crimes.

The most prominent recent case that upheld a restriction on crime-facilitating speech involved a lawsuit against the publisher of a murder-for-hire manual. The most prominent recent case striking down such a restriction involved a scientist trying to put his source code on a Web site, contrary to arms export laws.

The most prominent recent legislation aimed at such speech was a ban on certain online speech that described bombmaking techniques. And the most famous cases that implicate this issue are the classic hypothetical of the publication of the sailing dates of troopships and the injunction against the publication of information about building an H-bomb.

Moreover, even crime-facilitating speech that's focused on particular targets may involve information that few would consider especially private: For example, if a criminal is still at large, knows what a witness looks like, and would like to kill her in order to silence her, publicizing the name of the small business at which the witness works—hardly intimate information—may jeopardize her life almost as much as publishing her home address would.

Similarly, if we're concerned about speech that facilitates fraud or theft, publishing information about a business's security vulnerabilities or a list of the business's computer passwords may create as much risk of fraud as publishing a person's social security number would.

I will not try to resolve this question here, but only want to offer three observations. First, the fact that speech facilitates crime doesn't always justify restricting the speech (even if it sometimes might): Consider, for instance, normal chemistry books, which may be used by criminals to learn how to make explosives, or detective stories that describe particularly effective ways to commit a crime.

Second, the strongest argument for restricting speech that reveals crime-facilitating personal information is that the speech facilitates crime, not that it reveals personal information. It is therefore probably most useful to analyse such speech as a kind of crime-facilitating speech, rather than as a specimen of revelation of personal data.

Third, as Florida Star v. B.J.F. held, the crime facilitation concern at most supports narrow restrictions on the particular kinds of speech that materially risk facilitating crime. Whatever support there may be for a general right to suppress either speech that reveals embarrassing personal information or speech that reveals information about a person's purchases, the fact that a few kinds of such speech may facilitate crime can't justify these broad restrictions.

This chapter has made three arguments. First, despite their intuitive appeal, restrictions on speech that reveals personal information are constitutional under current doctrine only if they are imposed by contract, express or implied.

There may possibly be room for restrictions on revelations that are both extremely embarrassing and seem to have virtually no redeeming value, such as unauthorized distribution of nude pictures or possibly the publication of the names of rape victims, and perhaps for speech that makes it substantially easier for people to commit crimes against its subjects.

Even these, though, pose significant doctrinal problems. Second, expanding the doctrine to create a new exception may give supporters of information privacy speech restrictions much more than they bargained for. All the proposals for such expansion—whether based on an intellectual property theory, a commercial speech theory, a private concern speech theory, or a compelling government interest theory—would, if accepted, become strong precedent for other speech restrictions, including ones that have already been proposed.

The analogies between the arguments used to support information privacy speech restrictions and the arguments used to support the other restrictions are direct and powerful. And accepting the principles that the government should enforce a right to stop others from speaking about us and that it's the government's job to create "codes of fair information practices" controlling private parties' speech may shift courts and the public to an attitude that is more accepting of government policing of speech generally.

The risk of unintended consequences thus seems to me quite high. Third, this leaves people who are trying to make up their mind about information privacy speech restrictions with several options: Some people can wholeheartedly embrace some of the arguments for these restrictions, precisely because these arguments would help create precedent for cutting back certain free speech protections.

Thus, for instance, those who argue that the First Amendment should primarily cover speech that fairly directly furthers self-government may want to adopt information privacy speech restrictions as their poster child.

These restrictions are popular, they can to a large extent be defended using the "First Amendment only strongly protects speech relevant to self-government" theory, they are hard to defend under a more inclusive theory, and they can therefore produce substantial support for the theory among those who like the restrictions.

Others, who generally oppose any broad diminution of free speech protections but who think information privacy speech restrictions must be upheld, can try to set forth their proposed new exception and its supporting arguments as carefully and narrowly as possible. I hope their attempt to craft such a well-cabined, narrow rationale for any such new exception will be helped by this Chapter, which highlights some of the analogies that generally pro-speech-restriction forces might use to expand any exception that is created.

Maybe with a very carefully drawn exception, my fears about the unintended consequences of recognizing such exceptions won't come to pass. Still others may reluctantly conclude that the risk is just too great. We protect a good deal of speech we hate because we fear that restricting it will jeopardize the speech we value.

Some people may likewise conclude that it's better to protect information privacy in ways other than speech restriction—through contract, technological self-protection, market pressures, restraints on government collection and revelation of information, and social norms—than to create a new exception that may eventually justify many more restrictions than the one for which it is created.

Perhaps the Michigan Supreme Court's decision 100 years ago, in response to the Brandeis & Warren privacy tort proposal, was correct:

This "law of privacy" seems to have obtained a foothold at one time in the history of our jurisprudence, —not by that name, it is true, but in effect. It is evidenced by the old maxim, "The greater the troth, the greater the libel," and the result has been the emphatic expression of public disapproval, by the emancipation of the press, and the establishment of freedom of speech, and the abolition in most of our States of the maxim quoted, by constitutional provisions ....

We do not wish to be understood as belittling the complaint. We have no reason to doubt the feeling of annoyance alleged. Indeed, we sympathize with it, and marvel at the impertinence that does not respect it. We can only say that it is one of the ills that, under the law, cannot be redressed.

All three of these approaches have their strengths; the one approach, though, that I think is entirely unsound is to simply ignore the potential free speech consequences. The speech restrictions that courts validate today have implications for tomorrow. Only by considering these implications can we properly evaluate the true costs and benefits of any proposed information privacy speech restriction.

Chapter 4

The Construction of Images in the Popular Press

A social constructionist view suggests that much about the way we understand organizations, as reflected in our implicit theories, is likely to be controlled by our interactions with social agents who affect the availability, salience, vividness or value of the information we receive. Leadership concepts in particular appear as prominent features of these socially constructed realities.

Consistent with these views, we argue here that collective conceptions of organization, and of leadership in particular, are expressions of a national culture at large in which both leaders and followers are embedded and, as such, are open to those institutional forces that create and disseminate "business" news and information.

In this research we sought to explore the construction of leadership images as it is related to changing organizational performances. We focus here on the popular business press as an influential agent in this process.

THE IMPORTANCE OF MEDIA FOR THE SOCIAL CONSTRUCTION OF LEADERSHIP

Many social analysts have recognized the importance of mass media in shaping views of ourselves and the world around us. Research in mass communication has shown that the media influence people's cognition in a variety of ways. The media may determine what issues are important and set agenda for what the public thinks about, transmit knowledge and information, reinforce or crystalize existing beliefs, change existing beliefs, and cultivate perceptions of the nature of social reality.

The last decade has witnessed an unprecedented growth in the level and type of media coverage devoted to matters of organization and management. Interested publics are now routinely served by various business media outlets, perhaps most conspicuously by a business press with mass appeal.

According to the Standard Rate and Data Service, the six-month average circulation in 1989 of the Wall Street Journal was 1.93 million, that of Fortune, Business Week, and Inc. were.707.870, and.754 million, respectively. In addition to such dedicated business publications, popular newspapers and magazines, such as the New York Times and Time, with their own huge circulations (1.17 and 1.68 million), regularly feature business and management reports. Such mammoth figures are complemented by the extensive reach and appeal of television and other mass media outlets.

While an ostensible mission of the business media is to provide facts and information about business organizations, it is clear theat business journalism extends into areas well beyond simple reporting, transmitting to us a variety of deeper messages regarding organizations and their functioning. Media analysts have recognized its ideological and constructive aspects.

The media achieves its impact through its consideration of and interaction with the audience. News organizations are directly dependent on market forces and appeal directly to popular opinions. To maintain the allegiance of the audience, news selection and treatment has to take into account its viewing and reading behaviour and be responsive to its needs and gratifications.

Furthermore, the interpretation of meanings by readers is not passive reception or discovery of what is inherent in the news but active interaction with the text involving pre-existing cognition and attitudes, previous and current expectations, and the nature of the perceived social and physical environment. The relationships between the press and the audience are therefore indicative of a confluence of societal interests in supplying and consuming certain kinds of information.

In this regard, constructions of leadership are regularly and widely produced for our consumption, with transmissions often taking the form of portraits and images of great leadership figures, both in the public and private sectors. These images feed and expand our appetites for leadership products, appealing not only to our collective commitments to the concept but fixating us in particular on the personas and characteristics of leaders themsevels.

In this research we were interested in understanding how the business press, in conjunction with their reading publics, construct a leaders's image over time in light of radical changes in the fortunes of a firm. When we say "the business press" or "the media" we refer to a field of news organizations in general, not to individual news writers and reporters.

We keep in mind the fact that authors who are credited with having written some news article are only one part of the hierrarchy in typical news organizations, whose ranks include policymakers, top editors, section heads, writers, reporters, and researchers as well as support, dissemination, and business staffs.

Furthermore, news making is a process entailing news selection, editing, writing, information gathering, and information checking. Thus it is appropriate to treat news reports and articles as products of organizations rather than products of individual journalist.

Admittedly, newsworkers are not just organizational members but also professionals with professional norms and values. But, as Tuchman found, news professionalism has developed in conjunction with modem news organizations, and professional practices serve organziational needs.

Consequently, the dichotomy between organizational commitment and professional allegiance the characterized traditional professionals is very much obsolete in this domain. Previous research has studied the media in terms of political ideologies of different news organizations. For the purpose of the present study, however, we adopted a cultural perspective, examining how the news industry as a whole influences and shapes news consumers' cultural conceptions and beliefs. We therefore treated news organizations in aggregate as an organizational field that constitutes "a recognized area of institutional life" by sharing a rather homogeneous structure and values.

The basic question we sought to address was, Given the initial success of a firm, what image of the CEO will be constructed? And how will the image be reconstructed (if at all) with new, negative performance information that is also associated with the tenure of the same leader? We intended both to explicate the content of the leader image associated with given performance outcomes and to examine the degree of continuity and change of the image as the performance drama of a firm unfolds over time.

Organizational researchers have studied leadership attributions as a function of "performance cues," but they have not typically considered that, realistically, leaders can and often are associated with variable performance outcomes over time and that attributions made at any given time are often made within the historical context of previous attributions.

Although questions of the kind raised above typically have been studied at the individual level, we contend that they can also be explored at the collective level of news organizations, on the assumption that there is much communality in knowledge, assumptions, and routine practices. As we will argue, organizational credibility is the primary concern across news organizations, which makes both performance information and attribution history essential in the process of image construction.

A Construction-Constraint Model of Leadership Images

A traditional perspective on journalism is that news "mirrors" or "reflects" the actual nature of the world; journalists are thus objective reporters of actual events. A constructionist approach to social reality rejects the notion of an objectivity that is independently of social actors. In practice, business leaders are rarely observed and described as individuals per se but are seen as representatives or personifications of the organizations in their charge.

Thus, seeking "unbiased" knowledge of the actual activities and endowments of a leader and whatever consistencies exist therein is made less important. In any case, such knowledge cannot tell us much about the nature of the constructions that will emerge.

More important is what information will be used or ignored and how such information will be interpreted and given meaning in the constructed image. In theory, then, many alternative constructions are possible, and it would be difficult to predict a priori the contents of an image and the rules by which it is reconstructed over time.

In reality, however, the alternative reconstructions that are likely to emerge from the popular press and be tolerated by its reading publics will be constrained to a much smaller set of alternatives, so that the particular construction and reconstruction of leadership images is likely to be the joint product of forces that bear on the popular press and its readership.

We identified the following forces at work in the popular press:

- Antideterminism– a belief that individuals determine the fate of organizations;
- The effects of performance cues and antribution history;
- The professional values and ideology of news organizations; and
- Organizational routinization. These forces are explained in detail below.

Antideterminism

One can find evidence of more and less antideterministic perspectives being represented in the writings of organizational scientists, particularly around issues concerning the relative magnitude to the size of the leadership effect versus environmental factors on organizational performances. The antideterministic perspective is reflected in theories that suggest that the fates and fortunes of a firm can be understood in terms of the personal endowments of the leaders in charge.

A more deterministic perspective is presented by the so-called external-control models of management, by which a firm's performance is understood more in terms of the environmental and inertial constraints facing managements. A key differences in these two perspectives has been in the assumptions made regarding the extent to which managements are capable of exercising, through their unique endowments, control over an unruly environment in the service of organizational performance.

For the antideterminist, the principal significance of leaders lies in their substantive actions and activities, which effectively isolate their firms from the vagaries of environment or use environment to the advantages of their firms, or both, in direct proportion to their abilities and skills. For the determinist, leadership's role is largely symbolic, aimed at preserving among important constituencies the illusion of a more antideterministic world and continued support for the leaders' stewardships.

We argue that the business press is particularly prone to interpret organizational outcomes in terms of leadership. It is widely recognized by both practitioners and researchers that news focuses on individuals in general and leaders in particular: "In the mass mediated reality, organizations, bureaucracies and movements—in fact all larger and more enduring social formations—are reduced to personifications".

While there are practical reasons for the news to emphasize leaders (such as perceived importance of the news), there is an implicit theory of society that the social process, above all others, is shaped by leaders.

Western journalism has sometimes been portrayed as a sort of cult of personality that largely discounts anonymous social, economic, and political forces: journalism shuns these forces, proposing instead that great men and women still alive among us and that it is they who make history.... the media's celebration of personality stems more deeply from a belief in voluntarism—of will—that attributes social change to the deliberate actions of individuals. Journalism, in other words, is strongly antideterministic.

This antideterministic view of organizational performance will orient the business press to attribute organizational outcomes to personal qualities and activities of the leader, leading to a very positive image as the organization performs well. The image will be constructed in a way that accounts for that performance while reflecting the professional values of the news press.

PERFORMANCE CUES AND ATTRIBUTION HISTORIES

Studies of performance-cue effects suggest that the construction of leader images is mainly a process of matching leader characteristics with performance outcomes. The direction of performance outcomes (positive versus negative) therefore determines that of leader images. We call this view of attribution the outcome-primacy approach.

According to this perspective, the CEO of a successful firm will be depicted with positive personal qualities, but if the firm subsequently experiences performance failure, the same leader will now be stigmatized with an image of failure and be depicted with negative image characteristics. The new leader image, constructed to match the performance failure, would depart radically from the original one, which was well-fitted to the performance success.

The obvious omission in this argument is the prestructuring effect of attribution history. If, as we argue, attribution making in real life is often a continuous rather than a one-shot process, past attributions should influence new attributions.

First, past attributions may serve as schema through which performance cues would be selectively processed. Second, as Salanick's theory of commitment would suggest, the very act of attribution has a binding effect on future attributions to the extent that the action is explicit, irrevocable, volitional, and public. Attribution makers are therefore pulled in two different directions. One is to update and revise the leader image to fit the drastically different performance information, the other is to affirm the initial leaders image to maintain consistency with past attribution. Some kind of compromise will have to be reached.

Although the above discussion on attribution thory is typically applied to individuals, news organizations frequently face a similar dilemma. The dilemma arises from the prevalent organizational concern for credibility. As a Bristish newscaster put it, "Credibility in the minds of the audience is the sine qua non of news".

Apart from any professional concern for ethics, news institutions' dependence on market forces makes it essential for them to cultivate a credible image in order to compete for readers and advertisers. How, then, is credibility gained and maintained? Research on journalism mostly points to rules and procedures aimed at the objectivity or factivity of news.

In addition, Gans observed that journalists were very reluctant to change opinions because inconsistency undermines credibility. Accordingly, we argue that consistency is another means by which news organizations maintain credibility. Credibility through objectivity and consistency seems to reflect newsworkers' strategy toward "hard" and "soft" news, respectively. Objectivity implies tending to hard news, such as buying, merging, selling of business, and changes in stock price and profit.

Consistency requires coherent continuity in interpreting those hard events. Interpretation and construction occur more fully in soft news, such as feature stories of successful business leaders.The ideal of objectivity coupled with the antideterministic perspective of journalism predicts the construction of a very positive leader image in the soft feature stories that account for the hard events of business successes.

Once this positive image is formulated and publicized, consistency for the sake of credibility predicts continuation of the positive leader image. However, as time goes on and the company experiences performance failure, the radical development calls for radical revision of the original leader image. The question is whether the positive leader image should be supplanted by a negative one to fit the new performance outcome or whether the highly publicized positive image should be kept intact to maintain consistency.

This is no easy dilemma, because achieving one goal will cost the other. This may be resolved by reducing leadership attributions or by making more external attributions for performance. In veiw of our discussion of antideterminism, this alternative is less than satisfactory, since it would paint the leader as a rather passive actor in the process.

The more preferable alternative is to modify the image to the extent that the initially positive image is still preserved and yet the recent performance failure is also accounted for.

PROFESSIONAL VALUES AND IDEOLOGY

News selection and treatment are not free from values and ideology. From the ideological hegemony perspective, the media is seen as part of the poltiical system, specialized in formulating and distributing the ideology of the dominant social power. Scholars from a cultural perspective, however, seek to identify in the media values of the culture at large, in which journalism is imbedded. The aggregate of the values may be called ideology, which, however, does not necessarily imply hegemony of the dominant ruling coalitions with a system of deliberate and integrated values.

Gans summarized the journalistic values he identified in the national new as the journalistic para-ideology, which both reflects the existing values and shapes future values of the national culture. If news contains values and ideology, the will certainly find expressions in leader images constructed in the news. And since values and ideology are stable and enduring, news organizations will attempt to preserve the image of the leader who is regarded as the embodiment of their cultural values and ideology.

ORGANIZATIONAL ROUTINIZATION

News organizations are professional bureaucracies and

journalists are organizational members. News selection and treatment are a function of oganizational structures and requirements.

Topics are assigned downward to reporters, stories are reviewed and selected hierarchically, essential facts are verified by special checkers, and records are kept for future assignments. The process routinization produces consistency and predictability.

Furthermore, the formal and informal control mechanisms of the organization reinforce uniformity and consistency. Viewed from this inertial perspective of news organizations, a positive leader image, once constructed, is likely to be preserved, even in face of organizational performance change.

Considering the above forces, we formulated a tentative model from which we could derive expectations about the continuity and revision of leadership images in the popular press. Such forces operate as a set of constraints that define the characteristics of the reconstructions that will take place. Initially, performance cues will carry great weight in determining early constructions of the leader's image.

Information about the leader is likely to be used in a way that accounts for or otherwise explains the performance outcomes of the firm. The constructed image will tend to focus on the special endowments of the leader, particularly those consistent with cultural values.

As time passes and as new information on the changing fortunes of the firm are received, an interaction of performance information and elements of the originally constructed image will determine the characteristics of the reconstruction.

This suggests that the reconstructive process yields products that are continuous with the past. It describes a conservative process that does not contradict but, rather, preserves the original image, limiting revisions to the introduction of amendments that render the new performance information interpretable from a leadership point of view. To explore this model, we did a case study of the reports by the popular press on a business leader whose company experienced dramatic changes of performance: Donald Burr, the founder and chairman of People Express Airlines Inc.

Business leaders associated with dramatically performing organizations are often covered extensively by the popular press. Burr and his airline enjoyed very prominent and extensive coverage in popular journals and newspapers during the 1980s. Business Index alone recorded about 50 entries under Burr over a period of six years.

Burr was featured as Man of the Year by Time in 1985 and was further honored in cover stories by Inc., Business Week, Time, and others. In the initial success period, Inc. devoted eight full pages to reporting on Burr and his company. When the company was in trouble, the New York Times organized a case study of Peope Express attended by professionals and academics. Not only was Burr a celebrity in the popular press, he became a model of humanistic management for business school academics.

The long-time prominence of Burr in the popular press ensured a well-portrayed image for analysis. In addition, Burr had been in charge of People Express throughout its six years of operation, thereby making possible a direct and strong association between leader image and organizational performance.

Finally, the ups and downs of the company's performance were very dramatic, presenting us with an ideal context for examining the dynamic development of leader image. Following is a brief introduction to the state of the airline industry at the time and to Donald Burr and People Express, as depicted in two prominent sources: the U.S. Industrial Outlook and Current Biography 1986.

DEREGULATION AND THE AIRLINE INDUSTRY

Prior to 1978, airlines were subject to the economic regulatory jurisdiction of the Civil Aeronautic Board (CAB). Competition was restricted and rates and fares were tightly controlled. After 1978, when the Airline Deregulation Act was passed, many new airlines were certified, and 1983 greeted all airlines with complete freedom of pricing. As a result of the deregulation, the airline industry entered into a period of fierce competition, characterized by a rapid increase in the number of air carriers and rapid reduction of fares.

The new entrants, taking advantage of low operating costs, quickly expanded their markets by offering low prices. The major pre-deregulation carriers, in an effort to retain their traditional markets, offered discount fares that were even below their cost of providing services. Fare wars thus ensued. The industry as a whole operated at a loss between 1979 and 1982.

The fare wars, on the one hand, stimulated air travelling by luring passengers who might otherwise travel by rail or bus, but, on the other hand, forced the major airlines to streamline their operating costs. The industry started to recover financially in 1983 and continued into 1984 and 1985. Other factors that contributed to the recovery and continued economic growth of the airline industry included the general national economic growth, the decreasing and stabilizing of jet fuel prices, and labour concessions.

As the fare wars continued, the sustained price discounts seemed ultimately to hurt more the newer and smaller air carriers. Merger activities started in 1985 and became widespread in 1986. As a result, the industry was becoming highly concentrated, and by 1987 nine major passenger carriers accounted for 90 per cent of all revenue passenger miles. At the time, U.S. Industrial Outlook predicted that the airline industry would evolve into a few mega-carriers, with numerous smaller carriers controlling secondary markets and providing supplementary service in selected major metropolitan centres.

DONALD BURR AND PEOPLE EXPRESS

Taking advantage of industry deregulation, Donald Burr resigned from his executive position in Texas International Airlines Inc. to found People Express Airline Inc. Although credited with saving Texas International from going under, Burr publicized that he was not at all happy with the way it was run. Through People Express he wanted to demonstrate "a better way of doing things," "a better way for people to work together within the American system of democracy".

At People Express, every employee was required to buy 100 shares of the company. There was no corporate hierarchy and no rigid job specialization. Everyone was an owner-manager: a pilot was a "flight manager," and a flight attendant a "customer-service manager." Everyone was "cross-utilized": The flight manager might do inventory control and the customer-service manager might work at the ticket counter.

Burr himself had no secretary, and he often pitched in to fill whatever happened to be a vacancy. The company also did away with traditionally standard services such as free meals, free baggage handling, and comfortable lounges. Consequently, the high employee motivation, low labour cost, and elimination of the "frills" made it possible for People to offer very cheap fares that made flight a popular product for the people.

In April 1981, the company made its first flights. After an initial loss of $9.2 million in the first year, People began to earn a profit somewhere between $500,000 and $1 million in 1982. By 1983, the company was servicing 19 cities in the U.S. and, in May, started its foreign service to London.

Owing to its skyrocketing sales volume, People's shares hit an all-time high of nearly $50 in July 1983. And the company appeared in the 100 Best Companies to Work for in America. People's participative management became case-study models for business schools. Burr summarized his "six precepts" of People Express:

The first, of course, is service, growth and development of people. The second is to be the best provider of transportation for people. The third is to develop the best leadership. The fourth is to be a role model. The fifth is simplicity. And the sixth is to maximize profits.

Although sales continued to grow, 1984 witnesses a loss of profit, and stock prices tumbled to as low as $8 a share. There were also increasing passenger complaints about delayed flights, lost luggage, and overbooking. People Express was known as "People Distress." Internally there was growing disenchantment with Burr, which culminated in the departure of the company's chairman, Pareti, who was quickly joined by adozen other key employees.

People managed to come back from this nosedive by curbing expansion and cutting expenses. Profit for the second quarter of 1985 jumped to $13 million and $16.5 million in the third. To meet the challenges from major airlines that reduced fares as a way to cut into People's market, the company decided to expand its geographic base by buying a number of smaller airlines.

The major acquisition of Frontier Airlines made People Express the fifth largest airline in the U.S. The explosive growth of People coupled with its ensuing debt load and increasing competition from the full-service carriers sent the company into another tailspin in 1986. During the first quarter, the company suffered a crushing loss of $458 million. The management tried to save the airline by selling some of the larger planes and by upgrading service to attract a wider range of customers.

When this failed to work, People agreed to sell Frontier to United Airlines. But the sale was canceled because of United's wage dispute with the pilots' union. People had to file for bankruptcy for Frontier. Finally, in September 1986, People Express was sold to Texas Air, whose predecessor was Texas International. Burr therefore went full circle, back to his original company to be the executive vice president.

A few months later he resigned to "pursue independent business interests," thus bringing the story to an end. Based on People's performance and on major organizational events, the history of People Express can be divided into three periods. The first period covered 1981 to 1983, which, despite the initial loss, was one of great success.

The second period, from 1984 to 1985, witnessed great expansion, great loss, and great gains. This period can be seen as a period of mixed performance. The last period started in 1986 and ended with the merger of the company to Texas

Air in September of the year. This is clearly a period of failure. It is against this backdrop that our analysis takes place.

METHOD

Two analyses were conducted on magazine and newspaper articles about Burr. The first followed traditional content-analytic methods, identifying leader-characteristic themes, recording frequency, and analyzing trends of these themes. The second analysis focused on metaphors about Burr, using the theory and method proposed by Lakoff and Johnson. By design, much of the analysis is interpretive.

Although the mechanics of conducting the content analysis, described below, are quite conventional, the first analysis was performed on image descriptions by 72 readers of the published nmews articles. Involving respondents was primarily aimed at educing possible research bias and improving the reliability and validity of the findings. This assumed a reasonable linkage between the original stimuli of the news articles and the responses of the readers.

Our assumption was supported by previous mass-media research findings that news media have the power to hape news consumers' opinions, especially on topics about which they are ignorant. Furthermore, it was our belief that for the interpretation of image contents in the popular press, the reading public has an equal if not greater claim to reliability and validity than two academic researchers.

Some ethnographic researchers have argued that, since culture is a collective phenomenon, culture as discerned by researchers alone is inevitably more biased than if the researchers work as facilitators with a group of the cultural members. Following this argument, we had reason to expect that the collective judgment of the 72 respondents would help us interpret image meanings in the news articles more objectively.

But objectivity itself may be an illusion. Leader images in the press are more than explicit statements readily collected from the original writings. More often they have to be inferred from writings about the leader. To the extent that an image is impressionistic and holistic, its inference would depend on who makes the inference. As research on uses and gratifications has found, people with different motives (needs, beliefs, and values) may experience different media effects.

If news publishers, editors, and writers have audience considerations for story selection and production, business students would be more typical of their readership than researchers. Hence the readers' image formations may be closer than the researcher's to that of the news producers.

Lastly, the portrayed reality in the press is both an influence on and a reflection of the reading public. Given this collusive relationship, an analysis of the construction of Burr's image can proceed by focusing either on the writer or the reader. Analyzing both may serve as a cross-check of the finding.

ANALYSIS OF READERS' DESCRIPTIONS

In this first analysis we focused on the images formed by readers in response to the news articles selected as stimulus data by the following procedure.

STIMULUS DATA

The search for information about People Express and its CEO, Donald Burr, started with all the sources available to the authors, including Business Periodical Index, Business Index, Infotrac Academic Index, National Newspaper Index, and Magazine Index. In addition, computer searches were done on Business Data Base and Popular Magazine Review Online. A huge volume of information about the airline company was identified.

Business Index alone recorded 295 People Express entries by about forty business journals over six years. To make this information manageable, we decided to search only entries under Donald Burr. This trimmed the articles down to about 100, split almost evenly between journals and newspapers.

A quick look at the articles, however, showed that the indexing was far from stringent: many of the articles under the entry of Donald Burr in fact provided little information about him. It was therefore decided that we collect only articles that made references to Burr in their titles.

In addition, we retained those articles that had been contributed by news organizations that reported on Burr over all three periods. The rationale for this criterion was that journals or newspapers that carried reports about Burr over the total life of the company were appropriate for testing the self-consistency expectation.

Finally, we dropped those articles that had fewer than ten descriptive clauses on Burr. A descriptive clause on Burr was one that had as its topic Burr, his characteristics, his activities, or any other reference to him. The resultant stimulus data comprised 22 articles representing five journals and two newspapers.

These included the New York Times, Wall Street Journal, Business Week, Fortune, Inc., Newsweek, and Time. This material was divided into three groups according to the historical periods in which they were published. The entire procedure netted a total of about 10,000 words of text per period. The material for each period was subdivided into two groups so that the reading load for any individual was not more than 5,000 words of text.

IMAGE DATA

Before the stimulus data were presented to respondents, they filled out a questionnaire about whether they had read or heard about People Express nd Burr and, if yes, whether they thought People Express and Burr had been successful. Most of the respondents (86 per cent) reported having read or heard about People Express. Twenty per cent thought the airline was a success, 33 per cent thought it was not a success, and 47 per cent were not sure.

There were no differences among the three groups of respondents regarding their familiarity with the company and their perceived success of the company. Although the majority of the respondents showed some familiarity with the airline, very few reported knowledge of Donald Burr: 91.4 per cent of the respondents had not read or heard about Burr, and 90 per cent did not know whether he was successful or not. Of the 10 per cent who reported they did, 5.7 per cent considered Burr a success, and 4.3 per cent considered him not a success.

The stimulus data of three historical periods were randomly presented to 74 undergraduate business students, with 25 respondents for each period. Respondents were asked to write a description of Donald Burr both as a person and as a CEO, based on the materials they had just read.

To ensure that each and every article in the package was read, a question was placed after each article: "Have you read the whole article? Did you understand the article? If No, please read it again. If Yes, go on the the next chapter." Three of the descriptions were discarded because the respondent failed to write about Burr. Seventy-two portrayals served as the image data on which our analysis was performed.

CONTENT ANALYSIS

The image descriptions were first read for their generl structure of presentation. They were then screened for descriptions of Burr, which could be a word, a phrase, or a sentence. The descriptive units were similar to what some content analysts call "propositions". These propositional descriptions were then grouped into more superordinate theme categories.

For example, "a man of drive" and "he worked very hard" would be grouped under the theme of Motivation. Other examples of the Motivation theme included "ambitious," "a need for achievement," "desire to be the best," "high spirited," "energetic," "enthusiastic," "aggressive," "commitment," "determined," etc. When questions arose concerning the meaning of a linguistic unit, we consulted respondents again for clarification.

Across three periods, 14 different themes were abstracted. The propositions and themes provided qualitative data for examining the structure of the leader image within and across the performance periods. In this procedure, twenty original descriptive units from each category were randomly selected and each was recorded on a card. A total of 120 cards were given to each of the five judges, in random order, to be classified into six categories. Agreement of individual categories by the judges with those by the researcher ranged from 80 per cent to 100 per cent, with the average being 91 per cent.

In addition, coeffient Kappa, which takes into account the level of chance agreement, was calculated for each judge's overall categorization agreement with the researcher. The average of the Kappa coefficients was .89. Frequencies. Two types of theme frequencies were counted. One was the percentage frequency of propositions in a given theme for a given performance period.

This frequency by propositions provided statistics for examining the relative salience and importance of individual themes within the performance periods and for analyzing the trend of the themes across the periods. The second theme frequency was the percentage of respondents in a period that made reference to a given theme. This frequency by individuals served as an index of consensus, indicating the convergence of the leader image among the readers. We will refer to this frequency as the consensus rate.

RESULTS

The presentational structure of the articles of period 1 followed a pattern of attributes, achievements, and means. Burr's attributes were introduced as causes of the success of People Express, followed by details about how the success had been achieved. Eight image themes for period 1 were extracted.

Those themes that had an above-average frequency of references (12.5 per cent) were People, Motivation, Ability, and Innovation, constituting altogether 86 per cent of the total propositions. People, which denoted Burr's humanistic management philosophy and practice and his charismatic appeal, was the most salient theme.

All image themes were positive and complemented each other. The descriptions were permeated with exuberant praise and admiration, such as "very versatile," "extremely intelligent," "with people's interest at heart," "created a family in his organization," "a dreamer who realized his dreams," "noted for his unorthodox style of management ideas and innovations," "a man with a mission," and "oozes enthusiasm and optimism," etc.

The image themes formed a pattern, with substantive themes denoting the leadership traits of Burr and methathemes commenting on the substantive themes. The metatheme in the first period was Balance. It pointed out that Burr not only possessed positive characteristics, but these fitted his mission as well as each other perfectly to make him an ideal business leader. The balance theme consisted of propositions that were typically presented in pairs of couplets.

For example, Burr was seen as not only ambitious but also capable and willing to work hard; not only willing to take chances but also possessing a fundamental understanding of the business; not only wanted to do well for himself but also for others, employees and customers alike; not only a perfectionist but also a businessman who wanted to make a profit, etc.

The high consensus rate (the first three themes were all above 90 per cent) indicates that there was high consensus among the respondents that Burr was an all-around ideal leader: charismatic, innovative, dedicated, and competent. In the second period, the general presentational structure followed a sequential pattern of positive attributes, achievements, problems, and causes.

While illustration of the positive personal characteristics and great achievements continued, problems began to emerge and were traced by some to Burr's weaknesses. There were ten themes, six of which were positive and four negative. Yet none of the negative reached the average frequency of 10 per cent or the consensus rate of 50 per cent, whereas the major themes remained positive, with equal or above-average frequency and higher than 50 per cent consensus rate.

The most salient theme was still People. There were two metathemes. One was Overdone, which consisted of propositions that Burr had too much of some otherwise positive characteristics, such as desire to succeed and idealism. The other was Change, which suggested that as the company expanded, Burr had altered some of his previously good leadership ideas and styles or developed some undesirable attitudes. However, as pointed out above, they were of quite low salience.

Compared with the image constructed in period 1, the metatheme of Balance was replaced by Overdone, and all four of the added themes were negative. These negative themes, although with low frequency and consensus rates, introduced some minor contradictions to the exclusively positive themes generated in the first period. Overdone confliected with Balance, Unethical with Ethical, and Autocratic with People.

Change did not represent a rejection of any of the previous attributions but claimed that the leader himself had changed. Nevetheless, the four most prominent themes were all positive ones and enjoyed the highest four consensus rates; the total number of positive propositions constituted 80 per cent, whereas the total number of negative propositions accounted for only 20 per cent.

All in all, the leader images had gone through considerable reconstruction; however, despite the questions and doubts about the previously constructed image of an ideal leader, the image of the second period was still overwhelmingly positive. When it came to the failure period, period 3, the general structure of presentation in the articles consisted of an ordering of positive attributes, negative attributes, and failure.

That the positive descriptions preceded the negative ones seemed to indicate an obligation not to forget Burr's strengths while pointing out his weaknesses. There were nine images themes, four of which were positive and five negative. The four themes that had an above-average frequency rate (11 per cent) were People, Overdone, Motivation, and Innovation.

They constituted 76 per cent of the propositions of the third period. The major themes were no longer all positive. The negative theme, Overdone, which emeged from the second period, was prominent second only to the People theme. There seemed to be a greater deal of reconstruction resulting in a rather negative image. However, semantic analysis revealed some significant qualifications on the negativeness.

First, the most prominent theme was still People, and within the major themes, only 28 per cent of the propositions were negative. Second, two of the five negative themes were metathemes, which constituted 67 per cent of all the negative propositions. Overdone, as mentioned above, referred to an excessive amount of otherwise good personal qualities.

Some of the Overdone propositions were negative in view of the changed situation. The "too much of a good thing" was conceived by respondents as a state not solely caused by an absolute oversupply of the leader's endowment, but by its interaction with a changed external situation.

This was articulated by the second metatheme, Ill-adaptation, which emphasized the insufficiency of attributes and skills relative to the changed demands of the environment. So, although the previous all-positive image in terms of major themes was now broken, the negative themes of Overdone and Ill-adaptation did not directly conflict with the positive substantive themes.

The consensus rate of period 3 showed high agreement on all the major themes, with Vision and Overdone scoring highest, followed by People and Motivation. Ill-adaptation also showed a marginal majority rate. The overall image of the leader was of an admirable leader with otherwise basically good qualities that unfortunately ill-fitted a changed environment. The message conveyed through the image was that the cause of the failure by and large lay not in the inherent quality of the leader but in the changed situation.

Looking across the performance periods, images were reconstructed as performance varied. As problems arose and performance suffered, the total number of positive propositions decreased, whereas the total number of negative propositions increased.

Yet throughout the periods, positive propositions outnumbered negative ones. Furthermore, the aggregate percentage frequency of positive propositions in major themes did not show a significant over-time difference.

The percentage frequency of the negative propositions in the major theme Overdone differed significantly over time. These statistics and the semantic features of the major negative attributions presented above revealed a serious effort by the press to account for the performance failure without rejecting previous positive leader attributes.

TRENDS OF THE MAJOR THEMES ACROSS PERIODS

As performance fluctuated, the percentage frequency of the positive major themes of People, Innovation, and Motivation did not change significantly. The most noticeable theme change, in addition to the negative theme Overdone, was in Ability, the frequency of which decreased sharply. What's more, its very opposite, Inability, was developed in the third period. The consensus rate of Ability also decreased significantly over time.

On the basis of performance-cue studies, one might have expected Inability to emerge as a probable leader characteristic in the mixed period and a major dimension in the failure period. Yet there were no Inability propositions for the second period and only 6 per cent for the theme in the third period. This suggests that instead of overt negative attributions, there was a playing-down of the issue of competence by avoiding the topic (lowering the frequency of the positive propositions of Ability).

Furthermore, a semantic examination revealed that 80 per cent of the Ability propositions in the first period made reference to global propositions, such as "a genius," extremely intelligent," and "very versatile," while only 20 per cent confined Ability to specific areas of knowledge, skill, or expertise.

By contrast, in the failure period, the Inability propositions were mostly restricted to more specific areas, such as "not an organization genius" or "lacked the knowledge to change." Interestingly, only one reader used the globally negative term "a poor businessman" to describe Burr. Furthermore, many Inability statements were presented together with acknowledgments of Burr's past successes and strengths in motivating people.

Although chi-square analysis of both proposition frequencies and consensus rates showed no significant difference over time with People, Innovation, and Motivation, analysis of the content of the themes revealed subtle differences in People and Motivation. Throughout the three periods, the theme People was perceived as positive; but in the first period, it was presented as a personal quality with strong ethical tones: trusting and trustworthy, fair and caring for people.

In the second period, as the company was growing larger and more depersonalized, people orientation become more instrumental, a motivation skill. In the failure period. Burr's people orientation was admired but viewed as ill-fitting to the changed internal and external situations. Motivation in the success period was conceptualized in terms of ambition, need for achievement, enjoyment of the work, mostly intrinsically derived. But in the failure period, Motivation meant more determination, endurance, and courage, a quality demonstrated when confronting externally adverse conditions.

These changes told us again how past attributions interacted with current performance cues to determine the reconstruction of the leader's image. Instead of being rejected, the themes were modified by the injection of new meaning. The resultant new images were subtly different yet consistent with and traceable to the old ones.

ANALYSIS OF METAPHORICAL EXPRESSIONS

We sought to look directly into the original news articles to find independent evidence of the dynamics of leader-image construction. In order to do so, we analysed the metaphors used in the same news stories on which the respondents had based their own descriptions of Burr. We considered the study of metaphors appropriate because of the role of imagery associated with them. As Pondy highlighted, metaphors provide compelling, symbolic images that can link past and present. Journalists' metaphorical descriptions of Burr could help them reconcilek the great initial success with the subsequent decline of People Express.

Finally, according to Lakoff and Johnson, linguistic metaphors are not mere poetical or rhetorical embellishments but reflect the way the world is systematically conceptualized. Metaphors about Burr, besides adding vividness to the story, represent a crystallized image of the leader depicted in the popular press. To the extent that they are effective means to image presentation, metaphors might be an important linguistic means that had influenced our respondents in their image portrayal of Burr.

A metaphor, as defined by the Random House Dictionary, is "the application of a word or phrase to an object or concept it does not literally denote in order to suggest comparison with another object or concept, as in 'A mighty fortress is our God'." Lakoff and Johnson, however, had a more general definition, which includes both literal and nonlinteral metaphors.

Literal metaphorical expressions are those comparisons of two objects or concepts that are generally accepted and used as part of the normal literal language. Nonliteral ones are novel comparisons that are figurative, the understanding of which requires some nonliteral imagination. For example, using the metaphor "Theories are buildings," the sentence "He has constructed a complex theory" is a literal expression, whereas the sentence "His theory has thousands of little rooms and long, winding corridors" is a nonliteral expression.

The nonliteral type of metaphors seem to correspond with Random House's more restrictive definition of metaphor, and it was on these metaphors that our analysis focused. The reason for excluding literal metaphors was that, as part of normal langugae, they were much less distinictive and more difficult to pinpoint without controversy. The nonliteral expressions, however, owing to their novelty, were relatively easy to identify and convey sharper imagery for comparison.

Lakoff and Johnson argued that one important function of metaphor is structuring, i.e., using one concept (usually the known) to structure another (usually the new). Two key characteristics of structuring metaphors are stressed. One is that the conceptual structuring is partial. This is necessary because, if structuring is complete, the two concepts would be identical.

The partialness allows metaphor users or creators to relate certain aspects of one domain selectively to the corresponding aspects of the metaphorically defined or structured domain. Furthermore, partialness gives the metaphor user some freedom of downplaying or hiding certain other aspects of the defining domain. The second characteristic of metaphorical structuring is systematicity.

Despite the partialness, the authors argued, the selected aspects or the selection process is often systematic. So, or example, "organization," when conceived as an "organism," gives rise to a structured system of concepts: organization is analysed in terms of internal coordination and external adaptation; there are young and old organizations; and organizations have high or low birth or mortality rates, etc.

In analyzing metaphors about Burr, we did not assume systematicity in the fullest sense that the metaphors constituted one well-integrated conceptual system of leadership. Rather, we looked for more or less consistent interrelatedness among a variety of metaphorical expressions.

Given the license of highlighting and hiding in metaphorical structuring, we could observe how the overall conceptual structure of Burr's images would be modified through metaphors in accordance with the changing performance of his firm.

Metaphor identification. A metaphorical expression was identified as a nonliteral description of Burr if the description had to be understood and interpreted nonliterally. For example, "Burr gave birth to People Express" is a metaphor because, interpreted literally, Burr has to be a female and People Express has to be a baby. We interpret the statement metaphorically and infer from the discourse context that it means that Burr was the founder of the company and that he endowed the business company with a human character. We screened, sentence by sentence, the same sampled journal articles that were presented to the respondents.

Those words, phrases, or clauses that metaphorically described Burr's personality, his behaviors, or his impact were identified as metaphorical expressions. Altogether, 46 such expressions were identified.

METAPHORICAL CONCEPTS AND SYSTEMS

The metaphorical expressions were grouped according to the performance periods in which they were printed. In each period, they were further classified into the metaphorical concepts that were conceptually similar to the respondents' image themes. Depending on whether or not a concept had multiple, interrelated expressions, individual concepts were labeled as a system concept or nonsystem concept.

A system concept consisted of multiple yet interrelated metaphorical expressions, whereas a nonsystem concept had only one single expression. System concepts, by definition, had higher frequency than individual, nonsystem concepts. The most frequent concept would be considered the dominant concept.

However, since all metaphorical concepts identified here, systems or nonsystems, were about the same person, we looked for any possible structure that might interrelated them. We then compared and related all the concepts to discern a pattern of relationships. Finally, the metaphorical concepts were related to the image themes of the readers to assess the degree of correspondence.

Results

Period 1. In the first period, Burr was compared to a preacher, a parent, a builder, a wizard Mr. Peanut, and a competitor. Of all the metaphors, the preacher metaphor stood out as the most salient, vivid, and elaborate.

Half of the metaphorical expressions about Burr were devoted to the preacher concept. Following is a sample listing of the preacher expressions: He could've been a preacher. They don't say "minister," or "reverend," or "clergy," they say "preacher" because it convyes exactly the right sense of sweat-in-a-hot-tent, evangelical fervor that makes the pulse race. Burr works hard when he talks.

He paces, he sits; he stands; he throws out his arms; he condemns and praises, implores and jokes. The glue is Burr himself, who dashes about preaching his horizontal-management style with messianic zeal. Within the new structure, though, Burr will go on preaching his unorthodox management approach.

Then another question was posed and suddenly the evangelical fervor was back in his voice. "It takes almost a messiah," William Hambrecht says: "that's the glue that holds it together." The above expressions contained various aspects that constituted a system of the preacher concept.

Highlighted in this system were the specification of a message (horizontal-management philosophy), the unorthodox nature (not a minister or reverend or clergy), a strong sense of morality (he condemns and praises), the whole-hearted dedication and commitment (fervor, zeal, sweat-in-the-tent), and the spiritual hold (evangelic, the glue, the messiah) the preacher had on his followers.

Other concepts did not have as many expressions for us to formulate separate conceptual systems. Nevertheless, comparing and relating them with the preacher metaphor one could discern that the latter concept was the most fundamental and was capable of incorporating and entailing the other concepts. The parent metaphor stressed that what Burr had created was not a company but a family, which was reinforced by the builder metaphor, pointing to the priority Burr gave to people.

The wizard metaphor referred to Burr's charismatic hold on his employees; Mr. Peanut characterized his unorthodox management style; and the competitor metaphor here referred to competition of doctrine more than that of business.

We therefore considered leader-as-preacher as the theme that unified various metaphorical expressions and that the various preacher qualities represented characteristics of an ideal leader.

Period 2. Metaphors in the second period described Donald Burr as a preacher, a father, a maverick, an entrepreneur, a Spartan, a visionary, a whiz, and a competitor. The preacher concept again was dominant. more than half of the expressions identified referred to Burr as a preacher. The preacher theme became more elaborate and systematic.

The company was referred to as a "commune," "utopia," and "cult,; Burr's colleagues and employees as "disciples," "flock," and "band of renegades"; Burr as "teacher," "evangelist," "fervent," and "visionary"; his office as "pulpit"; and his speeches as "delivering sermons."

The unorthodoxy concept was reiterated by the metaphors of maverick, Spartan, and entrepreneur. The preacher concept was systematically fleshed out by expanding from personal qualities to the organization: his office, his colleagues and subordinates, and the company as a whole.

In view of the great expansion of the company and the successful survival of crises, the highlighting and elaboration of the messianic features of Donald Burr could be expected. However, the period was also one of growing pains and internal tensions. Accordingly, a new aspect of the preacher concept was employed, namely, that of fanaticism.

Hence, Burr was described by some as "Reverend Jim Jones" or "Guyana Jones," the religious cult leader whose followers committed mass suicide in Guyana in 1978. Here we witnessed an indication of the negative aspect of a preacher, which might prove fatal to his mission.

As we progressed into the third period, despite the difficulty and failure the company was facing, the preacher theme persisted, as was evidenced in the following metaphorical description: "People Express sometimes seemed more cult than company.

Donald Burr, chairman and co-founder, was spiritual leader. The thousands of travelers who crowded its planes at unthinkably low fares were its flock." Yet, in addition to the preacher metaphor, there emerged another salient set of metaphors, namely those of fighting. While Burr's competitiveness was stressed in both the first and second periods, the fighter metaphor in the third period stresses his strong will and heroism in the face of adverse situations.

Donald Burr was depicted as a "fallen hero" and a "Luke Skywalker" (the protagonist of the science fiction movie, "Star Wars"); People Express was described as a "victim of the competition," its activities as a life-and-death struggle in the skies, and its failure as "plunging"; other airlines were referred to as "foes" and likened to "the dastardly Darth Vader" (leader of the evil empire in "Star Wars"); the airline industry was seen as the sky of "a Darwinian environment," characterized by "fare wars," and "dominated by giants."

The fighter metaphor was compatible with the preacher metaphor, in the sense that "heroism" in the face of failure could be construed as creating an important nuance in the connotative image of Burr as a preacher. We witnessed a confrontation of the preacher and the brutal reality of the Darwinian environment. The result was that Donald Burr and People Express failed. Nevertheless, Burr was portrayed as heroic fighter for what he believed to be the just cause.

That he was a preacher rather than a traditional business manager effectively explained both his great success in the first and second periods and his tragic failure in the third period. Compared with the first- and second-period descriptions of Burr, the metaphorical expressions in the third period highlighted the hostility and adversity faced by Burr. The supportive metaphors of parent, builder, wizard, maverick, and visionary were absent; the fundamental aspect of spiritualism, however, persisted.

In general, this analysis evidenced the metaphorical construction and reconstruction of Donald Burr and a conceptualization of managerial leadership in the popular press. In this case, the role of leader was consistently likened to that of an unorthodox preacher who was visionary, charismatic, and dedicated to his mission.

What was emphasized about the mission was giving people (customers and employees alike) the first priority.

Although this new type of leadership had weaknesses, such as the double-edged idealism and dedication, and failed to survive the more powerful orthodox forces, it nevertheless represented in its mission, as one journalist put it, "the future of management."

A comparison of images constructed through metaphors with those by readers revealed a high degree of correspondence. Most of the image themes in the analysis of readers' descriptions had their expressions in the metaphors; for instance, Ability in wizard or wiz; People in preacher, parent, and father, Innovation in maverick, visionary; Motivation in preacher, competitor, and fighter; Thrifty in Spartan; Profit in Mr. Peanut; Overdone in Guyana Jones.

The descriptions given by the respondents were to a large extent the literal version of the metaphorical expressions used in the original news articles. There was also a correspondence between the general structures of the images revealed in the two analyses.

As with the metaphorical concepts, the image themes were all positive in the first period; in the second period, negative image themes co-occurred with the metaphors of fanaticism; and in the third period, the determination aspect of the Motivation theme corresponded with the fighter metaphorical concept, and the emphasis on the ill-fit between Burr and the Darwinian environment was present in both the description themes and the metaphor concepts.

Over time, the most striking resemblance was the persistance of the People theme and the preacher concept. We have observed in this study how the image of Donald Burr was constructed and reconstructed as the performance drama of People Express unfolded.

Our content analyses revealed a number of complexities and subtleties regarding how Burr was portrayed in the popular business press and gave us a reasonable degree of confidence in the changing image it provided. The results of the analysis of the readers' leader descriptions showed that the image of Burr over time achieved a certain consistency with the past at the same time that it was modified to accommodate new and radically different information regarding the fortunes of People Express. In addition, a direct analysis of the metaphors collected from the news accounts about Burr buttressed the above finding.

The symbolic and partial nature of metaphors permitted significant reconstruction of Burr without creating discontinuities with the past. We discovered a consistent, dominant concept that ran across all three time periods. The way the metaphorical system around the preacher concept was elaborated in successive historical periods served to retain an essential commitment to Burr's leadership as a way to understand both the initial success and the ultimate demise of People Express.

This analysis can be used to make some tentative statements about the popular business press. One might consider that journalistic reports are a main product of this industry. In the effort to meet the demands of consuming publics, the reporting of hard, factual news is enhanced via soft constructions of various organizational processes and attributes, including images of organizational leaders.

The production of these images is committing and thus exposes press organizations to risks that could damage their credibility. Such risks are present when the implications of hard facts are dissonant with the soft constructions that have been sold to consumers. Credibility is generated out of a consistency with past constructions and the ability of those constructions to accommodate current realities.

Stakes in credibility are, undoubtedly, common to many industries. However, unlike other industries, in which major revisions to products and services seem to carry the implication of innovation and, hence, more desirability for consumers, revisions to journalistic products seem, instead, to more easily carry the connotation of unreliability.

This point is poignantly illustrated in a recent ad campaign by Forbes magazine, which was run during the few months prior to the failed coup atttempt in the Soviet Union. The page-long ad was headlined "While the world has changed its opinion on Gorbachev, we haven't." To underscore the point, the ad cited four Forbes journalists at four points of time over eight months to illustrate the consistent position they all held on Gorbachev. What was highlighted was consistency across time as well as across individual reporters.

Our analysis also has the potential to offer some insights into the functioning of organizations in general. The commitment to images displayed by the popular press has its counterpart within organizational contexts, in the form of commitments displayed by various constituents to their own leaders. Issues of credibility, commitment, and reconstruction are a part of the process that determines the relative longevity of CEOs and other corporate executives in the face of lagging firm performances.

Not all constituents are in the position to form images of the leader to which they will be committed, and one plausible hypothesis is that evidence of initial soft-imaging of a CEO, on the part of various and powerful organizational constituents, may to some extent forecast the leader's tenure in office following indications of declining organizational performance.

The political viability of a leader riding a downturn in the fate and fortunes of a firm may depend heavily on the extent to which interested parties have been willing or able to construct a favorable image of the leader early one. Organizational constituents who have formed their own images of the leader may find them difficult to discard.

The effectiveness of public relations campaigns designed to keep incumbents in office may in fact depend on their ability to capitalize on this process: generating initial positive constructions during good times, fostering commitments to them, and causing them to be resistant to change during less fortuitous periods in the life of the organization.

Of course, dramatic performance downturns, as in the case of People Express, will put pressure on the initial constructions, and the commitments to them may eventually necessitate at least some image reconstruction in light of new and hard realities. Drastic organizational performance changes are themselves compelling enough to prompt the process of reevaluation and reconstruction of the leader image. Whether performance changes alone can significantly affect the content of subsequent images depends on their interaction with other forces.

In our case, the pressure of performance information was tempered by forces that favored continuity. By and large, the new images was continuous with the past but at the same time could account for the changed fate of the organization. This sort of continuity and conservative revision was in keeping with the constraining forces of self-consistency, values, and organizational routine.

We view this as a general process that could apply to different patterns of performances and initial constructions. Further research, however, should be conducted to test whether initial negative leader attributions follow a similar pattern of continuity.

With respect to leadership studies, it can be said that the static, one-shot attribution context in which previous performance-cue effects have been found does not approximate closely the on-going, continuous aspect of performance, attributions regarding it, and the resultant images of leaders that are constructed.

Simple performance-cue effects in isolation cannot adequately account for the dynamics and complexities of leader-image perceptions. Images of leadership are constructed and reconstructed within a context of organizational performance histories.

Accordingly, attributions based on performance must also have a history. While organizations may not perform consistently (always successfully or always poorly), organizations and members strive for consistency in their judgment of the leader to maintain credibility as well as a sense of control. Yet attribution consistency is not to be achieved at the expense of its power of accounting for the ups and downs of performance.

Part of the commitment to the success image of Burr, one might suggest, is linked to his embodiment of certain cherished values. Burr is an idealized representation of the American entrepreneurial spirit: a visionary, daring to dream and daring to pursue the dream until it comes true. Who would ever want or even dare to destroy such a spirit?

The positive leadership characteristics abstracted from the two separate analyses in our study showed great overlappings with the journalistic values identified by Gans. His research on national news media over two decades identified eight clusters of enduring values that reflect value preferences of journalists as a profession and, to some extent, also those of news sources and audiences. Of the eight clusters of values, we found the following four to be closely related to the leader-image themes in our study.

1. Altruistic Democracy: Politicians, officials and democracy are expected to be honest, efficient, dedicated to acting in the public interest, Spartan in their tastes, and citizens should participate to eliminate the need for government;
2. Responsible Capitalism: Moopoly is evil, smallness and family-owned business is viewed favorably; business officials are expected to be honest and efficient; business news is dedicated to entrepreneurs and innovators as well as able corporate managers' innovation and risk taking are seen as more desirable in business than in public agencies;
3. Small-town Pastoralism: a specification of the desirability of nature and smallness; bigness is impersonal and inhuman; the ideal social organization should reflect a human scale; and
4. Individualism: The ideal individual struggles successfully against adversity and overcomes more powerful forces; self-made men and women remain attractive; hard and task-oriented work is valued.

Three out of the four positive image themes about Burr, namely, People, Innovation, and Motivation overlapped greatly the above four clusters of values, and these were the themes that were stable across the performance periods. More specifically, the following information made salient in the press about Burr and his company showed close links to the journalistic values.

Burr was an entrepreneur (Responsible Capitalism), a self-made man (Individualism); People Express was the product of the Airline Deregulation Act and a challenger of the big monopolies (Responsible Capitalism, Small-town Pastoralism, and Individualism); at People, there was no corporate hierarchy—employees were owners, everybody was a manager, and Burr had no secretary (Altruistic Democracy, Responsible Capitalism, Small-town Pastoralism).

These overlappings provide evidence of the impact of values and ideology on the initial construction and subsequent maintenance of the positive leader images. In addition, a scan of recent business publications, from newspapers and magazines to best sellers, reveals that American business places similar values on transformational and charismatic leaders who are reputed to empower employees and achieve performance "beyond expectations."

To test directly the impact of values on image construction, future research can examine how news agencies with different value orientations report the same leader. For example, the present study could be redesigned to explore differences in reports of Burr by the general press (New York Times and Time) versus the business press, the more liberal versus the more conservative.

Alternatively, research can also focus on differing reports by the same news agency on different kinds of leaders: the entrepreneurs versus the big corporate executives, or charismatic versus noncharismatic leaders, such as Burr versus Frank Lorenzo, the technician-like CEO of Texas Air and Eastern Airlines. These kinds of studies would throw light on how value orientations influence people's conceptualization of organization and leadership.

The reconstruction of Burr's image, as we have been able to observe it, can be portrayed as a process that began with highly positive features but ended not with a denial or replacement of those endowments but with a revised image in which those very same endowments were portrayed as being responsible for his demise. The "downside" of Burr's idealism and motivation gradually came into relief for news readers and writers as the performance drama of his firm unfolded.

This particular sort of reconstruction is reminiscent of a theme in classic Greek tragedies, that of the fatal flaw of character. The early Bible-stumping imagery during Burr's ascension gradually turned into overzealousness during his fall from grace.

Burr's magnificent endowments as a leader were tragically flawed in a way that accounted for his ultimate failure with People Express. In this respect, the reconstructed image of Burr's persona is similar to the likes of characters such as Oedipus and Medea.

Such constructive and reconstructive efforts seem to be consistent with the notion of the romance of leadership. The collective commitment to leadership represents perhaps another important constraint on the images of leaders that will be set forth by news press and tolerated by reading publics.

Whatever particular reconstructions emerge, their general themes must not diminish the significance of leadership as a way of understanding performance. The media—in the present case, the business press in particular—with its antideterministic bent, makes an important contribution to that kind of reassurance.

Just as buyers and sellers, through their influence on supply and demand, determine prices in the marketplace, writers and readers, who traffic in images of leadership, influence each other to determine how leaders are talked about and, in the end, how these images are systematically reconstructed so as to preserve leadership as a concept.

In doing so, we rescue ourselves from the threats of a dangerous and capricious world and the disconcerting prospects of uncontrollable, if organized, human systems.

Chapter 5

Journalists' Perceptions of Audience Trust

Recent research has explored the causes and consequences of plummeting audience trust in news media institutions. For example, it has been demonstrated that audience mistrust moderates media influences, such as agenda-setting effects or effects on the perception of opinion climate. It has also been argued that mainstream media skepticism is related to audience exposure patterns. Mistrusting audiences tend to diversify their news diets and consume less mainstream and more alternative news.

Most research has hi therto focused on audience mistrust of the news media. Conversely, this chapter explores the way this trust is felt by journalists. Psychological research demonstrates that trust and mistrust are important for the trustee, as well as for the truster. This literature implies thai feeling trusted matters for those receiving trust.

If this is indeed the case, journalists' perceptions of audience trust in the news media need to be investigated, and differences between journalists perceiving audience trust and those perceiving audience mistrust need to be explored. The current investigation uses survey data collected from a sample of Israeli journalists (n = 209) and examines possible correlates of perceived audience trust.

TRUST AND AUDIENCE TRUST IN THE NEWS MEDIA

Trust is defined as a voluntary expectation on the part

of one party (the trustor) that he/she will benefit from the interaction with another (the trustee) rather than be hurt by it. Trust is "an attitude which allows for risk taking decisions."

Because trust encompasses secular norms, like professionalism, trust in journalism is based on the audience's belief in the professionalism of journalistic practice.8 It is possible to apply the concept of trust to the relationship between journalists and audiences, because news deals with the impersonal world, and hence the uncertainty of the audience with regard to media reports is embedded in the relationship.

The concept of trust has received a tremendous amount of scholarly attention in various disciplines, ranging from international relations to social psychology. Trust is "the bedrock perception upon which society is possible." It allows individuals to establish cooperative relationships whenever doing so is mutually beneficial.

Sociologists and political scientists alike share the notion that trust is an essential form of what they call "social capital." Trust is a social resource not only because it helps people achieve common goals, but also because it helps to reduce the costs of arbitration and enforcement. Putnam argues that trust is a key ingredient in economic dynamism and government performance.

However, feeling trusted, not merely trusting others, is also important in trust relations. For example, mistrustful forms of supervision, in which supervisors make frequent checks on subordinates, have been shown to lead to anger and aggression toward the supervisor.

In general, experimental psychological research has demonstrated that feeling mistrusted is related to the greater propensity of trustees to violate trust. Thus, social trust becomes "social capital" not only through the increased motivation of trusting people to cooperate, but also through the reduced motivation of trusted people to betray trust.

If one applies this social psychological principle to audience relations with journalists, one might expect that journalists would make every effort to maintain trust if they sense that they are trusted. On the other hand, when journalists sense audience mistrust, they might become less committed to the audience. Their loyalty to professional journalistic norms dictating factualness, verification, objectivity, and balance might be adversely affected.

If journalists feel mistrusted, but still want to maintain psychological consistency, they may belittle audience trust as a professional value altogether. Hence, it is possible to predict that perceptions of audience trust will be related to journalists' identification with classic trust-related professional norms; similarly, perceptions of audience mistrust should be related to reduced levels of identification with these professional norms.

TRUST IN THE CULTURE OF JOURNALISM

An association between perceived audience trust and journalistic professionalism is expected not only given social psychological knowledge regarding felt trust, but also granted that trust is a central element in the professional ideology of journalism. The centrality of audience trusts to journalistic professionalism can easily be noticed when one looks at journalists' codes of ethics. Such documents often mention the trust of the audience as the rationale for many journalistic decrees, such as neutrality and objectivity, and even for not accepting gifts.

Audience trust is often mentioned and referred to as "an asset" presently enjoyed by journalists, but potentially threatened by ethical misconduct. Conditional sentences such as "without the trust of our readers, we will be unable to adequately perform our mission of providing news" are prevalent in formal codes of journalistic ethics. Such sentences, along with the frequent use of terminology referring to the "retaining" and "maintaining" of trust, all point to the fact that journalistic professional discourse treats trust as something enjoyed at present, and at the same time as the raison detre for journalistic professionalism.

The centrality, or even sanctity, of audience trust for journalistic professionalism can also be inferred from the reaction of the journalistic community to events potentially damaging for audience trust, such as the Janet Cooke scandal, or more recently the Stephen Glass or Jay son Blair affairs. In such cases, most journalists respond to the violations of the norms of credibility and factualness by stressing the centrality of audience trust to the profession.

As Eason argues, journalists felt "assaulted," "humiliated," and "befouled" in the wake of the Janet Cooke scandal because the violation of trust potentially reflected upon what journalists see as a profession with "only one credential": credibility.

As columnist Ellen Goodman put it in the aftermath of the affair: "This is a society running short on trust... Most journalists deal with this fact every day. We're assigned the role of public trustee. So we are all affected by any single reporter who fuels the public wonder: Is this true? Do I believe them?... It makes our jobs harder. It makes our lives harder. We feel it."

In sum, audience trust plays a vital role in the occupational culture of journalists. This trust is an aim, an important tool, an asset, and the rationale behind most professional credos. Journalists adhering to professional norms do so partly because they wish to maintain audience trust. Those less committed to professional norms might rationalize that these principles are unimportant, since the audience does not trust media reports anyway.

However, in recent years journalists have had reasons to doubt the validity of the professional assumption regarding the trust of the audience. Survey data in the United States point to the fact that public trust in the media is eroding. While there has not been much academic research into journalists' reactions to survey data tracking the declining trust of the audience, abundant professional discourse reacting to such reports can be found in professional magazines and conventions.

Some journalists have dismissed survey findings about diminishing audience trust as representing nothing more than responses people give to pollsters, bearing no relation to reality. Others have pointed to the various methodological problems that might impair the validity of such surveys. Others still simply argue that it should not matter for journalists whether a growing number of citizens do not trust the press.

As Ben Bradlee, former editor of the Washington Post, argues, "We journalists are not there to be loved. And I don't know that other professions are getting more respect. Not Congress. Not politicians. Not businessmen." As Brace Sanford maintains, however, journalists may simply be resisting survey findings about dwindling audience trust by saying that they are not in the business of being popular.

In sum, some reports indicate that journalists ignore survey findings regarding shrinking audience trust. However, social psychological research about trust seems to indicate that when trustees feel mistrusted, they tend to betray trust. This leads to the contrary expectation, that when journalists sense audience mistrust, they might become less committed to the audience.

The central role of audience trust in journalistic professional ideology also suggests that perceptions of audience trust should be correlated with journalistic professionalism; but in this case, audience trust is such an essential part of the professional culture that it is impossible to speak of a causal direction.

Given this conflicting reasoning, it seems sensible to ask: RQ1: Will perceptions of audience trust or mistrust be related to identification with professional journalistic norms? This will be the main research question examined in the following pages. Because this is the first exploration to date of journalists' perceptions of audience trust, it seems warranted to ask who those journalists who feel trusted are. Are they demographically or professionally different from journalists who feel mistrusted?

Therefore, the second research question seeks to explore the demographic and professional characteristics of journalists who feel trusted by the audience: RQ2: What is the profile of journalists who feel trusted, based on demographics, professional ascription and status, and the evaluation of the audience?

THE CONTEXT: JOURNALISM IN ISRAEL

Since its inception in 1948 and for more than three decades, Israel, a state with a centralist governmental structure and a social-democratic tradition, had a media map dominated by government-controlled public radio (and since 1968, television), accompanied by party-controlled newspapers, with virtually all political parties owning newspapers.

As a result of the collapse of the social-democratic ethos, as well as the rise of privatization and globalization, and the strengthening of neo-liberal tendencies, the nature of the media market has completely changed. Since the 1970s, party newspapers have lost their status and their readership, and three independent papers have come to dominate the scene: two tabloids (Yedioth Ahronoth and Maarw) and the highbrow Haaretz.

Television broadcasting has been transformed from a system based on one monopolistic public channel (Channel One of the Israel Broadcasting Authority, or IBA), to a multi-channel structure, with the launch of the commercial and privately owned Channel Two and Channel Ten (the former commenced operation in 1993, the latter in 2002).

Radio news is still dominated by the state owned Kol Israel (Voice of Israel, operated by the IBA) and the military-operated Galey Tzahal. Since the 1980s, local newspapers, mainly syndicated and privately owned, have flourished in many localities. Local television news, broadcast through cable only, began operation during the 1990s.

As in other settings, the Israeli mainstream national and local media are supplemented by "small," alternative media outlets, owned and operated by members of minority groups and co-cultures, and made for their consumption. These include a variety of newspapers and (mostly pirate) radio stations targeted at populations such as Arab Israelis, Ultra-Orthodox Jews, extreme right wing ideological groups, and

Mizrachiyim (Jews of Middle Eastern origin). Unlike the United States, where the main reason for fragmentation was the desire of producers and advertisers to reach a clearly defined niche for selling their products, in Israel the motivating force was the development of identity politics, and the desire of co-cultural groups to express themselves, largely due to the fact that as "mute communities," they had been excluded from the national media.

These alternative media are mostly small-scale, underfunded and understaffed news productions. While some of these channels are very popular among their target audiences, most of their audiences consume alternative media in addition to, rather than instead of, mainstream news channels.

A thriving journalistic professional community has evolved in Israel over the years, especially since the 1960s, with the establishment of formal journalists' associations. The most prominent of these, the Israel Press Council (IPC), was able to acquire semi-formal acknowledgement by the legal system.

The professional community of Israeli journalists has codes of ethics, ethics courts, and various publications dedicated to professional discourse.The journalists' associations have been somewhat effective in combating legislation that sought to curb the freedom of the press, but much less effective in preventing the erosion in salaries, and the move from employment arrangements based on tenure and uniform wages to those based primarily on personal contracts.

Despite the legacy of "mobilized journalism," loyal to national or party causes, recent studies seem to point out that most Israeli journalists at present adhere to the objective "gatekeeper" journalistic model, rather than to alternative models of advocacy, public, or "new" journalism. Interestingly, survey data show that the Israeli public maintains moderate levels of trust in the media.

Perhaps the Israeli public is more trusting of news institutions due to the ongoing IsraeliPalestinian conflict:

institutional trust is known to be higher during times of crisis, due to "rallying" effects.

Method

Data: The research questions will be examined in survey data collected from a sample of Israeli journalists between September and December 2002. As in previous survey research, a journalist was defined as a person who makes decisions directly affecting hard-news content.

This category includes reporters and editors, but excludes camerapersons, graphic editors, copy editors, and the like. Also excluded were journalists who concentrate on soft news, for example, sports, entertainment, travel, and fashion. Stratified sampling was used to build a diverse sample of reporters and editors.

Journalists were sampled from every Hebrew language national news outlet (including print, television, and radio), and from a sample of local newspapers. Each outlet was further stratified by respondents' seniority to ensure that the sample included senior reporters and editors, on the one hand, and more junior reporters, on the other.

A separate stratum was created for journalists from alternative media targeting specific populations (including news outlets in Arabic, English, and Russian, and news media targeted at religious and right-wing groups). The list of Israeli journalists that was used as a sampling base was obtained from the Ifat Media Information Centre. This list was updated and completed using bylines and credits, and in a few cases using lists of journalists obtained from editors of the various news media.

Some of the questionnaires were sent by mail to journalists who had previously been contacted and had agreed to participate in the study. Other journalists were interviewed by telephone. The Dahaf Institute for public opinion research conducted the interviews for this portion of the study.

Of the 389 journalists contacted, only 13 (about 3%) refused to participate. However, an additional 167 journalists (about 43%) who had agreed to participate in the study did not return the questionnaire by mail (even after they were re-contacted by the research assistant).

The rest, 209 journalists, completed the questionnaire by either phone or mail. Hence, the overall response rate was 53.7%. This response rate is comparable to those achieved by other scholars using questionnaires to investigate journalists worldwide.

The sample included 201 Jews and 8 Arabs (about 4%). The average age was 39. Approximately 79% of the respondents defined themselves as "secular," 8% as "religious," and an additional 12% as "traditional." About 90% of respondents were Israeli-born, 45% identified themselves as Ashkenazim (Jews of European or American origin), and 14% identified themselves as Mizrachiyim (Jews of Middle Eastern origin).

The rest of the Jewish respondents stated that neither category applied to them, or that they were of mixed origin. Approximately 61% had an academic education, 20% had studied in schools of communication or journalism, and an additional 20% had degrees in fields of study related to the subjects they covered (political science, economics, Middle Eastern studies, etc.).

The sample somewhat over-represented male journalists (71%, while estimates of the proportion of female journalists in the Israeli media range from 35% to 40%), probably because it over-represented senior journalists (101 of the 209 respondents were "senior").

Measures

Identification with Professional Norms. Respondents were asked to rate the importance of a series of professional journalistic norms. The question was worded, "Please indicate whether you think each of the following is an important principle of journalism." Response categories ranged from 1="not at all important" to 4="very important."

The items included "always remaining neutral," "getting the facts right," "not publishing rumors," "getting both sides of the story," "providing at least two sources to corroborate a story based on anonymous sources," and "keeping some distance from the people you cover." The items were averaged to create a scale.

Perception of Audience Trust was measured using two items. Respondents were asked whether they agree with the statements, "The Israeli audience trusts the Israeli media" and "My audience is very trusting of my journalistic work and the journalistic work of the news organization I work for."

The latter question was intentionally doublebarreled to allow the inclusion of relatively anonymous reporters and editors in the study (who would probably not be able to respond to questions about audience trust in their particular work). Response categories ranged from 1="do not at all agree" to 4="strongly agree."

The correlation between the items was only moderate. Hence, results will be reported for two separate measures [one measuring perceived general trust in the Israeli media as a whole, and the other tapping perceived particular trust, as well as for a joint perceived trust measure calculated as the sum of both items.

Evaluation of the Audience. Respondents were also asked whether they agree with the following statements: "The Israeli audience cares only about sensationalism" and "The Israeli audience is very interested in news". Response categories ranged from 1="do not at all agree" to 4= "strongly agree." The correlation between both items was moderate ($r = .29$, $p < .001$, after reverse-coding the first statement), and hence they will be treated separately, as well as jointly, in the following analysis. The joint measure, calculated as the sum of both items, had a mean of 6.08, and a standard deviation of 1.14.

Results

Israeli journalists perceived low levels of audience trust in the Israeli media in general, but high levels of trust in their own news organizations. While only 5.4% strongly agreed with the perceived general trust statement, 35.2% strongly agreed with the perceived particular trust statement. Only one respondent (.5%) strongly disagreed with the perceived particular trust item. In comparison, 16.6% of respondents strongly disagreed with the perceived general trust statement.

A paired sample f-test was used to test for the statistical significance of the difference between the answers to the particular and general trust items. Results showed that the perceived general trust scores were significantly lower than the perceived particular trust scores. RQ1 asked whether journalists who perceive audience trust would adhere to professional norms relating to audience trust.

To examine the association between the constructs, the perceived trust items were correlated with the professional identification scale. Significant correlations were found for both perceived general trust, perceived particular trust, and the joint perceived trust measure. That is, the more the journalists sensed that audiences trusted the Israeli media in general and their own news organization in particular, the more they thought that journalistic values such as neutrality and verification were important.

Bivariate analysis, however, is not sufficient in order to demonstrate a connection between perceived trust and identification with journalistic norms. The bivariate association could be spurious, e.g., caused by potential correlates of both constructs.

To negate the possibility that the association between perceived audience trust and adherence to professional norms is entirely caused by an association between both and a third variable, multivariate analysis is required. For this purpose, Ordinary Least Squares regression was run, with the professional identification index as the dependent variable. Factors potentially related to professional identification were entered as covariates.

These included formal training in communication or journalism, working for local vs. national media, working as a senior or junior journalist, journalists' perception of the audience, their own trust in the Israeli news media, and a range of demographic variables. The model explains 22% of the variance in the professional identification scale. Age was associated with the professional identification scale. Older journalists exhibited a tendency to identify more with professional norms such as factualness and balance. Personal trust in the media was significantly associated with professional identification: the more journalists trust the media, the more they tend to identify with trust-related journalistic norms.

Formal training in journalism or communications, seniority, and education were all positively, though not significantly, related to professional identification. Religious journalists identified less with professional norms, and females identified slightly more. Again, both latter effects were not statistically significant.

Our main interest here is the coefficient for perceived trust. Even after controlling for all other variables, the association between perceived audience trust and professional identification remained statistically significant. That is, the more journalists identified with professional norms, the more they felt trusted.

The same regression model was run twice more, with the particular and general trust items instead of the joint perceived trust measure (all other variables were kept as covariates in the model). Results show that the general pattern reported above holds for both perceived general trust and perceived particular trust separately.

The more people perceived particular trust, the more they identified with professional norms. The same was true for perceived general trust, though this time the coefficient was only borderline significant. Who Feels Trusted? Since this is the first exploration of journalists' perceptions of audience trust, it seems worthwhile to ask what characterizes journalists who feel trusted.

For this reason, the association between the perceived trust variables and other phenomena was examined. Perceived audience trust was statistically unrelated to most demographic variables. The differences between males and females on both perceived trust items (particular and general) were not significant. Both perceived trust items were not significantly correlated with age, education, or ethnic origin. The only demographic variable departing somewhat from this pattern was religiosity, which correlated positively and significantly with perceived particular trust. More religious respondents felt that their audience had more faith in their news media outlet than did secular respondents.

Perceiving audience trust was also uncorrelated with variables relating to respondents' seniority in the journalistic community. Senior reporters and editors did not differ from more junior journalists in the levels of perceived general and particular audience trust.

Journalists working in national media outlets did not differ from journalists working in local media outlets. There were also no significant differences in the perceived trust items among journalists working in different types of broadcast media-print, radio, television, Internet, and news agencies. In sum, it seems that perceived trust could not be predicted by any type of occupational or demographic variable, except for religiosity.

For this reason, the correlations between the perceived trust items and additional variables were tested. The perceived trust items were positively correlated with journalists' own trust in the Israeli media. This item was worded, "Personally, I am very trusting of the Israeli media." Perceived audience trust was also correlated with journalists' evaluations of the audience.

The more the journalists felt trusted, the more they agreed with the statement, "The Israeli audience is very interested in news". The more the journalists felt that Israelis trusted the media, the less they agreed with the statement, "The Israeli audience cares only about sensationalism". The correlation between the joint perceived trust measure and the joint audience evaluation measure was r =.25.

Discussion

This study was designed as a preliminary and exploratory investigation of journalists' perceptions of audience trust. Results show that feeling trusted is correlated with the identification of journalists with professional norms relating to trust-principles such as telling both sides of the story, remaining neutral, getting the facts right, and not publishing rumors.

When interpreting this finding, we should keep in mind that the correlation between perceived audience trust and adherence to journalistic norms does not imply causation. Social psychological research and theories about trust advance the interpretation that felt trust leads to greater professional identification.

However, it was argued that audience trust is embedded so strongly within journalistic professional ideology that we cannot determine what causes what. Arguably, the direction of the association could even be reversed, with professional identification leading to perceptions of trust, rather than the other way around.

The association between perceived audience trust and identification with journalistic norms remained significant even after controlling for potential intervening variables. This was true especially with regard to perceived particular trust. However, it is important to note that the absolute size of this association was not very strong.

The difference between journalists perceiving the most and the least audience trust translates to a difference of.40 on the 1-4 journalistic identification measure. Still, perceived trust was one of the strongest predictors of identification with journalistic norms, second only to age, and stronger than some more likely determinants of professionalism, e.g., formal training, seniority, and demographics.

The findings are, of course, limited to Israeli journalists, and hence cannot be generalized to other contexts, given enormous cultural differences between Israel and other developed societies. Though slightly more trusting of the media, Israelis are less trusting in general, and therefore probably less likely to feel trusted than Americans.

Thus, they might dismiss perceived mistrust more easily by thinking that trust is not important. More research needs to be carried out in order to determine whether Israeli journalists are the exception, or whether the association between perceived mistrust and professional identification is the rule.

As the first exploration of journalists' perceptions of audience trust, this study provides us with an opportunity to probe into these potentially important perceptions. The data revealed that Israeli journalists sense a low level of audience trust in the Israeli media in general, but a high level of trust in their own news organizations and in their own journalistic work.

This finding, perhaps similar to Davison's thirdperson perception of the audience, should probably be interpreted as a "self-preserving bias." Psychologists tell us that people tend to perceive the world in ways that preserve their own self-evaluation. For journalists, perceiving that "I am trusted," while "other journalists are not," is certainly human.

Feeling mistrusted was associated with believing that the audience was uninterested in politics and sought only sensational stories. This attitude could also be a self-preserving bias: "If the audience is mistrustful, then the audience is probably shallow."

The study also explored other potential sources of journalists' perceptions regarding audience trust in addition to their evaluation of the audience. However, both measures of perceived trust were not associated with most demographic variables, with the reporters' rank in the journalistic hierarchy, with the medium in which they operate, or with their employment by a national or local media outlet.

The only significant predictor of perceived trust, outside religiosity and the evaluations of the audience, was the journalists' own trust in the media. When journalists had faith in the Israeli media, they exhibited a tendency to think that audiences trusted the media, and vice versa for journalists mistrusting the Israeli media. We tend to think that others see the world as we do.

This "looking glass effect" is probably the explanation for the associations between journalists' perceptions of audience trust and their own trust in the Israeli media. As one top producer told Gans in his seminal study of news organizations, "The conception of our audience is a reflection of ourselves."

Additional potential sources for journalists' perceptions of audience trust in their news organization or in the Israeli media in general were not measured in this study. Some editors and journalists probably read market research that frequently reports on audience trust.

Others may be aware of academic research documenting audience trust in the media, especially research that has been quoted by news outlets. Journalists' sense of audience trust or mistrust may also be influenced by informal feedback.

Journalists probably vary in their exposure to formal and informal audience feedback, and the content of such feedback varies between and within news organizations. These differences, which were not measured in the current study, may account for the differences among journalists regarding perceived audience trust.

More religious journalists sensed a higher level of audience particular trust. This finding is interesting given the fact that among the Israeli population in general, religious audiences tend to mistrust the news media.

Perhaps religious journalists simply do not feel the antagonism and alienation of religious audiences toward mainstream media because these sentiments are targeted mostly at secular journalists, in addition, some religious journalists probably do not personally feel audience mistrust, since they work for alternative niche-targeted media, and hence they enjoy their religious audience's trust (while their audience's mistrust is targeted toward mainstream news media).

A major limitation of this study has to do with measurement problems in both main constructs. The reliability of the professional identification scale was rather low, and the correlation between the two components of perceived audience trust was only moderate.

However, the main findings were replicated when analyzing general and particular trust components separately and by and large when separating the professional identification scale into single items. Furthermore, when interpreting the results, one should consider the fact that measurement error typically biases correlation estimates downward.

If weak measures worked in the above analyses, then the associations reported could probably be replicated with more accurate measures. In sum, this study demonstrated that journalists' perceptions of audience trust are correlated with their identification with professional norms, their general evaluation of the audience, and their own trust in the media. The design of this study limits our ability to reach conclusions with regard to the causal mechanism explaining these associations.

Future research should explore these mechanisms using a superior (perhaps longitudinal) design and improved measures. The results of the current exploration suggest that doing so should be worthwhile. On the afternoon of April 11, 2007, attorney James Cooney, who represented one of the "Duke Lacrosse case defendants," spoke to a group of students, family and supporters of the defendants, and the news media.

Just minutes before, North Carolina Attorney General Roy Cooper, after an exhaustive investigation in the case, dropped all charges and declared the defendants, Reade Seligmann, Collin Finnerty, and David Evans to be "innocent of all charges." While excoriating the performance of the Durham Herald-Sun in its coverage of the case, Cooney then declared that one cannot win by suing "people who buy ink by the barrels." In other words, while the attorneys and defendants clearly were unhappy with the newspaper, there would be no libel suit forthcoming.

The decision by the attorneys not to sue the Herald-Sun, as well as other media outlets, such as CNN's "Nancy Grace Show," which especially had been quick to pronounce guilt for the Duke Three has its roots in a series of decisions made by the U.S. Supreme Court more than four decades ago. The first of these decisions, Times v. Sullivan, which was decided in March, 1964, in essence rewrote all of state law regarding the libeling of "public officials."

In subsequent decisions, the High Court added most government employees and later included "public figures" as well. There is no doubt that modern libel law is a product of what the court led by Earl Warren decided during the tumultuous Civil Rights Era and did much to change the landscape there.

In a 2004 report, the Media Law Resource Centre noted that over the past 25 years, the media firms have been increasingly winning libel lawsuits filed against them. Media firms are winning more trials, and even the number of libel trials is falling, according to the report1 Furthermore, even large jury awards often are substantially reduced on appeal, the report noted.

It would seem that these developments would bode well for the freedom of the press, and many people have given the U.S. Supreme Court much of the credit for this change in the legal landscape. The U.S. Supreme Court under Chief Justice Warren was well known for its decisions that changed much of the legal landscape in this country.

From Brown v. Board of Education to the Miranda case, the high court reshaped the direction of government policy in its issuances from the bench, triggering a debate on "judicial activism" that resonates to the present day. Although the Warren Court was not known to be particularly friendly to private enterprise, it did act decisively to protect one set of private firms - newspapers and other print media companies - from the ancient tort of libel.

Beginning with its landmark 1964 decision, Times v. Sullivan, to its 1967 decisions of Associated Press v. Walker and Butts v. Curtis Publishing Company, the court in effect rewrote libel law for the entire nation, setting down new and extensive burdens that "public officials" and "public figures" had to overcome in order to win libel suits.

The litigation that began the Sullivan chain of events came from the South during the turbulent Civil Rights Era. A police commissioner from Montgomery, Alabama, claimed that an advertisement in the New York Times libeled him, and a local jury agreed, awarding him $500,000, at that time, according to Lewis, the largest libel judgment in Alabama history. Other officials in southern states were also seeking damages from the Times and other media outlets they considered to be "unfriendly."

The Warren Court overturned that decision - and much of state libel law - and permanently changed the legal environment for libel. For the most part, the court's action is portrayed as an ideological attempt to expand the bounds of freedom of speech and to affect public discourse in this country.

Yet, we believe that this is a rather short-term view that does not take into account the interests of the various players in the courtroom dramas. Indeed, the issue was not simply about free speech, but also how the courts were to deal with what essentially was a strategy by southern politicians to win large libel judgments against northern-based news organizations.

As we see it, there were gains from trade to be obtained from the court's decision: the court protects the newspapers, which simultaneously help to protect the courts from adverse public opinion. James Buchanan and Gordon Tullock began the Public Choice revolution in which researchers have examined government through the lens of interests of the participants. For the most part, the analysis has been of legislatures, since it is rather easy to do statistical analysis using votes.

Examination of the courts via analysis other than one of the "public interest," on the other hand, has been almost non-existent. Timothy Terrell took a Public Choice approach to the issue of standing for environmental groups, but little else has been written on this subject We attempt to add to this literature.

We add that a relatively new journal, the Journal of Empirical Legal Studies, does apply statistical analysis to the courts. It does not pursue a particular point of view but rather examines cases as they occur. For example, the November

2004 edition was devoted entirely to the trend toward civil settlements and criminal guilty pleas, but did not attempt to place it in anything like a Public Choice or interest group framework.

Besides raising questions about the intentions of the Supreme Court in these libel cases, this chapter also examines some of the changes brought about by the high court's decision, looking at the frequency of libel verdicts being reversed on appeal.

Our study shows that (1) the Sullivan decision and others following decidedly changed the patterns of libel awards and appeals, and (2) one can give an alternative explanation to the Gertz v. Welch decision, which we believe was decided, at least in part, because of the unpopular political positions of the John Birch Society.

In the end, we raise the interesting question as to whether or not the Supreme Court was more interested in protecting the "civil rights" and other "progressive" movements, as well as so-called mainstream news media, than it was actually protecting and promoting universal free speech.

Libel and Liability

Libel suits are occupational hazards of journalism, even in the wake of the landmark U.S. Supreme Court decisions. While the First Amendment protects the press from most government censorship, the peril of multimillion dollar losses through libel judgments can threaten the financial and reputational well-being of media organizations, along with reporters who write the offending stories.

Overbeck points out that "the fear of libel suits often leads journalists to suppress newsworthy stories they would otherwise publish, thus engaging in a form of self-censorship that is rarely in the public interest". Even if the libel claims are not legally valid, Overbeck says that "hostile juries sometimes hand out enormous punitive damage awards against newspapers, magazines, and broadcasters...."

He adds that a "single libel suit can be financially devastating even to a powerful media corporation". (In many cases, however, these damage awards are either severely reduced or overturned altogether on appeal, although Overbeck warns that courts do not overturn all multi-million dollar libel judgments.

We argue that the Sullivan and Walker decisions greatly reduced the likelihood of actual payment of huge libel judgments.) Even though newspapers carry libel insurance, the legal fees that newspapers must absorb, even if they win in court, can damage the firm, even in a post-rimes v. Sullivan legal climate.

The possibility of losses due to even the successful defence of a claim of libel can serve as a warning to residual claimants to monitor the content of their newspapers. If a media firm loses a libel case, the payout can be expensive, even if the firm has libel insurance.

Furthermore, there is also the loss of "reputational capital" that a news firm can suffer, and it can have a negative impact on the value of the firm's assets. Thus, one can expect residual claimants to set up a system that will attempt to intercept stories that might be regarded as libelous. Editors, publishers, and attorneys are the barrier to libel, an important line of defence set up by owners of the media firm.

Historical defence of libel has rested upon:

1. Truth: If a statement is true, no matter how harmful or hurtful it may be, it cannot be considered to be libel.
2. Privilege: "Fair and accurate" accounts of what happens during an official government proceeding (including legislative bodies and the courts), along with an accurate report of a government document.
3. Fair Comment: This is a statement of opinion regarding the performance of someone considered to be in the "limelight," including politicians, actors, or sports celebrities.

The U.S. Constitution is not the only legal document protecting freedom of the press. State constitutions also restrict civil authorities from suppressing news stories. Most libel suits have been filed in state courts, and libel cases rarely were overturned by U.S. Supreme Court review before Times v. Sullivan. In 1964, however, the U.S. Supreme Court changed the bounds of freedom of the press dramatically.

The court, led by Chief Justice Warren, continued its activist legacy in Times v. Sullivan, which Editor and Publisher declared to be "one of the most important decisions upholding freedom of the press in our time." It was perhaps the single most important court ruling on libel since the John Peter Zenger decision of 1735 in New York.

Literature on Libel

As one might expect, the legal literature on libel is immense and cannot be covered in a meaningful sense in this brief chapter. However, we use for our background two law journal pieces, including Logan and Franklin; communications law books; and communications books, including Overbeck and Nelson, Teeter and Le Due. However, the legal literature on libel fails to deal with the economic effects that libel cases have had on media firms.

The economics and business literature, unfortunately, is quite scant on this subject Anderson has covered the effects of libel upon asset values of newspaper firms, but most libel literature tends to deal either with the laws themselves or approaches the subject from an ideological viewpoint

According to Franklin, Times v. Sullivan along with Walker did, indeed, change the libel landscape. He writes about libel cases since 1964 that "From an overall perspective, the most striking conclusion is that plaintiffs win such a low percentage of appeals (5 per cent) compared to the success rate of 66 per cent for defendants." Although there have been numerous high dollar judgments given at the trial court level, they rarely stand, Franklin writes.

Logan is even more enthusiastic. Of the post Times v. Sullivan era, he says: Several decades later... we can now fully evaluate the Court's handiwork: few libel claims filed; many dismissed before trial by judges (both state and federal); a handful of trials; some plaintiff victories, but because of the close appellate oversight, only the occasional full affirmation of a jury award, especially punitive damages; and eventual payouts of only cents on the dollar. These are indicia of a significant victory for those who hoped to rein in, but not destroy, the deterrent effect of the law of libel.

As shall be shown at the end of the next section, one can argue that the Sullivan verdict proved to be very important for news organizations that were engaged in libel defenses, especially at the appellate level We first describe the case and then look briefly at its effect on libel verdicts.

Case of New York Times v. Sullivan

On March 29, 1960, the Committee to Defend Martin Luther King and the Struggle for Freedom in the South, a civil rights group, ran a full-page advertisement in the New York Times. Entitled "Heed Their Rising Voices," the advertisement alleged police brutality against civil rights demonstrators in several southern cities, including Montgomery, Alabama.

Nelson, Teeter, and Le Due write that "there were errors in the advertisement" The New York Times admitted in court that it had not checked the text of the advertisements against its own news stories, which gave conflicting accounts of the events. As Nelson, Teeter, and Le Due note, die controversy centered upon the following statement:

In Montgomery, Alabama, after students sang "My Country 'Tis of Thee" on the State Capital steps, their leaders were expelled from school, and truckloads of police armed with shotguns and tear-gas ringed the Alabama State College Campus. When the entire student body protested to state authorities by refusing to re-register, their dining hall was padlocked in an attempt to starve them into submission.

Actually, while police were present in large numbers, they did not surround the Alabama State campus. Furthermore, no one padlocked the dining hall. Although his name was not mentioned in the advertisement Montgomery Police and Fire Commissioner L.B. Sullivan took exception and claimed he was libeled by implication. He sued the Times in Alabama state court for $500,000 in damages. While only about 39 copies of the Times circulated in the Montgomery area (394 in the state of Alabama), according to Lewis, the trial judge in Montgomery ruled that that was a significant enough number for the case to be heard in Alabama Circuit Court.

Judge Walter B. Jones instructed the jury panel that Sullivan did not have to prove that he had suffered any financial damages due to the advertisement He said jurors only had to consider whether or not the statements in the advertisement were false and, if false, it they had adversely affected Sullivan's reputation. The jury returned a verdict for $500,000 in favour of the plaintiff.

The Times appealed to the Alabama Supreme Court which affirmed the lower court ruling. The court said that the verdict did not violate Alabama law, and that the amount of the judgment was fair, even though Sullivan did not prove financial damages. The Times appealed to the U.S. Supreme Court, which agreed to hear the case.

Indeed, the verdict was popular in the South at a time when the region was in the midst of the struggles of what now is called the Civil Rights Era. Even though a fellow newspaper had been financially damaged, the nextday editorial in the Alabama Journal, the Montgomery evening paper, declared that the decision "could have the effect of causing reckless publishers of the North... to make a re-survey of their habit of permitting anything detrimental to die South and its people to appear in their columns".

Emboldened by the decision, a number of other government officials from southern states filed libel suits against news media organizations. By 1964, according to Lewis, local and state officials "had brought nearly $300 million in libel actions against the press," or more than $1.7 billion in current dollars.

Overbeck writes that the U.S. Supreme Court historically had been reluctant to hear state libel cases, but this was no ordinary libel case, nor was this an ordinary Supreme Court. In the January 6, 1964, hearing, Sullivan's attorneys told the court that "the Constitution has never required that states afford newspapers the privilege of leveling false and defamatory 'facts' at persons simply because they hold public office. The great weight of American authority has rejected such a plea by newspapers."

Benjamin J. Stein writes that the court's decision was more about the social and political climate of the day, not about the law: There were two distinctive aspects to this advertisement. First it was largely false in its descriptions of brutality and repression, which turned out to be often made up (emphasis Stein's). second, the advertisement changed history.

He further writes: Legal realism has to be understood, at least glancingly, before one can even start to understand what happened when the Supremes got the appeal on New York Times v. Sullivan. The justices in their black robes were faced with an awesome legal realism problem. On the one hand, cleariy the lower courts were correct in Sullivan.

The advertisement had been not only false, but wildly, irresponsibly, cruelly false. A man had been called a lawless "violater" (sic) when many of the specifics of his bad acts were simply made of whole cloth. libel was a crucial part of the legal structure of America....As recently as 1952, the Supreme Court, per Justice Frankfurter, had said there was no First Amendment protection for libel.

The Supreme Court, Stein writes, was in a quandary. He says: all of the weight of authority stood for the proposition that Sullivan had been defamed falsely, had lost reputation, and collect. Note to author Is something missing in the quote, since "and collect" doesn't fit in Plus, the decisions of the lower courts are presumed to have some weight just because they saw the evidence and the witnesses with their own eyes.

On the other hand...the appellee, Mr. Sullivan, was a segregationalist, an official of George Corley Wallace's Alabama, and all of his friends and supporters were racists and bigots too, presumably. The appellants, and the libelers, so to speak, were kindly black clergymen allied with Martin Luther King, Jr. They were for racial justice. Also, one appellant was the New York Times, by far the most powerful newspaper in the world, a voice of enlightened racial harmony, a strong, important backer of the Warren Court in its most controversial decisions.

It certainly is true that the New York Times was a strong ally of those in the "civil rights" movement, and was on record as editorially supporting many of the controversial Warren Court decisions like Brown vs.

Board of Education. Furthermore, as already pointed out, the strategy of public officials and other outspoken opponents of civil rights for blacks suing New York-based news organizations for libel was proving to be a huge financial threat to these firms, and a decision that would have preserved the established pattern of leaving libel decisions to the states would have left newspapers and broadcast entities open to even more lawsuits.

In hindsight, it is not surprising that the court "saved" the Times, given the situation at that time and the activist nature of the Warren Court. On March 9, 1964, the High Court handed down a 9-0 reversal of the verdict, creating a whole new standard for libel when "public officials" were involved. Furthermore, the justices did not order a new trial, but rather closed the case in order to keep the suit from returning to Alabama.

Justice William J. Brennan wrote the decision for six members of the court (Three other justices, while agreeing with the majority, published their own decisions.) Brennan wrote that the Alabama verdict could not stand for three reasons. First, it gave public officials too much leverage in fighting newspapers with which they disagreed.

Second, it would truncate the "national debate" on controversial issues. Third, public officials voluntarily move into an arena that opens them to more public criticism than is given to private citizens. Brennan's decision declared that "debate on public issues should be uninhibited, robust, and wide-open."

While he agreed that such debate "may well include vehement, caustic, and sometimes unpleasantly sharp attacks on government and public officials," the First Amendment protected such debate, said Brennan. The court raised the burden of proof for public officials who sue for libel, making them prove that a defamatory statement "was made with 'actual malice', which is knowledge that it was false or given with reckless disregard of whetiier it was false or not," according to Justice Brennan's opinion.

"Times malice" requires that public officials who wish to win a libel suit must be able to demonstrate successfully in court that those who published the falsehood either knew the information they were publishing was false, or that the defendants acted recklessly in searching for the truth. Armed with its decision, the court expanded the "Times malice" requirement to nearly all government employees. In its Curtis Publishing Company v. Wallace Butts and Associated Press v. Edwin A. Walker decisions in 1967, a unanimous court extended libel protection to stories written about people who were "public figures." The court's decision granted extra protection to media firms, and potentially saved newspapers and broadcasters millions of dollars in libel judgments.

The Walker case was similar to that of Sullivan. Former U.S. Army Gen. Edwin Walker, who had been accused of circulating John Birch Society literature to his soldiers in the 24th Infantry Division stationed in Germany, later organized protests to the admission of James Meredith, an African-American., to what was then the all-white University of Mississippi in 1962 after Walker's resignation from the army.

Like Sullivan, Walker sued the Associated Press for its admittedly inaccurate coverage of his activities during the protests, which became so violent that President John F. Kennedy sent National Guard troops to enforce a desegregation order from the federal courts. And like Walker, he was awarded $500,000 by a sympathetic jury, a decision that was upheld until the Supreme Court overturned it by its decision to apply the "Times malice" standards to Walker, whom it determined to be a "public figure."

The numbers bear out the success of the Sullivan and Walker decisions in reducing libel claims. While the average verdict at the trial level rose significantly in the years following the decisions, the appellate courts clearly took the high court's rulings to heart and were much more likely either to reverse the lower court decisions or to substantially reduce the awards amounts. While jury awards did rise during the post-Sullivan era, the appeals courts were much more likely to overturn the jury decisions or at least shrink the judgments that juries awarded people they believed to be victims of libel. The Walker decision seemed to have settled the libel question, but the Warren Court also had generated much controversy.

First, jurists like William Rehnquist and Warren Burger believed the high court had erred in taking much of the libel authority from the states in the way that it did in Sullivan and beyond. Second, one can argue that the "liberalism" of the Warren Court also helped to energize conservative political groups who were against the court's decisions against prayers in public schools, school desegregation, the rights of criminal suspects, and criminal investigations.

Thus, when Republican Richard Nixon became President of the United States in 1969, conservatives hoped that he would make appointments that would push the courts in other directions. (Whether the Supreme Court under the leadership of Nixon appointee Chief Justice Burger was more "conservative" is a matter for discussion, but it is clear that Nixon and other conservatives wanted the court to change some of its ideological and legal directions.)

The case of Gertz v. Welch ultimately was a challenge to the earlier Warren Court libel rulings for two reasons. First, it offered the court the alternatives of either to continue its expansive rulings regarding libel or to scale them back; second, it offered the court another opportunity to examine the separation of powers between states and the federal government However, as is demonstrated in the next section, the high court took a third option: it relied upon what one might describe as a "legal technicality."

The Gertz v. Welch Decision

Gertz is similar to Butts and Walker in that Elmer Gertz, a Chicago attorney, was prominent in his profession.

However, unlike those two, the high court ruled in a 5-4 decision that Gertz was not a "public figure" and, therefore, did not have to meet the "Times malice" standard in order to win his lawsuit against American Opinion, which is published by the John Birch Society.

(Gertz, an attorney, successfully represented a family that brought civil action against a Chicago police officer who shot and killed their son. An article in American Opinion called Gertz a "Leninist" and a "Communistfronter," among other things and claimed the lawsuit was a "frame-up" against the police officer.)

As the numbers demonstrate, not all of the court agreed. Justices William O. Douglas and Brennan argued for expanding the "Times malice" standard to everyone, not just public officials and public figures in the course of public discussion. As in the situation of Sullivan and Walker, one of the parties in the lawsuit opposed the imposition of civil rights laws and policies.

However, unlike Sullivan and Walker, this time the anti-civil rights party was the plaintiff, not the defendant The John Birch Society was and is known for its "ultraconservative" views and was vehemently opposed to the Warren Court and many of its decisions, although, ironically, it was using one of that court's most famous decisions on libel as die basis for its appeal. If the standards used in the Butts and Walker decisions had been applied in Gertz, it is clear that the court would have deemed Elmer Gertz a "public figure."

Gertz, after all, had been involved in a number of prominent cases, including the winning of parole in 1958 of the notorious killer Nathan Leopold, and he ultimately succeeded in having the death penalty overturned for a famous client, Jack Ruby (who shot Lee Harvey Oswald to death on national television). Nor was the High Court united, as it had been with Sullivan and Walker, both of which were unanimous decisions, while the Gertz vote was 5-4.

Justices who were on all three courts included William O. Douglas, William Brennan, Potter Stewart and Byron White. Of these justices, only Stewart voted with the majority in Gertz. The four other votes came from justices appointed by presidents Lyndon B. Johnson and Richard M Nixon.

Public discussion in the aftermath of Gertz centered on the question of whether the high court was "giving back" protections that the Warren Court had given to the press. In his dissent, Douglas argued that the decision amounted to an "erosion of First Amendment protection" of journalists. While Chief Justice Warren Burger also dissented, he and White "argued that the Court had gone too far in the direction of protecting the press, and that common law rules should be left intact in libel cases involving private individuals."

Yet, the court ultimately based its decision on a small point: it ruled that Elmer Gertz was not a "public figure," so the court's rules established in Walker did not apply. However, as pointed out before, Gertz was well-known in legal circles around the country, not to mention in Chicago itself, and certainly was as much a "public figure" as others to whom the courts had given that designation.

The real difference was not in the nature of the plaintiff, but rather in the common thread of each of the defendants: they held to very different views on race and racial integration than did the majority of the Supreme Court-and the plaintiffs. American Opinion was not a mainstream publication, but rather an arm of the very conservative John Birch Society, which not only had called for resistance to the civil rights movement but also had been at the forefront in calling for the impeachment of Earl Warren during the 1960s.

The court clearly was not in favour of offering protection to an entity which-unlike the New York Times a decade earlier-was not on the same page with the Supreme Court when it came to civil rights issues. The Supreme Court not only upheld Gertz's claim that he was not a "public figure," but also remanded the case back for another trial. This time, instead of the $50,000 verdict which came from the first trial, the jury ordered the John Birch Society to pay Gertz $500,000.

Moreover, it is clear that the court's decision and the trial that followed afterward was popular with at least some advocates of press freedom. Perhaps the most telling example comes from the former New York Times columnist and reporter Anthony Lewis, who already has been cited at length in this chapter for his book that strongly supported the U.S. Supreme Court's Sullivan decision. Writes Gertz (1992):

Congratulatory letters and calls poured in following the extensive publicity of the (second) jury verdict....Anthony Lewis, the much-quoted columnist and Supreme Court reporter whose book Gideon's Trumpet is a classic in narrating a case in understandable terms, had been calling me from time to time during the long years of delay to learn the latest developments in my case. "You did it for many others besides yourself," he wrote.

This is the same Anthony Lewis who wrote the following about Times v. Sullivan and its aftermath: in the years following the Sullivan decision, the court resoundingly vindicated the promise of the First Amendment that in the United States there shall be "no law... abridging the freedom of speech, or of the press."

However, Lewis was willing to make an exception in the Gertz case, and if one has read Lewis' columns over the years, it is clear that he has a special dislike for people whose political positions are anywhere to the right of his, and, thus, he would not be sympathetic to the John Birch Society.

Furthermore, he claims that Elmer Gertz had his reputation "damaged" by the American Opinion piece, yet Gertz clearly was open about his left-of-centre political viewpoints and certainly would not have minded being called a "Leninist" or anything else by people on the right In fact, it would seem that in Gertz's circles,praise fromAmerican Opinion would have been much more damaging to his reputation than condemnation.

Moreover, Lewis specifically condemned the use of libel as a bankrupting tool elsewhere in Make No Law, yet when it was clear that the half-million dollar verdict was aimed at doing severe financial damage to the John Birch Society, that was acceptable to him.

Upon pocketing his award, Gertz took his wife and friends on an around-the-world cruise and sent "wish-you-were-here" postcards to the JBS headquarters from various ports of call.

Yet, if one gains a sense of the First Amendment, which Lewis claimed to be supporting, it was written to protect unpopular speech by unpopular people, and one would hope that includes members of the John Birch Society. In judging Lewis's post-Gertz actions, however, one gains the sense that it could be an example of what Nat Hentoff called Free Speech for Me, but Not for Thee.

The editorial response of the New York Times to the Gertz decision also gives us pause as to the newspaper's views on free speech. The June 26, 1974, a front-page article in the Times began with the following:

The Supreme Court ruled today that an ordinary citizen elevated to sudden prominence by news events can sue any newspaper or radio or television station that circulates a false and defamatory account of his role in those events....The high court left standing however, the protection of newspapers and broadcast stations against such libel suits when their reports deal with "a public official" or a "public figure," even if the articles are untrue and damage his reputation.

As noted earlier, Elmer Gertz hardly was an "ordinary citizen," given his penchant for representing high-profile clients, nor did American Opinion's information, as inaccurate as it might have been, damage Gertz's reputation in any meaningful sense of the word. Furthermore, an editorial in the New York Times dated June 27, 1974, fully supported the Supreme Court's decision: In a five-to-four decision, the Court made what impresses us as a sensible adjustment in its rules permitting private individuals, as distinct from public officials or other public personalities, to sue newspapers or television stations for libel. Under some past decisions it has appeared virtually impossible for ordinary citizens projected into sudden prominence by a particular event to protect themselves against false and defamatory reports.

Civil libertarians, not to mention organizations representing newspapers, had a much different opinion than did the Times, which apparently was all-too-happy to see the court backtrack when the defendants were of a different political persuasion than the Times editorial board.

As Gertz himself acknowledges, a number of organizations, including the American Newspaper Publishers Association, American Society of Newspaper Editors, Association of American University Presses, and the Authors League of America, among others, formed the Libel Defence Resource Centre in 1981 in part to deal with potential libel problems that arose, in part, because of the Gertz decision.

Whether or not ideology or a commitment to "fairness" drove the Times to take its supportive position of Gertz v. Welch is beyond the scope of our research. However, one does have to look somewhat askance at a journalistic organization that was willing to sacrifice "robust" speech because people whose political beliefs were inimical to that of the Times editorial board were in the dock.

The Impact of Sullivan and Gertz

By changing the ground rules of libel during the 1960s, the High Court lowered the risk newspapers face in publishing stories, as many news stories involve either public officials or public figures. Thus, the decisions significantly lessened the probability of someone successfully suing media firms. While media companies would still have to spend money for legal fees if someone chose to sue for libel, Times v. Sullivan reduced the chances of newspapers and broadcasters having to pay large judgments and also would be seen to be a deterrent to new lawsuits.

Even though libel insurance many pay a large portion of the judgment, the lessening of the chances of losing a libel suit would also serve to enhance the firm's "reputational capital" because a news outlet suffers in the public esteem after a jury returns a guilty verdict.

The court's actions fit an event study because because in hindsight this decision was not surprising, given the activist nature of the Warren Court and its sympathies for those in the Civil Rights Movement However, at the time the ruling was a bombshell. Even the attorneys for the New York Times, who had hoped the court at least would overturn the libel verdict never expected the justices to effectively rewrite libel laws for all 50 states. It was not just the new standards set by the court that turned libel law upside down, but also the fact that the High Court once again had trumped what once had been in the states' domain.

Up to the court's disposition of that case, many in the media believed that the Supreme Court had all but abolished state libel laws. Gertz, while reaffirming the court's public official/public figure position, left the libel door open for "private persons" to successfully sue by requiring less than the "actual malice" or "Times malice" standard in their case, yet one wonders if the application of "private person" status to Elmer Gertz was made arbitrarily because the justices on the U.S. Supreme court, as well as many of their political allies, did not wish to be seen as standing up for an organization like the John Birch Society..

But, as noted earlier, while private individuals did not have to prove the actual malice standard to win a judgment, they did have to prove actual damages, according to the court despite the small gain for those suing for libel, there was no returning to the pre-Sullivan legal climate. Thus, the case both kept vital protection for newspapers, but also left other media outlets vulnerable.

For example, on the same day, June 25, 1974, the high court struck down a Florida law that required newspapers in that state to print replies by people who believed they had been unfairly criticized by that particular paper, a newspaper version of the "Fairness Doctrine" that at the time applied to broadcasters. The unanimous ruling was an important victory for newspapers, and it further raises questions about the protections the court afforded established newspapers versus the publication of an unpopular political organization.

In examining the aftermath of the court's decisions on libel, one first must keep in mind that the court did not employ these rulings in order to provide financial benefits to newspapers. We contend that it was trying to protect certain news outlets from being sued into bankruptcy by segregationalist politicians and activists, and the court was trying to protect its own civil rights legacy by helping to ensure that news organizations that supported its actions were not silenced.

Thus, while it is clear that the decisions conferred at least some economic benefits upon newspapers, that hardly would have been the court's main purpose. Likewise, when the court in 1974 ruled that Ebner Gertz was a private figure, one result was that it created a temporary loss in the stock value of newspapers, and one doubts that the court meant to cause financial damage to all newspapers.

There is no doubt, however, that the Gertz decision did cause serious financial loss to the John Birch Society. Not only did the organization lose money, but it had to pay court costs and other expenses. As noted in the previous section, the immediate results also suggest that the limited nature of the court's decision in Gertz gives evidence that the action was not necessarily a backward turn on libel, but rather another example of the court protecting the civil rights legacy that it and others had established.

This, of course, is only speculation, but we do think the results do not necessarily lead us away from that line of thinking. As we pointed out in the introduction, libel suits do not provide the same danger to media firms that they once did, although, as MLRC Executive Director Sandra Baron does warn that the dangers from libel have not disappeared, either:

The good news is that there are fewer libel, privacy and related claims going to trial against media defendants, and that media are winning a higher percentage of those that do go to trial. But these cases remain a threat to the media. While most of these excessive trial awards are reduced on appeal, the expense of litigating can be daunting.

The danger is that excessive damage awards, and the cost of litigating and appealing them, may give editors and publishers pause when covering controversial people and topics. We have argued in this chapter that the decisions by the Warren and later Burger courts regarding libel certainly provided overall protection for media firms, although the protection was not complete, as the John Birch Society found out. We do believe that protection of speech-even if the court's decisions might have some political motivation-still is important to a free society, whatever reasoning the courts might give. In that, we agree with Franklin and others that the High Court's decisions of more than 40 years ago still resonate today.

Chapter 6

Conduit-Based Regulation of Speech

Architecture is destiny. As much as information today determines the contemporary wealth of nations, the physical world retains its relevance. Architecture affects crime rates, arguably even collegiality among professors. The interplay between the physical and the ethereal likewise shapes the constitutional doctrine that facilitates the free flow of ideas.

The structure of a communicative medium dictates its performance. Awareness of the structure of information markets improves the calibration of intellectual property and refines legal responses to potential electronic bottlenecks. This Chapter takes the next logical step: revealing the deep doctrinal structure of legal efforts to influence the design and maintenance of communicative conduits.

This Chapter's examination of free speech jurisprudence begins by describing how any communicative medium can be visualized as three distinct physical, logical, and content-based layers. End-to-end design, the Internet's operative ideal, also provides a crucial doctrinal metaphor.

Like the conduits through which communications pass, free speech jurisprudence can also be analysed layer by layer. Cases involving the regulation of the time, place, or manner of speech comprises the physical layer, in which regulatory prerogative generally prevail. By contrast, most forms of content-based regulation draw strict scrutiny.

In a perverse twist of the end-to-end principle, the intelligence in First Amendment jurisprudence resides at its edges. Though the Supreme Court has achieved doctrinal stability in reviewing content-based restrictions and time-place-manner rules, the Justices have behaved erratically whenever they have examined the intermediate logical layer—cases involving the regulation of specific communicative conduits.

The Court has not developed a cogent approach to regulations designed to structure channels of communication that mediate between physical space and eventual expression A generation ago, decisions affirming comprehensive federal power over broadcasting practically defined conduit-based regulation of speech. Broadcasting cases cannot be squared with strict scrutiny of content-based regulation of speech.

Since 1978 the Supreme Court has proved quite uneven in keeping pace with technological changes in communications. After locating the doctrinal baseline established in the broadcasting cases, this Chapter surveys more recent cases involving cable television and sexually explicit speech in a variety of media.

Four interrelated rationales for conduit-based regulation of speech have emerged: scarcity, regulatory intensity, the government's interest in enhancing voices, and a conduit's pervasiveness. Although each of these rationales is superficially plausible, deeper inspection counsels a skeptical regard for the notion that conduit-based regulation merits distinctive First Amendment treatment.

This Chapter accordingly disavows the strategy of adjusting First Amendment standards of review in response to putative differences among conduits in reviewing conduit-based restrictions on speech, courts should remain wary of disguised efforts to control content the end-to-end principle counsels simple standards for reviewing regulation aimed at the logical layer of speech Real information is ideally transmitted on simple protocols that allow speakers and listeners to control all intelligence within a network.

Likewise, a constitutional jurisprudence that minimizes reliance on conduit-based distinctions best protects free speech. Architecture is destiny. As much as information today determines the contemporary wealth of nations, the physical world retains its relevance. Even though firms in today's technology-driven economy derive much of their value from information and other "intangible resources," physical determinants of productivity remain critical.

Architecture affects crime rates, arguably even collegiality among law professors. Paradoxically, place may assume greater value in an information-based economy. "Place has become the central organizing unit of our time, taking on many of the functions that used to be played by firms and other organizations."

The interplay between the physical and the ethereal likewise shapes the constitutional doctrine that facilitates the free flow of ideas. "Physical settings shape expressive practices and expectations." The structure of a communicative medium virtually dictates its performance.

Wealth transfers within the new economy prompt "new efforts by the government to intervene in the marketplace to favour a particular outcome," and in due course courts will entertain "new constitutional claims" arising within the political economy of modern communications. Awareness of the structure of information markets improves the calibration of intellectual property and refines legal responses to potential electronic bottlenecks.

This Chapter takes the next logical step: revealing the deep doctrinal structure of legal efforts to influence the design and maintenance of communicative conduits. End-to-end design, the Internet's operative ideal, illustrates how logical architecture affects network performance and how the law in turn shapes architecture.

End-to-end design also provides a crucial doctrinal metaphor. Like the conduits through which communications pass, free speech jurisprudence can also be analysed layer by layer. Cases involving the regulation of the time, place, or manner of speech comprise the physical layer, in which regulatory prerogative generally prevails.

By contrast, most forms of content-based regulation draw strict scrutiny. In a perverse twist of the end-to-end principle, the intelligence in First Amendment jurisprudence resides at its edges. Though the Supreme Court has achieved doctrinal stability in reviewing content-based restrictions and time-place-manner rules, the Justices have behaved erratically whenever they have examined the intermediate logical layer—cases involving the regulation of specific communicative conduits.

The Court has not developed a cogent approach to regulations designed to structure channels of communication that mediate between physical space and eventual expression. A generation ago, decisions affirming comprehensive federal power over broadcasting practically defined conduit-based regulation of speech. In The Mobius Strip of the First Amendment, William Van Alstyne argued that the broadcasting cases could not be squared with strict scrutiny of content-based regulation of speech.

Since 1978 the Supreme Court has proved quite uneven in keeping pace with technological changes in communications. Four interrelated rationales have emerged: scarcity, regulatory intensity, the government's interest in enhancing voices, and a conduit's pervasiveness. Although each of these rationales is superficially plausible, deeper inspection counsels a skeptical regard for the notion that conduit-based regulation merits distinctive First Amendment treatment.

In reviewing conduit-based restrictions on speech, courts should remain wary of disguised efforts to control content. The end-to-end principle counsels simple standards for reviewing regulation aimed at the logical layer of speech. Real information is ideally transmitted on simple protocols that allow speakers and listeners to control all intelligence within a network. Likewise, a constitutional jurisprudence that minimizes reliance on conduit-based distinctions best protects free speech.

FREE SPEECH JURISPRUDENCE, END-TO-END

The structure of any communications conduit reflects the tripartite division of human enterprise between production, transmission, and distribution. Implicit in the structure of the

Internet, among other conduits, is the end-to-end principle. By simplifying communicative protocols, end-to-end design drives all intelligence within a network toward its edges, where speakers generate ideas and audiences respond.

Free speech jurisprudence should be understood as operating within physical, logical, and content layers. Section A elaborates the three-layered structure of the Internet. Section B shows how the law of free speech falls into three corresponding layers.

THE INTERNET AS DEVELOPMENTAL PARABLE

Industria est omnia divisa en tres partes. Virtually every industry in an age of mass production and consumption, "like ancient Gaul, is divided into three parts": production, wholesale transmission, and retail distribution. What is true of chrysanthemums and "the flow of wheat from the West to the mills and distributing points of the East" applies with greater force to electronic networks.

A similar tripartite model governs the spatial, legal, and social infrastructure of communications. Network architecture dictates how speakers and listeners interact. Every conduit consists of a physical layer, a logical (or code) layer, and a content layer. The physical layer of the Internet consists of network infrastructure. Common logical protocols within a packet-switched, interconnected network transforms the physical Internet into "a unique medium... located in no particular geographic location but available to anyone, anywhere in the world."

Atop lies a rich content layer, the fertile output of the "most participatory form of mass speech yet developed." Rife with "material about topics ranging from aardvarks to Zoroastrianism," that content "is as diverse as human thought." Standard accounts of economic development describe property as the engine of growth. In an information-driven economy, intangible property plays the heroic role of spurring innovation.

But closer examination reveals the modest contribution of intellectual property to the Internet's inventive potential, at least relative to the network's open architecture. The Internet's most distinctive logical features have arisen from the explicit eschewing of proprietary standards.

Most elements of the Internet's logical architecture, such as HTML and the TCP/IP protocol, lie in the public domain. Only on the desktop, the technological frontier at which most users encounter Internet content, do proprietary markers begin to divide the terrain.

At the heart of the Internet lies its operating ideal, the end-to-end principle. End-to-end architecture seeks to accomplish two related goals. First, the higher-level layers, "more specific to an application, are free to organize lower-level network resources to achieve application-specific design goals efficiently."

By contrast, "[l]ower-level layers, which support many independent applications, should provide only resources of broad utility across applications," while enabling applications throughout the network to share resources and resolve conflicts over resources.

End-to-end design places a network's "intelligence" at its ends while keeping all intervening protocols as simple and general as possible. Providers and consumers of content may express themselves creatively, whereas the network itself is "stupid." The resemblance to parsimonious computer programming is unmistakable. "By keeping the network simple, and its interaction general, the Internet has facilitated the design of" unanticipated applications such as "Internet telephony, digital music transfer, and electronic commerce."

End-to-end design also promises neutrality vis-a-vis "new uses of the network": "[N]on-discrimination... invites innovation. It is a guarantee... that innovation will be rewarded if the innovation is one that markets respect." The absence of a "centralized distribution point" makes it difficult for "network operators or government regulators" to "stifle independent information sources."

The "abundance generated by... an open-access network eliminates one of the key First Amendment diversity difficulties found in mass media." That the Internet currently strives to maintain the end-to-end ideal does not mean that every conduit naturally achieves this streamlined architecture.

The debate over the application vel non of real property doctrines to Internet traffic fiercely disputes whether access to websites should be governed by a rule sounding of nuisance within a commons, or, alternatively, whether "a rule of consent supported by judicial injunctions" should constitute the "default rule" for "access to websites and proprietary networks connected to the Internet."

Neither end-to-end nor proprietary design arises without deliberate legal intermediation. Just as every form of intellectual property is dictated by positive law rather than by nature, the law consciously crafts the architecture of every conduit in order to achieve some set of regulatory goals. No less than interpretation, network architecture is "normative all the way down."

By regulating a conduit's operative logic, the government can control its content. That potential in every other setting attracts serious judicial attention. It also warrants a closer look at the logic of free speech jurisprudence.

A NEW HOPE FOR FREE SPEECH JURISPRUDENCE

One can condense American constitutional law into a struggle to reconcile two standards of review articulated in the early years of the Republic. One standard prescribes deference to legislative prerogatives; the other calls for strict scrutiny of suspect laws. The former standard operates as a rubber stamp; the latter is "'strict' in theory" but "fatal in fact." Real confusion arises when the Supreme Court attempts to bridge these extremes.

Constitutional protection of speech is no exception. Much of free speech jurisprudence represents an exercise in drawing categorical boundaries. The three prevailing categories correspond closely to the three layers of a communicative conduit. On "track one,", content-based regulation triggers strict scrutiny unless the speech at issue is worthless, less valuable or more dangerous than "core" speech, or not really speech at all. These exceptions aside, track one is very protective. On this track, "government has no power to restrict expression because of its message, its ideas, its subject matter, or its content." "Subject only to narrow and well-understood exceptions," track one forswears "governmental control over the content of messages expressed by private individuals" in favour of "the principle that each person should decide for himself or herself the ideas and beliefs deserving of expression, consideration, and adherence."

Giving "government the choice of permissible subjects for public debate" would concede an unthinkable official monopoly "over the search for political truth." Track one's dedication to the proposition that "one [person's] vulgarity is another's lyric" vindicates the axiom "that no official, high or petty, can prescribe what shall be orthodox in politics, nationalism, religion, or other matters of opinion."

At the other extreme, "time, place, and manner regulations are acceptable so long as they are designed to serve a substantial governmental interest and do not unreasonably limit alternative avenues of communication," unless the government has dedicated its own property for use by private speakers or the public at large has acquired some sort of speech-related easement.

Weak scrutiny in most physical layer cases typifies "track two" controversies in which "government is concerned with the noncommunicative impact of speech, not the message that is being conveyed." Courts sometimes apply no meaningful scrutiny at all. For instance, when government shuts an adult bookstore to ban prostitution on the premises, the government's valid interest in fighting the sex trade drains all constitutional relevance from the incidental closure of the bookstore.

First Amendment doctrine contemplates a third track. Government endeavors at times to speak in its own right, either by operating its own communicative institutions or by subsidizing private parties who propagate officially sanctioned ideas. "Track one and one-half [blends] track one's concern with government's control of messages [with] track two's concern with government's allocation of resources."

Expressive conduct cases epitomize this track. The aesthetic and legal significance of clothing illustrates how "a message may be delivered by conduct that is intended to be communicative and that, in context, would reasonably be understood by the viewer to be communicative."

By the same token, if a message hinges on the expressive value of "sleeping in symbolic tents" on public parkland, the government may assert a countervailing "interest in conserving park property" through "measures such as the proscription of sleeping that are designed to limit the wear and tear on park properties."

Given that the expressive conduct test of United States v. O'Brien "asks so little in principle, it should not be surprising that it means so little in practice."Public forum cases likewise typify track one and one-half. In theory, public forum doctrine represents a departure from minimal scrutiny of burdens on the time, place, and manner of speech. Yet the doctrine settles far less than it promises.

It resolves nothing to assert, as public forum doctrine does, that the government may regulate the time, place, and manner of speech in order to advance significant objectives unrelated to the message being conveyed, as long as the government neither bars speech altogether nor extinguishes adequate alternative channels of communication.

Because alternative channels are never fully adequate, all regulations of public forums "will entirely suppress speech with respect to some potential audience and with a particular cognitive and emotive impact." To describe the central problem of public forum doctrine as "whether the manner of expression is basically incompatible with the normal activity of a particular place at a particular time" is emphatically not to answer this "crucial question."

The same conflict between space and expression pervades "captive audience" and "no place like home" cases, which attempt to reconcile speech-related uses of circumscribed spaces with nonspeakers' interests in privacy, peace, and quiet. Situated between the physical and content layers, the logical layer lies squarely on track one and one-haft.

Insofar as the logical layer in communications intercedes between physical infrastructure and ultimate expression, regulation of that layer combines an official interest in resource allocation with an interest in content. Logical layer cases oscillate between the relatively skeptical attitude toward content-based regulation and the comparatively deferential approach to laws affecting the time, place, or manner of speech. This facile jurisprudential taxonomy begs a critical question: which decisions comprise the logical layer?

Contemporary communications analysis treats "code" as synonymous with the logical layer. And "code" in real space consists of the "constitutions, statutes, and other legal" prescriptions that shape human conduct. Any expressive "medium" consists of the "set of social conventions and practices shared by speakers and audience." The logical layer of free speech jurisprudence comprises controversies in which the law structures the use of a communicative conduit in putatively content-neutral fashion and in ways beyond those dictated by the conduit's physical characteristics.

The logical layer transcends strictly physical constraints and addresses regulatory interests independent of content. Correspondingly, official responses to a conduit's logical characteristics, as opposed to its physical or expressive traits, represent conduit-based regulation of speech. I will treat the "logical layer" and "conduit-based regulation" as synonymous.

Consider conventional broadcasting. Yochai Benkler describes "radio frequency spectrum" as part of the "physical infrastructure level" of "the information environment." This is not quite right. Spectrum "is not a thing but a force (or more precisely a 'disturbance in the force,' to employ Star Wars terminology)." A spectrum license grants the right to transmit information, for a fixed period, at a stipulated frequency, and in or to a particular location.

Spectrum does not exist of its own accord; it gains legal life once the FCC "determines the quantity and location of frequencies to allocate for a given service," decides how to divide "the frequencies allocated for a given service," and ultimately "assigns licenses to particular entities" by comparative hearings, auctions, or lotteries. Rights in spectrum are not "purely a natural phenomenon, because the number of broadcast stations is more a function of regulatory policy choices than a function of radio frequency constraints."

Official decisions to divide wavelengths "into discrete parcels and [to] licens[e] them for use so that interference is minimized" effectively "create" spectrum. In a notorious instance of the interplay between legal policy and spectrum's physical characteristics, the FCC's relentless pursuit of localism fixed the number of national television networks at three for decades. Only the FCC's decision to relax its restrictions on television networks' programming options broke the grip of CBS, NBC, and ABC.

The problem of crafting a First Amendment approach to the logical layer transcends broadcasting. Whenever courts ponder whether to adjust First Amendment analysis by conduit—FM radio, cable television, the Internet, or direct broadcast satellite—the interplay between regulation and the conduit's physical attributes engages the free speech jurisprudence of the logical layer. Content-based restrictions that would receive withering scrutiny in any other setting (especially in print media) suddenly enjoy greater vitality if portrayed as conduit-based regulation.

To the extent that the entire First Amendment corpus can be recharacterized either as content-based or as content-neutral-after all, laws assertedly directed to "values unrelated to communication, such as noise, congestion, property, aesthetics, or privacy," ultimately "have information effects" insofar as they "affect what gets said, by whom, to whom, and with what effect" —the concept of conduit-based regulation provides merely another channel by which courts may switch between track one's libertarian jurisprudence and track two's pro-governmental stance.

At least two-thirds of free speech jurisprudence is as cogent as any other constitutional doctrine. "[D]espite its difficulty, complexity, and controversiality," track one is reasonably stable. By and large, content-layer decisions are quite protective of speech. Regulations targeting the time, place, or manner of speech face a different fate. Intermediate scrutiny in the physical layer purportedly differs from "the rule of rationality which will sustain legislation against other constitutional challenges," but the results suggest otherwise. "The sole consistency" within track two "is that... the Government [almost] always wins."

Everything else defies description. Track one and one-half follows no predictable, normatively defensible set of doctrines. Cases on speech subsidies offer all the theoretical satisfaction of any body of law involving potentially unconstitutional conditions. The logical layer cases similarly confound ordinary comprehension.

By failing to incorporate awareness of any communicative system's layers, the Supreme Court's free speech jurisprudence has ironically come to resemble an end-to-end network: intelligent edges connected by a dumb pipe oblivious to the content being transmitted within it. Free speech jurisprudence can also be understood in terms of the Star Wars movies. Content layer cases decidedly favour individual speakers, as though Luke Skywalker were the protagonist in every controversy.

Luke offers good company to the war protesters whose tribulations gave birth to contemporary free speech law. If only the Rebel Alliance would trade its lightsabers for gavels, this mythically grandiose body of law, filled with valiant nonconformists, iconoclasts, and dissenters, could be called "The Hero with a Thousand Cases." Track one has completed the cosmic cycle of "a separation from the world, a penetration to some source of power, and a life-enhancing return."

Other cases consistently uphold the government's regulatory interests. Darth Vader best personifies the physical layer decisions. Especially when the government controls physical terrain cloaked in emblems of sovereignty, rebellious uses such as protests harbor no hope. All other cases are so outlandishly cryptic and so corpulent and ugly that they might as well have been rendered by Jabba the Hutt. There is another way to characterize the Court's least satisfying decisions. Their reasoning can be deciphered, but only after great strain, and what the Court has to say is trivial and ultimately quite annoying.

Perhaps Jar Jar Binks would be a better mascot. Alas, either of these George Lucas creations would aptly symbolize the logical layer cases. In addressing these logical layer cases, this Chapter will tackle the daunting task of translating from Hutt or Jar Jar Speaks into English.

THE LOGICAL LAYER OF FREE SPEECH JURISPRUDENCE

Cases contesting conduit-based regulation of speech have varied, as one might expect, by conduit. As of 1978, when William Van Alstyne wrote The Mobius Strip of the First Amendment, this jurisprudential "logical layer" consisted almost entirely of cases involving broadcasting.

The intervening quarter-century has confounded the Supreme Court's views of conduit-based regulation. This Chapter will now examine the logical layer cases in three conduits: broadcasting, cable, and the Internet.

BROADCASTING'S SPECIAL CONSTITUTIONAL STATUS

Courts routinely use technological changes to dilute constitutional protection for speech in a new conduit. At a minimum, "differences in the characteristics of new media justify differences in the First Amendment standards applied to them." Justice Jackson proclaimed that each conduit "is a law unto itself": "The moving picture screen, the radio, the newspaper, the handbill, the sound truck and the street corner orator have differing natures, values, abuses and dangers." Justice Kennedy has advocated analyzing laws affecting new conduits "by reference to existing elaborations of constant First Amendment principles."

This habit has proved surprisingly durable. In conduit-based controversies, courts often try to derive "the operative metaphor for freedom of speech" from "an appropriate analogy for the technology." Rooted in broadcasting, this analogical technique eventually yielded a comprehensive "Broadcast Model."

"Of all forms of communication, it is broadcasting that has received the most limited First Amendment protection." Conventional wisdom traces broadcasting's diminished constitutional status to Red Lion Broadcasting Co. v. FCC, the 1969 decision that upheld a federal right-of-reply regime within broadcasting. To begin an examination of broadcasting's special status with Red Lion, however, is to neglect more than a quarter-century of constitutional history.

In the 1940s, the FCC recognized that an increasing amount of programming was not locally produced, but "transmitted by wire... from their point of origination" by a national syndicate "to each station in the network for simultaneous broadcast." The FCC's "chain broadcasting" rules eventually evolved into longstanding rules regarding network affiliation and station ownership, territorial exclusivity, the division of the broadcast day, and network influence over programming and advertising.

In National Broadcasting Co. v. United States, the Supreme Court upheld the chain broadcasting rules. Much of NBC has fallen to the deregulatory axe. Even that decision's most dramatic consequence, the divestiture of NBC's "Blue" network into ABC, probably would not happen today. NBC's constitutional legacy, however, is considerably greater. In rejecting the network's First Amendment challenge, Justice Frankfurter reasoned: "Freedom of utterance is abridged to many who use the limited facilities of radio.

Unlike other modes of expression, radio inherently is not available to all. That is its unique characteristic, and that is why, unlike other modes of expression, it is subject to governmental regulation." Characterizing "the facilities of radio as limited and therefore precious," NBC concluded that spectrum "cannot be left to wasteful use without detriment to the public interest."

If any decision deserves credit as the origin of conduit-based regulation's "scarcity" rationale, it is NBC and not Red Lion. In strictly doctrinal terms, Red Lion represents a modest extension of NBC. Yet Red Lion's greater prominence vis-a-vis NBC is readily understood. Whereas NBC involved the degree of vertical integration and coordination in which a network could engage with local affiliates, Red Lion targeted expressive, editorial decisions by broadcasters.

The rules in Red Lion subjected broadcasters to "broad rights of access for outside speakers" that, in almost any other setting, would be "antithetical... to the discretion" that the Constitution guarantees to publishers. The Supreme Court evaluated "the requirement that discussion of public issues be presented on broadcast stations, and that each side of those issues must be given fair coverage."

The personal attack rule provided that "[w]hen a personal attack has been made on a figure involved in a public issue... the individual attacked himself [must] be offered an opportunity to respond." The political editorializing rule required a broadcaster who endorsed or opposed a political candidate to offer all disfavored "candidates... reply time to use personally or through a spokesman." Unlike "the general fairness requirement," the personal attack rule and the editorializing rule gave a broadcaster "the option of presenting the attacked party's side himself or choosing a third party to represent that side."

Red Lion upheld the fairness doctrine. Because of spectrum's physical limits, the Court surmised, "only a tiny fraction of those with resources and intelligence can hope to communicate by radio at the same time." Thereupon the Court recited the classic formulation of the scarcity rationale: "Where there are substantially more individuals who want to broadcast than there are frequencies to allocate, it is idle to posit an unabridgeable First Amendment right to broadcast comparable to the right of every individual to speak, write, or publish."

Although the FCC abandoned the personal attack and political editorializing rules in the late 1980s, the scarcity rationale endures. The broader interest in a pluralistic media market of numerous independent voices likewise survives. A mere five years after Red Lion, Miami Herald Publishing

Co. v. Tornillo invalidated a state right-of-reply law practically identical to the fairness doctrine. That law unacceptably compromised a newspaper publisher's "exercise of editorial control and judgment."

Tornillo also condemned the compulsory access law's compliance costs, measured not only "in terms of the cost of printing" but also in terms of the opportunity cost of forgoing "material that the newspaper may have preferred to print." The Court endorsed Zechariah Chafee's warning that "[l]iberty of the press is in peril as soon as the government tries to compel what is to go into a newspaper." The "kind of forced response" at issue in Tornillo—or, for that matter, in Red Lion—is "antithetical to the free discussion that the First Amendment seeks to foster."

The dissonance between Tornillo and Red Lion suggests that many of the rules imposed on broadcasters would be unconstitutional if they were applied to print journalists. Attempting to square both cases "with a single view of the first amendment" has proved "a terrific academic strain." Rather notoriously, however, Tornillo never even cited Red Lion. It is Tornillo, and emphatically not Red Lion, that expresses Othello's attitude toward intrusions on exclusivity and control: "I had rather be a toad/ And live upon the vapour of a dungeon,/ Than keep a corner in the thing I love/ For others' uses."

Red Lion did not claim that the fairness doctrine or broadcast regulation in general has no impact on broadcast content. NBC acknowledged that the chain broadcasting rules transcended mere "supervision of [broadcast] traffic"; they effectively "determin[ed] the composition of that traffic." Altering broadcast content, however coarsely or subtly, is the raison d'etre of structural regulation.

For example, expected differences in content were the only justifications for the affirmative action policies in Metro Broadcasting, Inc. v. FCC and Lamprecht v. FCC. Metro Broadcasting upheld race-conscious comparative licensing and distress sale policies on the assumption that a "broadcasting industry with representative minority participation will produce more variation and diversity than will one whose ownership is drawn from a single racially and ethnically homogeneous group."

Lamprecht struck down comparable rules designed to increase female ownership and participation. Red Lion, by contrast, involved a far more direct restraint on editorial freedom. In the abstract, it is hard to gauge whether NBC or Red Lion upheld the more aggressive programme. Although comprehensive structural restraints are arguably more confining than an overtly content-based set of rules targeting an isolated set of editorial practices, NBC suggested that structural regulation warrants less concern.

That case, and not Red Lion, established the federal government's greater discretion to regulate horizontal and vertical integration in broadcasting, relative to the same economic phenomena in other media markets. NBC so thoroughly sanctified the federal government's presumptive power to structure broadcasting that a major 1956 challenge to the FCC's multiple ownership limits in radio passed with nary a hint of constitutional infirmity.

The 1978 decision in FCC v. National Citizens Committee for Broadcasting (NCCB) embraced NBC's deferential posture toward structural regulation of broadcasting. NCCB upheld the FCC's ban on "common ownership of a radio or television broadcast station and a daily newspaper located in the same community."

After extolling the need to regulate a market whose "finite... frequencies" are "far exceeded by the number of persons wishing to broadcast," the Supreme Court blessed the allocation of "licenses so as to promote the 'public interest' in diversification of the mass communications media." The Court cited both NBC and Red Lion, even though NCCB's cross-ownership rule much more closely resembled NBC's chain broadcasting rules than Red Lion's fairness doctrine.

NCCB emphasized that its deferential approach would insulate efforts to "'enhanc[e] the volume and quality of coverage' of public issues" in broadcasting, but not necessarily "similar efforts to regulate the print media." Despite conceding that "'the issue... would be wholly different' if 'the Commission [were] to choose among applicants upon the basis of their political, economic or social views,'" NCCB flatly denied that the cross-ownership ban was "content related."

Averring that the cross-ownership restrictions would "promote free speech, not... restrict" the Court asserted that the ban and broadcast licensing at large "preserve[] the interests of the 'people as a whole... in free speech.'" NCCB even praised structural regulation as a noncensorial means for "'enhanc[ing] the diversity of information heard by the public without on-going government surveillance of... content." By comparison, Red Lion set firm limits on scarcity as a defining characteristic of broadcasting.

Red Lion recognized the technologically volatile nature of scarcity. Well before Red Lion, the Supreme Court had identified the "rapidly fluctuating" and "dynamic [field] of radio transmission" as "a field of enterprise [whose] dominant characteristic" has been "the rapid pace of its unfolding." "Advances in technology," Red Lion acknowledged, "have led to more efficient utilization of the frequency spectrum, but uses for that spectrum have also grown apace."

Improvements in consumer electronics substitute for spectrum by allowing stations to operate at closer frequencies and lower power. Today the average household can receive thirteen conventional television signals. Mindful of "[t]he rapidity with which technological advances succeed one another to create more efficient use of spectrum space on the one hand, and to create new uses for that space by ever growing numbers of people on the other," Red Lion thought it "unwise to speculate on the future allocation of that space."

The past four decades have fulfilled Justice Douglas's interrelated prophecies that "television viewers" would enjoy at least "400 channels through the advances of cable television" and that scarcity would become a "constraint of the past." Red Lion apparently tried to confine its analysis to the technological context of broadcasting circa 1969. Minimizing doctrinal damage, after all, is one of the languid virtues of deciding one case at a time. The modest protection of these dicta, however, yielded to the greater force of Red Lion's holding. The most enduring statement in Red Lion is not its formulation of the scarcity rationale, but the assertion that "differences in the characteristics of new media justify differences in the First Amendment standards applied to them." After Red Lion, courts assess "[e]ach medium of expression... by standards suited to it."

CABLE AS BROADCASTING S ECONOMIC AND LEGAL RIVAL

In Red Lion's immediate wake, the jurisprudence of conduit-based regulation focused on cable television. Despite its origins as a technology for extending broadcast television into "remote or mountainous communities," cable became a formidable competitive threat. In the late 1960s, the FCC asserted jurisdiction over cable in order to stem the flow of viewers and revenues away from UHF and educational stations.

Failing to anticipate that much UHF bandwidth would "sit around for years collecting electromagnetic dust," Congress buttressed the FCC's localism policy by entertaining its own proposals to curb cable's "unregulated explosive growth." These policies clashed in the 1968 case of United States v. Southwestern Cable Co. Decided one year before Red Lion, Southwestern Cable held that statutory jurisdiction over "'all interstate and foreign communication by wire or radio'" permitted the FCC to regulate cable.

The Court openly endorsed the Commission's objective of preserving UHF and educational stations as the foundations of "an appropriate system of local broadcasting."Having rested exclusively on a reading of the Communications Act of 1934, Southwestern Cable implicated but did not determine the appropriate First Amendment standard of review for regulations aimed at cable.

It remained unclear whether cable operators might enjoy the rights enjoyed by print publishers under Tornillo, as opposed to broadcasters' more restricted rights under Red Lion. In theory, the Supreme Court could have elevated both broadcasters and cable operators to Tornillo's more generous level of protection. The Court acknowledged in 1979 that "cable operators... share with broadcasters a significant amount of editorial discretion" over programming.

In 1986 the Court conceded that cable "plainly implicates First Amendment interests" and that the production of "original programming" and the exercise of "editorial discretion over... stations or programs" enable a cable operator "to communicate messages on a wide variety of topics and in a wide variety of formats." The Court nevertheless declined to embrace any specific standard of review.

A contemporaneous trilogy of tax cases, however, had already unleashed Red Lion in cable's realm. The 1983 case of Minneapolis Star & Tribune Co. v. Minnesota Commissioner of Revenue invalidated an ink-and-paper tax aimed at the print media, as distinct from other businesses. The Court condemned exemptions that placed the onus of this tax on the state's largest newspapers.

Four years later, Arkansas Writers' Project, Inc. v. Ragland struck a sales tax that covered general-interest magazines while exempting religious, professional, trade, and sports journals. Ragland "involved a more disturbing use of selective taxation than Minneapolis Star": a magazine's tax status in Ragland depended "entirely on its content."

Minneapolis Star and Ragland established two principles protecting the press. Singling out the press from other businesses and distinguishing among speakers within a class are both objectionable, even absent "evidence of an improper censorial motive." Minneapolis Star plainly spoke in "the language of strict, not intermediate, scrutiny." Ragland, however, did "not decide whether a distinction between different types of periodicals presents an additional basis for invalidating" a discriminatory tax as applied to the press.

Minneapolis Star, for its part, suggested that preferential taxation of the press might be unconstitutional. If preferential taxation of the press indeed offends the Constitution, then those four words in the First Amendment, "or of the press," may lose all significance. Perhaps "the freedom of speech, or of the press" lacks the elasticity of such constitutional phrases as "unreasonable searches and seizures," "cruel and unusual punishments," and "Commerce among the several States."

The Court completed its tax trilogy in 1991. In Leathers v. Medlock, Arkansas taxed cable services while exempting "newspapers, magazines, and satellite broadcast services." The Court rejected a cable operator's claim of "intermedia and intramedia discrimination," having found no evidence that "the tax was directed at, or presented the danger of suppressing, particular ideas."

By failing to distinguish "the information service provided by cable... from the information services provided by Arkansas' newspapers, magazines, television broadcasters, and radio stations," Leathers invited the very distinction that separated broadcasters in Red Lion from print journalists in Tornillo. By the 1990s, cable television emerged as "UHF's savior rather than its scourge" by finally giving UHF stations "technical parity with VHF stations."

As a legal matter, however, the Supreme Court stopped short of equating cable with broadcasting. In the first of two cases named Turner Broadcasting System, Inc. v. FCC, both involving a requirement that cable operators transmit the signals of broadcasters requesting carriage, the Court reasoned that its "distinct approach" to broadcasting rests on that medium's "unique physical limitations."

Turner I distinguished Red Lion and other broadcasting cases because cable "does not suffer from the inherent limitations that characterize the broadcast medium." Recognizing "rapid advances in fibre optics and digital compression technology," the Court predicted the quick elimination of "practical limitations on the number of speakers who may use the cable medium." The Court also downplayed "any danger of physical interference between two cable speakers attempting to share the same channel."

Turner I rejected the suggestion that the Court's broadcast jurisprudence rests not on "the physical limitations of the electromagnetic spectrum, but rather the 'market dysfunction' that characterizes the broadcast market." The "mere assertion of dysfunction or failure in a speech market, without more," the Court held, "is not sufficient to shield a speech regulation from the First Amendment standards applicable to nonbroadcast media."

Turner I nevertheless rejected strict scrutiny. "Given cable's long history of serving as a conduit for broadcast signals," the Court observed, "there appears little risk that cable viewers would assume that the broadcast stations carried on a cable system convey ideas or messages endorsed by the cable operator."

The Court placed even greater weight on "an important technological difference": whereas a "daily newspaper... does not possess the power to obstruct readers' access to other competing publications," the "physical connection between the television set and the cable network gives the cable operator bottleneck, or gatekeeper, control over most (if not all) of the television programming that is channeled into the subscriber's home."

In 1997 the Supreme Court reconsidered must-carry. Whereas "the state of the record" in Turner I confined the Court to assessing the government's interests solely "'in the abstract,'" an "expanded record" enabled Turner H "to consider whether the must-carry provisions were designed to address a real harm, and whether those provisions will alleviate it in a material way."

The Court found that Congress had garnered "specific support for its conclusion that cable operators had considerable and growing market power over local video programming markets."

"Must-carry," the Court concluded, "ensures that a number of local broadcasters retain cable carriage, with the concomitant audience access and advertising revenues needed to support a multiplicity of stations."

Justice Breyer's partial concurrence noted cable's "physical dependence upon the availability of space along city streets," which imposes "a kind of bottleneck that controls the range of viewer choice" and which therefore justifies "at least a limited degree... of governmental intervention." The

Turner decisions' narrow consensus dissolved in the chaotic 1996 case of Denver Area Educational Telecommunications Consortium, Inc. v. FCC.

No fewer than five opinions advocated distinct approaches to First Amendment review within a new conduit. None commanded a majority. Section 10(a) of the Cable Television Consumer Protection and Competition Act of 1992 permitted a cable operator to prohibit sexually explicit programming on leased access channels.

Section 10(c) granted an operator the same power over public access channels. Section 10(b) required operators to segregate sexual explicit programming on leased access channels, block it presumptively, and unblock it upon subscriber request.

Six Justices agreed that section 10(b)'s "segregate and block" requirements failed strict scrutiny in light of less speech-restrictive means for filtering sexually oriented programming.

Three Justices, led by Justice Breyer, voted to uphold section 10(a) under Turner I's intermediate scrutiny standard; a coalition led by Justice Thomas supplied three additional votes under a strict scrutiny approach.

Justice Breyer, joined by two other Justices, also used Turner I's intermediate scrutiny test to invalidate section 10(c). Of the five Justices who agreed to strike down section 10(c), only two—Justices Kennedy and Ginsburg—invoked strict scrutiny under the designated public forum doctrine of International Society for Krishna Consciousness, Inc. v. Lee.

Justice Breyer's plurality opinion declared that "no definitive choice among competing analogies (broadcast, common carrier, bookstore)" could justify "a rigid single standard, good for now and for all future media and purposes."

Justice Breyer hesitated to allow "a partial analogy in one context" to "compel a full range of decisions in [another] new and changing area."Justice Stevens's concurrence likewise declared it "unwise to take a categorical approach to the resolution of novel First Amendment questions arising in an industry as dynamic as this." He echoed his previously expressed sentiment that Congress should enjoy the flexibility to craft policies governing the "unusually dynamic" telecommunications industry.

Justice Souter, also writing in support of Justice Breyer's plurality, noted that "all of the relevant characteristics of cable are presently in a state of technological and regulatory flux." As broadcast, cable, and online technologies converge toward "a common receiver," Justice Souter surmised, "we can hardly assume that standards for judging the regulation of one of them will not have immense, but now unknown and unknowable, effects on the others."

Combining skepticism that "it will continue to make sense to distinguish cable from other technologies" with faith that "changes in these regulated technologies will enormously alter the structure of regulation itself," Justice Souter confessed "that 'if we had to decide today... just what the First Amendment should mean in cyberspace... we would get it fundamentally wrong."

Justice Kennedy excoriated the plurality's refusal to anchor its analysis to existing First Amendment models. "When confronted with a threat to free speech in the context of an emerging technology," he urged, the Court should "analyse the case by reference to existing elaborations of constant First Amendment principles.

He described "the creation of standards and adherence to them" as "the central achievement of... First Amendment jurisprudence." Despite disagreeing on the disposition of the disputed rules, Justice Thomas endorsed Justice Kennedy's adherence to established First Amendment models.

Condemning the "doctrinal wasteland" to which the Court had consigned cable operators, Justice Thomas suggested "that cable operators should enjoy the same First Amendment rights as the nonbroadcast media."

He throttled Red Lion's dictum that "it is the right of the viewers and listeners, not the right of the broadcasters, which is paramount."

Concluding that Turner I had undermined Red Lion's

emphasis on "the rights of viewers" Justice Thomas declared that "it is the cable operator's fight that is preeminent."

THE NAKED AND THE LEWD: CONTENT-BASED REGULATION ONLINE

The Turner cases and Denver plunged free speech doctrine into chaos. Yet the resulting "clash of doctrines is not a disaster—it is an opportunity." Indeed, subsequent cases have hinted at a promising solution. The key lies in the contrast between conduit-based and content-based regulation.

Recent cases adjust First Amendment review according to whether the law targets content, focuses solely on the physical context of speech, or straddles these worlds by controlling the legal operations of a particular conduit.

The direction of policy "in electronic media cases" is arguably "driven by a renewed concern for access interests, rather than indecency issues." As a matter of doctrinal development, though, the reverse is true. Almost all of the decisions regarding conduit-based regulation of the Internet have involved sexually explicit but nonobscene speech. Speech of this sort warrants constitutional protection.

As a "great and mysterious motive force in human life," and as the most "intimate and personal" of acts at the core of "one's own concept of existence, of meaning, of the universe, and of the mystery of human life," sex runs through United States Reports as if "emblazoned on the very heavens in skywriting." Due process entitles "two adults" to engage in "private sexual conduct" with "full and mutual consent."

The First Amendment protects an adult's "right to read or observe what he pleases" and "to satisfy his intellectual and emotional needs in the privacy of his own home." At least when it portrays consensual adult sexuality with some artistic flair, pornography has provided a constitutionally sanctioned outlet for those who suffer "the tragic feeling of being endowed with a larger-than-usual capacity for love, without a single person on earth to offer it to."

What enhances pornography's impact on the Internet, as opposed to any other conduit, is creeping discomfort about parents' technological incompetence relative to their children. Ever since 1984, when home television viewers won a de facto privilege to record programs and heightened their interest in the ability to programme VCRs, me" Supreme Court has entertained a parade of controversies in which children's grasp of communications technology has exceeded their parents'.

An embarrassing proliferation of media now eclipses what was once broadcasting's distinctive trait of being both "uniquely pervasive" and "uniquely accessible to children." The Internet's ubiquity and user-friendliness—even Supreme Court Justices believe that "n avigating the Web is relatively straightforward"—make it a fearsome means by which "children may discover... pornographic material."

Congress tries to prevent "the widespread availability of the Internet" from providing "opportunities for minors to access materials... in a manner that can frustrate parental supervision or control." Justice Breyer has doubted not only the willingness of parents to monitor what children watch and where they watch it, but also the ability of parents to enforce the decisions they do make.

By contrast, Justice Stevens "would place the burden on parents to 'take the simple step of utilizing a medium that enables' them to avoid [sexually explicit] material."This preference reflects a "growing sense of unease" with "the interest in protecting children from prurient materials... as a justification for using criminal regulation of speech as a substitute for, or a simple backup to, adult oversight of children's viewing habits."

These cases thus hinge on judicial instincts regarding parental supervision in a technological environment that emphatically favors the young. Contemporaneously with Denver, Congress delivered fresh legislation that would enable the Supreme Court to reformulate its approach to conduit-based regulation.

The Telecommunications Act of 1996, widely condemned for hobbling "a crucial segment of the economy worth tens of billions of dollars" with statutory "ambiguity" and "self-contradiction," notoriously ignored the Internet except as a transmission vector for porn.

Title V of the Act, better known as the Communications Decency Act of 1996 (CDA), addressed the online transmission of sexually explicit speech. The passage of the CDA sparked a collision between the strategy of adjusting First Amendment review by conduit and the imperative of applying strict scrutiny to content-based regulation of speech.

Reno v. ACLU, the first of the Supreme Court's Internet-specific free speech controversies, not only invalidated the CDA as a transparent assault on speech but also reinstated Red Lion's multifaceted approach.

Reno held that the Internet lacked three key features that justified broadcasting's deferential First Amendment standard: "the history of extensive Government regulation of the broadcast medium; the scarcity of available frequencies at its inception; and [broadcasting's] 'invasive' nature."

Justice Stevens observed that "the vast democratic forums of the Internet" have never "been subject to the type of government supervision and regulation that has attended the broadcast industry." In light of this medium's relative freedom from regulation, he detected no risk that users "might infer some sort of official or societal approval of" online content. He also noted that "the Internet is not as 'invasive' as radio or television."

"Finally," Justice Stevens added, "unlike the conditions that prevailed when Congress first authorized regulation of the broadcast spectrum, the Internet can hardly be considered a 'scarce' expressive commodity." In 2000, the Court got a chance to reconcile Reno with Denver and the Turner cases.

United States v. Playboy Entertainment Group, Inc. treated restrictions targeting "signal bleed" from imperfectly scrambled cable channels offering sexually explicit programming as a transparent instance of content-based regulation: "The speech in question is defined by its content; and the statute which seeks to restrict it is content based."

Even Justice Breyer, writing in dissent, agreed that "this case involved the application, not the elucidation, of First

Amendment principles."Playboy did continue the habit of drawing comparisons to broadcasting: "Cable television, like broadcast media, presents unique problems, which inform our assessment of the interests at stake, and which may justify restrictions that would be unacceptable in other contexts."

The Court, however, used "a key difference" between cable and broadcasting to reinforce rather than dilute strict scrutiny. Observing that "cable systems have the capacity to block unwanted channels on a household-by-household basis," the Court held that Congress had unconstitutionally favored broad-gauged measures against signal bleed over the feasible, effective, and less speech-restrictive strategy of "targeted blocking."

Technology in private rather than official hands, the Court concluded, enables "esthetic and moral judgments about art and literature, [to] be formed, tested, and expressed." In two cases styled Ashcroft v. ACLU, the Supreme Court reviewed the statutory successor to the CDA. In response to Reno, Congress passed the Child Online Protection Act of 1998 (COPA).

Ashcroft I, decided in 2002, deflected a facial challenge to COPA's overt use of the three-part obscenity test of Miller v. California, particularly that decision's reliance on "contemporary community standards" in defining a work's appeal to the prurient interest. The challengers argued that COPA would subject online work, otherwise globally available, to the suffocating standards of America's least tolerant community.

A three-Justice plurality led by Justice Thomas concluded "that COPA's reliance on community standards... does not by itself render the statute substantially overbroad for purposes of the First Amendment." Justice Thomas rejected the contention that the Internet's "'unique characteristics'" justify an approach distinct from prevailing doctrine on obscene and indecent speech.

Hamling v. United States upheld a federal ban on obscene materials delivered via United States mail. Sable Communications of California, Inc. v. FCC upheld a similar federal statute as applied to obscene telephone calls but invalidated the statute as applied to indecent, nonobscene communications.

Justice Thomas concluded that Congress could place "'the burden of complying with [its] prohibition on obscene messages'" upon a producer of online speech reaching "different communities with different local standards."

Concurring in the judgment, Justice Kennedy again insisted that the "unique characteristics" and "distinct attributes" of "each mode of expression" should guide First Amendment analysis. In a stark departure from Turner I, however, Justice Kennedy emphasized factors beyond physical scarcity.

"The economics and the technology of each medium," he wrote, "affect both the burden of a speech restriction and the Government's interest in maintaining it." Rejecting Justice Thomas's reliance on Hamling and Sable, Justice Kennedy stressed that "[t]he economics and technology of Internet communication differ in important ways from those of telephones and mail."

"Paradoxically," he observed, "it is easy and cheap to reach a worldwide audience on the Internet, but expensive if not impossible to reach a geographic subset." Unlike mail and telephony, regulating Internet speech without regard to "national variation in community standards" would impose an unacceptable burden. Justice O'Connor likewise disputed the plurality's use of Hamling and Sable. Concurring in the judgment, she endorsed Justice Kennedy's position that "Internet speakers' inability to control the geographic location of their audience" warranted a departure from standards on mail and phone communications.

Also concurring in the judgment, Justice Breyer urged the Court to interpret "the statutory word 'community' to refer to the Nation's adult community taken as a whole" in order to avoid "the serious First Amendment problem that would otherwise" arise if the statute were construed to "provide the most puritan of communities with a heckler's Internet veto affecting the rest of the Nation."

Alone in dissent, Justice Stevens stressed the technological aspects of the Internet as "a medium in which speech cannot be segregated to avoid [specific] communities" and in which a speaker, having spoken "everywhere on the network at once," can neither "control access based on the location of the listener, nor... choose the [precise] pathways" of transmission.

Justice Stevens argued that the "fundamental difference in technologies," which enables a single law effectively to prohibit transmission of a message to every American with Internet access, should preclude the analogical use of constitutional "rules applicable to the mass mailing of an obscene montage or to obscene dial-a-porn."

Whether Ashcroft I supports a conduit-specific approach to Internet speech depends on the tenuous process of deciphering decisions so "fragmented" that "no single rationale explaining the result enjoys the assent of five Justices." What passes as "'the holding of the Court may be viewed as that position taken by those Members who concurred in the judgment on the narrowest grounds.'"

Counting to five in Ashcroft I yields unsatisfactory results. Justice Thomas's plurality of three effectively equated the Internet with the Postal Service and the public switched telephone network as transmission vectors for sexually explicit speech. Four of the Justices concurring in the judgment—Justices O'Connor, Kennedy, Souter, and Ginsburg—did favour a conduit-specific approach reminiscent of Red Lion.

Justice Breyer, though sympathetic, adopted a statutory resolution that kept him from addressing COPA's constitutionality. Justice Stevens would likewise have supplied a fifth vote for Justice Kennedy's technologically sensitive methodology, but he stood alone in dissent.

On remand, the lower courts reinstated the preliminary injunction against COPA. In a second case styled Ashcroft v. ACLU, the Supreme Court sustained the injunction. The shift between Ashcroft I and H from a facial attack to a preliminary injunction markedly favored COPA's foes. Characterizing COPA as overtly content-based regulation, Ashcroft H readily imposed strict scrutiny. Because the government bore "the burden of proof on the ultimate question of COPA's constitutionality," the injunction would stand as long as COPA's challengers could establish at least one "plausible, less restrictive alternative."

Writing for the same coalition of five that decided Playboy, Justice Kennedy concluded that "[b]locking and filtering software is... less restrictive than COPA, and, in addition, likely more effective as a means of restricting children's access." Justice Kennedy praised filters for imposing "selective restrictions on speech at the receiving end, not universal restrictions at the source."

He speculated that filters might be "more effective than COPA," insofar as filters operate without regard to geography and cover "all forms of Internet communication, including e-mail." Justice Kennedy drew an explicit comparison to Playboy. Both Playboy and Ashcroft H, he wrote, "involved a content-based restriction designed to protect minors from viewing harmful materials."

In each instance, Congress had to choose "between a blanket speech restriction and a more specific technological solution that was available to parents who chose to implement it." The record in Playboy was "silent as to the comparative effectiveness" of the anti-signal bleed statute and the alternative of consumer-initiated requests to block specific cable channels.

In Ashcroft II, the government likewise "failed to introduce specific evidence proving that existing technologies," such as filtering software, are less effective than COPA. In both cases, the availability of technological alternatives defeated content-based regulation. The Supreme Court has consistently preferred consumer-level controls, even if imperfect, over categorical restrictions on speech at its source.

For example, the ratings system mandated by the Telecommunications Act of 1996 undermines any comprehensive ban on indecency within any conduit able to exploit the V-chip. Indeed, the development and diffusion of "user-control technologies" should have the effect of invalidating all "intrusive government restrictions."

Justice Kennedy drew an explicit comparison to Playboy. Both Playboy and Ashcroft H, he wrote, "involved a content-based restriction designed to protect minors from viewing harmful materials."In each instance, Congress had to choose "between a blanket speech restriction and a more specific technological solution that was available to parents who chose to implement it.

"The record in Playboy was "silent as to the comparative effectiveness"of the anti-signal bleed statute and the alternative of consumer-initiated requests to block specific cable channels. In Ashcroft II, the government likewise "failed to introduce specific evidence proving that existing technologies,"such as filtering software, are less effective than COPA.

In both cases, the availability of technological alternatives defeated content-based regulation. The Supreme Court has consistently preferred consumer-level controls, even if imperfect, over categorical restrictions on speech at its source. For example, the ratings system mandated by the Telecommunications Act of 1996 undermines any comprehensive ban on indecency within any conduit able to exploit the V-chip.

Indeed, the development and diffusion of "user-control technologies"should have the effect of invalidating all "intrusive government restrictions."

Judicial assessments of technology are contestable, to say the least. In his Ashcroft H dissent, Justice Breyer berated filtering software's "serious inadequacies."He preferred COPA over filtering "that underblocks, imposes a cost upon each family that uses it, fails to screen outside the home, and lacks precision."

In United States v. American Library Association, Inc., Justice Stevens similarly observed that software based "on key words and phrases"cannot exclude a precisely defined category of images. In Ashcroft II, however, Justice Stevens endorsed "filtering software"as a "user-based"alternative to

COPA. Greater judicial receptiveness to consumer-level technology will yield further outcomes similar to Playboy and Ashcroft II.

In right of the government's burden to overcome strict scrutiny of content-based restrictions, evidentiary deadlock favors the challenger. "The 'starch'in our constitutional standards cannot be sacrificed to accommodate the enforcement choices of the Government."

THE IMPLICIT LOGIC OF CONDUIT-BASED REGULATION

Having defined the Supreme Court's approach to conduit-based regulation of speech, this Chapter will now criticize that jurisprudence. Section A will reexamine Red Lion, which remains the quintessential statement of this body of law. Contrary to its caricature as the origin of a senseless "scarcity"rationale, Red Lion in fact articulates almost all of the rationales invoked in examinations of legislative efforts to structure a specific conduit.

Section B will dissect Red Lion's three interrelated rationales: scarcity, enhancement of underrepresented voices, and overall regulatory context. Section C will examine a factor added by later decisions: the social meaning that emerges from a conduit's pervasiveness.

RED LION RECONSIDERED

"A science which hesitates to forget its founders is lost. By this standard, constitutional law fares poorly. The jurisprudence of conduit-based regulation has not yet transcended its origins in broadcasting. This entire body of law "has a musty odor"even though Red Lion, "its chief source of constitutional authority,"has not yet reached its fortieth anniversary.

No one besides the Supreme Court actually believes the scarcity rationale. Dissatisfaction with Red Lion has spawned an academic cottage industry. Lower courts have urged the Supreme Court to overrule Red Lion. Even the FCC repudiated Red Lion (though the Commission later renounced this heretical stance). Yet Red Lion still matters because the Supreme Court says it does.

Lower courts inclined to declare that Red Lion "no longer makes sense"acknowledge, as they must, that they are "not in a position to reject the scarcity rationale."The high court consistently invokes Red Lion when it dilutes First Amendment review of laws having some connection to broadcasting.

Though much of the criticism of Red Lion has focused on the scarcity rationale, the decision's treatment of technological innovation looms much larger. In many settings, technological innovation demands reinterpretation of the Constitution. Even originalist theories accommodate "technological changes."

Mindful of the government's ability to exploit "subtler and more far-reaching"technologies, the Supreme Court monitors how "the advance of technology"may affect "the degree of privacy secured to citizens by the Fourth Amendment."Wary of "leaving the homeowner at the mercy of advancing technology,"the Court considers not only "relatively crude"technology in use, but also "more sophisticated systems ... in development."

Fear of technological erosion of rights should trigger a similar alarm in free speech jurisprudence. What Chief Justice Warren observed with respect to "the television camera"applies equally to Fourth and First Amendment liberties: "technological innovations [are] not entitled to pervade the lives of everyone in disregard of constitutionally protected rights."

The special status of technological innovation as "a singularly uncontroversial justification for modifying established doctrine"warrants heightened vigilance. Far from embracing new channels of expression, lawmakers routinely respond to unfamiliar technologies by suppressing them. Putative "technologies of freedom"could in fact represent the First Amendment's "Trojan horse."

Armed with Red Lion's declaration that "differences in the characteristics of new media justify differences in the First

Amendment standards applied to them,"courts routinely exploit technological differences between older and newer modes of communication in calibrating constitutional protection within the newer medium.

It is unclear whether systematic reliance "on reference points provided by older, established technologies"has advanced the constitutional understanding of conduit-based regulation.

A jurisprudential engine fueled so heavily by "principles operating at a low or intermediate level of abstraction"is bound to yield "incompletely theorized judgments."Worse still, these controversies'factual records rarely "reflect current technological reality--a serious flaw in any case involving the Internet"or any other emerging technology.

Nor is there anything doctrinally neutral about the exercise of paying obligatory homage to Red Lion. Given the doctrinal baseline for content-based regulation--strict scrutiny absent affirmative debasement of the speech at issue--Red Lion's invitation to examine "the characteristics of new media"represents a one-way, downward ratchet.

As Red Lion itself illustrated, invoking a conduit-specific approach to the First Amendment tends, perhaps inexorably, to degrade constitutional protection for speech. Throughout the logical layer of free speech jurisprudence, judicial consideration of a conduit's traits rarely if ever enhances constitutional protection.

In United States v. American Library Association, Inc., for instance, parties challenged the Children's Internet Protection Act's requirement that libraries install filtering software on Internet access terminals as a condition of federal funding.

A plurality of Justices rejected the argument that Internet access converts a public library into "a 'designated public forum'"enjoying heightened protection against governmental restrictions on the time, place, and manner of speech. According to Chief Justice Rehnquist, a library "provides Internet access, not to 'encourage a diversity of views from private speakers,'but ... to facilitate research, learning and recreational pursuits by furnishing materials of requisite and appropriate quality.

"The Chief Justice echoed the Senate's sentiment that the Internet was nothing '"more than a technological extension of the book stack."'

An accurate assessment of the free speech jurisprudence of conduit-based regulation begins with a proper refutation of Red Lion's mythically implausible scarcity rationale. The opinion's concluding paragraph and footnote identify three interrelated rationales.

In addition to "the scarcity of broadcast frequencies,"the Court cited two distinct factors counseling judicial acquiescence in the regulation of broadcasting: "the Government's role in allocating those frequencies, and the legitimate claims of those unable without governmental assistance to gain access to those frequencies for expression of their views."

Red Lion also presented two intriguing "related arguments"beyond the admittedly temporary "technological scarcity of frequencies."First, the Court acknowledged that legally induced "economic scarcity"arising from actual or potential "limits on entry to the broadcasting market"might justify "the fairness doctrine or its equivalent"on behalf "of those excluded"from the airwaves.

Other passages plainly reveal the Court's awareness that scarcity in broadcasting was a technologically volatile phenomenon. Red Lion took pains to confine its holding to the state of communications technology as of 1969.

Second, the Court hinted that it might uphold "legislation that directly or indirectly multiplies the voices and views presented to the public through ... devices which limit or dissipate the power of those who sit astride the channels of communication with the general public."

Careful exegesis of Red Lion therefore reveals no fewer than three distinct justifications for tailoring First Amendment protection by conduit. First, a nuanced understanding of scarcity and its technological context might justify governmental intervention.

Second, the history and thoroughness of regulation may warrant greater deference to the legislative structuring of a conduit. Third, a conduit's vulnerability to monopolization may merit official efforts to mute louder voices so that softer ones might be heard.

Cases after Red Lion supplied a fourth rationale: some media are "uniquely pervasive,"able without warning to shatter privacy even at home, and "uniquely accessible to children, even those too young to read."The leading authority for the pervasiveness rationale, FCC v.

Pacifica Foundation, upheld the FCC's power over the timing of potentially offensive broadcasts such as George Carlin's "Filthy Words"routine without relying "on the notion of 'spectrum scarcity.'"

Red Lion, as it turns out, came dangerously close to articulating a comprehensive (if not altogether coherent or credible) theory on conduit-based regulation of speech.

Aside from an inchoate expression of enhancement theory and a failure to anticipate pervasiveness, its justifications conform quite closely to the multifaceted approach that the Supreme Court would eventually summarize in 1997: "the history of extensive Government regulation,""the scarcity of available"avenues for expression, and the contested medium's "'invasive'nature."

The First Amendment jurisprudence of conduit-based regulation therefore hinges on four interrelated rationales: scarcity, regulatory context, enhancement, and pervasiveness.

ENHANCING THE LEGAL UNDERSTANDING OF RIVALROUSNESS AND REGULATION

- *Enhancement theory:* Among the rationales marshaled in defence of conduit-based regulation, the so-called "enhancement theory"is the easiest to dismiss. First Amendment jurisprudence has struggled mightily with the urge to enhance the voices of the "many people who have ideas ... but who do not have enough money to own or control publishing plants, newspapers, radios, moving picture studios, or chains of show places."Congressman Charles E. Bennett argued in 1949 that the antitrust laws were "one of the greatest bulwarks against Communism"because they protected ordinary Americans "from domination by business interests so large and monopolistic that the voices of average people cannot be heard in their thunder.

"Some analysts today advocate overtly content-based regulation, arguing that the failure "engage an imperfect "marketplace of ideas"favors the privileged. These critics fear that deregulation of access to the most lucrative conduits--whether through a retreat from the regulatory status quo or by vigorous First Amendment review--could winnow "the field of otherwise eligible applicants strictly according to their ability to pay"and eliminate "those who lack dollars to put in an effective bid."

Enhancement theory assumes that an unregulated speech market will fall victim to "biases that skew, distort, and corrupt"public discourse.

Regulating speech in the public sphere, from this perspective, is no less objectionable or necessary than applying the law of evidence in criminal cases.

Wealth may be the most dreaded influence: accelerating "the age-old human drive for self-gratification through "exploitation of highly advanced electronic technology" allegedly "trivializes public expression and ... undermines the traditional aims of the First Amendment.

"From this perspective, "the right prize"at stake in making "regulatory choices"for "the Internet and the digitally networked environment"is "not the Great Shopping Mall in Cyberspace,"but rather "the Great Agora--the unmediated conversation of the many with the many."

No matter how badly scholars want enhancement, though, courts disagree. Most free speech cases spurn "the concept that government may restrict the speech of some elements of our society in order to enhance the relative voice of others. "Favoring one speaker over another is "wildly at odds with the normal First Amendment belief that more speech is better."The instinctive rejection of the enhancement theory grows from the suspicion that "government intervention is as likely to suppress diversity as to promote it."One of the exceptional areas of First Amendment jurisprudence that does accommodate the enhancement theory is conduit-based regulation.

The Supreme Court's frequent observation that "the broadcast media pose unique and special problems not present in the traditional free speech case"allows the enhancement theory to flourish within broadcast regulation. The limited nature of spectrum putatively justifies an aggressive federal role in "secur[ing] a reasonable equality of opportunity in radio."

In the clearest endorsement of enhancement theory, NCCB declared that ""efforts to enhance the volume and quality of coverage"of public issues'through regulation of broadcasting may be permissible where similar efforts to regulate the print media would not be."This dictum has never proved dispositive in any subsequent Supreme Court case; as with the scarcity rationale, broadcasting law's exceptional treatment of the enhancement theory has never dictated the resolution of other conduit-based disputes.

A shows, lower court decisions involving structural regulation of communications have consistently confined NCCB to broadcasting. Cases involving must-carry obligations and ownership restrictions in nonbroadcast media have applied a tougher brand of scrutiny. NCCB therefore provides no firm support for the proposition that enhancement theory pervades the jurisprudence of conduit-based regulation.

Confining this deviant theory to a single, historically circumscribed setting merely isolates the law of broadcasting as an aberrant branch of First Amendment jurisprudence. Rejecting enhancement theory does not resolve the yearning for greater competition in the marketplace of ideas. The "great fear"that motivates the jurisprudence of conduit-based regulation is "a fear not of one but of many."This body of law embodies a concern that uncoordinated speech markets would drown in a "cacophony of competing voices, none of which can be clearly and predictably heard."

The challenge lies in reconciling this anxiety with the "profound national commitment to the principle that debate on public issues should be uninhibited, robust, and wide-open,"with "the assumption that the widest possible dissemination of information from diverse and antagonistic sources is essential to the welfare of the public."

Enhancement theory's putative justification, scarcity, simply does not distinguish broadcasting from any other conduit. First Amendment doctrine presumptively rejects enhancement as antithetical to self-governance through the free flow of ideas. That presumption has historically been reversed, or at least suspended, in the context of broadcasting facilities whose peculiar scarcity supposedly warrants a deviant approach. If the scarcity rationale collapses, either with respect to broadcasting or across a diverse range of conduits, its fall similarly dooms enhancement theory.

- Scarcity as rivalrousness and the government's regulatory response. The contradictions of enhancement theory therefore demand a more careful definition of "scarcity."Scarcity in the sense of rivalrousness is not equivalent to the economic definition of scarcity as a constraint on consumer choice. The latter notion of scarcity, as "a universal fact, ... can hardly explain regulation in one context and not another,"let alone "justif[y] content regulation of broadcasting in a way that would be intolerable if applied to... the print media."Because "[a]ll economic goods are scarce,"not "everyone who wishes to publish a newspaper ... may do so."Invoking scarcity in this sense represents at best an exercise in spurious market definition. Not only is scarcity universal; it is marvelously contingent and elastic. Any technologically driven expansion in available channels of communication can defeat a claim of scarcity. Absent a convincing demonstration of "physical interference,"the government lacks "an essential precondition"that might otherwise justify "an umpiring role."

Clarifying the scarcity rationale begins with a careful distinction between rivalrous and nonrivalrous resources. In stark contrast with the rivalrous nature of most tangible goods, whereby gainful use by one party leads directly to another party's loss, use of a nonrivalrous good "by one entity does not necessarily diminish the use and enjoyment of others."Although ideas are as "free as the air to common use,"the frequencies on which ideas may be transmitted are not free from physical conflict.

"Every transmitter creates some interference": whenever a consumer "uses a cordless telephone, or even turns on a light,"the resulting emission of energy creates some "interference for nearby users of nearby frequencies."Because simultaneous use of spectrum is inescapably rivalrous, "organizing that resource within a system of control makes good sense."Within broadcasting, that system consists of a "regulatory mechanism to divide the electromagnetic spectrum and assign specific frequencies to particular broadcasters."

The constitutional significance of the "limited"availability of "radio facilities"cannot be distinguished from the regulatory interest in preventing "the confusion that would result from interferences"among competing uses of spectrum. What the jurisprudence of conduit-based regulation has called scarcity is better understood as rivalrousness, which justifies governmental efforts to dismantle barriers to competition and freedom of movement within the marketplace of ideas.

So rehabilitated, the scarcity rationale even restores a hint of enhancement theory: "The logic of the scarcity rationale is that there are not enough opportunities for speakers to express themselves, and that the government has a role to play in ensuring that these limited opportunities be put to the most valuable uses for society."If nothing else, broadcast licensing's awareness of rivalrousness boasts a long legal pedigree. The Supreme Court has characterized any "attempt by a broadcaster to use a given frequency in disregard of its prior use by others, thus creating confusion and interference,"as a dastardly act that "deprives the public of the full benefit of radio audition."Broadcast "pirates"enjoy no meaningful right to free speech. Indeed, rivalrousness effectively defines the law of broadcast licensing.

The Ashbacker right to comparative licensing proceedings eases a conflict created by the law itself: the decision to award any license precludes another broadcaster from using the same frequency in the same locality.

Although alternatives to licensing, such as auctions or common law resolution of claims by "spectrum squatters,"would offer different solutions to rivalrousness, they could never cure the mutual exclusivity of competing uses. Conducting an auction, as the law now often demands, would still require the FCC to set power limits and frequency ranges, which in turn would affect the number of licenses and their uses.

Reliance on the common law would require nonexpert, generalist courts to perform the same task, ex post rather than ex ante. This choice between a liability rule and a property rule, though justifiable on other economic grounds, does not settle or eliminate rivalrousness.

The heated debate over licensing and its alternatives thus hinges solely on a question of remedies, even as underlying conflicts among uses of spectrum remain unresolved. Licensing as a remedy does carry constitutional consequences. Approval of broadcast licensing represents a significant departure from the Supreme Court's deep and historically validated suspicion of licensing as the quintessential prior restraint.

"The struggle for the freedom of the press was primarily directed against the power of the licensor."Early in constitutional history, "a law requiring the licensing of printers"was recognized as the "archetypical censorship statute." The sixteenth and seventeenth century "licensing laws"that the Bill of Rights targeted as a "core abuse"have a contemporary analogue in broadcast licensing. Even when courts allow licensing schemes, they impose stringent conditions, lest the unscrupulous licensor achieve censorial objectives through "post hoc rationalizations"and "shifting or illegitimate criteria.

"In another instance in which "equal protection" considerations are "closely intertwined"with free speech, constraints on licensing consider the "specific sequence of events leading up to the challenged decision,"especially departures from procedural or substantive norms.

Not even extensive tailoring, however, can excuse most licensing schemes. "It is not merely the sporadic abuse of power by the censor but the pervasive threat inherent in its very existence that constitutes the danger to freedom of discussion."In speech as in other endeavors, "the main value of the sword of Damocles is that it hangs, not that it drops.""Measured against the criteria"prescribed for prior restraints, "the broadcasting regime clearly fails."

Moreover, the longstanding practice of using comparative licensing to resolve spectrum conflicts effectively merges the scarcity rationale with solicitude for regulatory schemes. The Supreme Court "has recognized the strong governmental interest in certain forms of economic regulation, even though such regulation may have an incidental effect on rights of speech and association."

Although broadcasters have been regulated on terms distinct from those imposed on common carriers, what matters is that the government does restrict entry into and exit from these industries, and does so tightly. Though neither "owned by the federal government"nor subjected by it to rate regulation, "spectrum is subject to strict governmental regulation."Regulation of entry, even if not of rates, gives the government freer rein over an entire conduit.

The Court has distinguished laws targeting "the structure of market"from laws "regulating the content of speech."To the extent that they can be characterized as structural rather than content-based, conduit-based regulations escape searching scrutiny. Just as neither half of "the Commerce Clause protects the particular structure or methods of operation in a ...

market,"the Supreme Court "sees nothing in the First Amendment to prevent"measures that "promote the 'public interest'in diversification of the mass communications media." Accommodation of existing regulation gives wide berth to broadcast licensing and kindred schemes for structuring communications markets.

In many other settings, the grant of a license may injure other competitors but does not perforce exclude them from the market. In those circumstances, regulation creates no entitlement to a comparative hearing.

Regulatory law distinguishes between programs that confer licenses on all "fit, willing, and able"applicants and schemes such as broadcast licensing or cable franchising, which follow the public interest, convenience, and necessity standard articulated in statutes such as the Communications Act of 1934.

Although licensing presumes that "the broadcasting field is open to anyone"who "shows his competency, the adequacy of his equipment, and financial ability to make good use of [an] assigned channel,"this nominally open opportunity is constrained by a crucial contingency.

There must "be an available frequency over which"the would-be entrant "can broadcast without interference to others."What broadcasting law calls scarcity is merely the recognition that every license precludes all other contemporaneous uses of spectrum. Cable franchising likewise guarantees that a single operator will serve a particular locality.

Physical restraints do govern both settings--as spectrum limits the number and strength of distinct signals, so will cable operators encounter some limit on their ability to lay wire. In both settings, however, the more important constraint is legal rather than physical.

To repeat: scarcity as rivalrousness is not equivalent to the economic definition of scarcity as a constraint on consumption. Before Ashbacker, the Supreme Court held that "economic injury to an existing station is not a separate and independent"consideration in broadcast licensing. It takes but a small sleight of hand, though, to transform injury to rival broadcasters into a relevant element of the public interest: "economic injury to an existing station, while not in and of itself a matter of moment, becomes important when on the facts it spells diminution or destruction of service."

If anything, treating scarcity as synonymous with economic injury yields perverse broadcasting policy. Incumbent protection, once anathema in broadcast regulation, has become the raison d'Etre of licensing in the public interest. Incumbent licensees eventually secured a presumption favoring renewal, ultimately codified in 1996.

"Preserving the effective over-air use of the radio spectrum had been the basis of regulatory policy, but once the policy was established it became an end in itself, to be preserved even against a new medium that eliminated the need for the policy in the first place."Like holders of taxicab medallions, incumbent broadcasters seek to limit the number of licenses.

They usually succeed. Efforts by the broadcasting industry to protect its interests at cable's expense demonstrate that "[n]ew regulations, ostensibly defended as public-interested or as helping viewers and consumers, will often be a product of private self-interest, and not good for the public at all."What is bad for broadcast is good for America.

- Divergent regulatory approaches to different communications conduits. The communications industry reflects many of the traits that justify regulation of other failed or flawed markets. In media markets, speakers deviate substantially from the romantic, "Luke Skywalker" vision of speakers as boardwalk painters, soapbox orators, and subway guitarists. "Speakers are not numerous, nor are they fungible." Regulating communicative conduits in pursuit of perfect competition—a model based on numerous small firms freely entering and exiting a market for fungible goods and competing solely on the basis of price—is neither possible nor desirable. Substantial economies of scale preclude a communications market of atomistic, independent actors. Because an "industry with a larger number of owners may well be less efficient than a mA technologically savvy jurisprudence of conduit-based regulation would classify DBS and the Internet according to their real-world performance. But it is clear that these conduits' legislative status is driving their constitutional status. Such treatment effectively creates "one long [legal] bootstrap." Longstanding regulatory provisions have now "become part of the constitutional baseline used to determine whether a particular regulation violate[s] the First Amendment." The notion that the social meaning of a thoroughly regulated conduit justifies further regulation not only engages in the circular illogic of "basing government control on government control"; it also "fails to distinguish spectrum from forms of property" beyond the government's reach.

Rights in other scarce resources, most saliently land, are determined by "a mode which neither necessitates nor tolerates a regime like that of the Fee." In a constitutional tradition that tempers many rights accorded to owners of property but protects speech forthrightly, certain communicative conduits are regulated more stringently than land. In a polity where "government control is not a justification for government control, but a response to some other justification," regulatory disparities should rest on legitimate factual differences.

The jurisprudence of conduit-based regulation reflects no such rationality; it rests exclusively on historic path-dependency. Even though land and spectrum present identical issues of scarcity and rivalrousness, "it is only because the legal devices used in respect to land have been so vastly different from those represented by the FCC that we unthinkingly suppose that there must be some intrinsic differences."

Over time, conduit-based regulation's bootstrap becomes even longer and more pernicious. Any explicit inclusion of regulatory intensity in a constitutional test "creates a somewhat perverse incentive for legislatures—regulate a medium in its infancy or lose your chance to regulate at all."

Try as the law might in an industry's embryonic stage to avoid "an all or nothing-at-all choice," any solicitude for ongoing regulation, however modest, will favour preemptive regulation. From the perspective of a legislator or regulator who can rationally anticipate constitutional jurisprudence, "all other things will not be equal if waiting means forfeiting the right to regulate." In dynamic terms, this "sinister" jurisprudence allows "regulation [to] serve as a constitutional justification for more regulation" and to "reinforce an overriding culture of regulation for its own sake."

- Compelled speech as an illustration of a regulation's constitutional significance. Perhaps the most vivid illustration of the interplay between regulation and free speech jurisprudence comes from the seemingly distant doctrine that concerns compelled speech through cooperative marketing. The First Amendment bars the government from compelling individuals to express views contrary to their beliefs. The government may not coerce individuals to subsidize speech to which they object, or even to be saddled with unwanted associates. Notwithstanding the compelled speech doctrine, the 1997 Supreme Court case of Glickman v. Wileman Bros. & Elliot, Inc. rejected a First Amendment challenge to marketing orders that required producers of tree fruit to pay assessments for generic advertising. Wileman stressed "the importance of the statutory context"; nectarines, plums, and peaches are marketed under the Agricultural Marketing Agreement Act of 1937, which "displaced many aspects of independent business activity." The tree fruit programme forced producers to contribute funds to cooperative advertising "as part of a broader collective enterprise in which their freedom to act independently [was] already constrained by the regulatory scheme."

Indeed, the Agricultural Marketing Agreement Act "displaced competition" so thoroughly that tree fruit marketing orders issued under that statute's authority and actions pursuant to those orders were "expressly exempted from the antitrust laws."Four years after Wileman, the Court again revisited the constitutionality of compulsory cooperative advertising. The 2001 case of United States v. United Foods, Inc., contested a cooperative marketing programme for mushrooms. Unlike the marketing scheme in Wileman, the Mushroom Promotion, Research, and Consumer Information Act imposed "no marketing orders that regulate how mushrooms may be produced and sold, no exemption from the antitrust laws, and nothing preventing individual producers from making their own marketing decisions."

Indeed, the Mushroom Act dedicated "almost all the funds collected under [its]... mandatory assessments" to the exclusive purpose of "generic advertising." The regulatory gap between the Agricultural Marketing Agreement Act and the Mushroom Act proved constitutionally decisive. Because the tree fruit programme in Wileman "to a large extent deprived producers of their ability to compete and replaced competition with a regime of cooperation," it enabled the government to demand and collect "compelled contributions for germane advertising... in furtherance of an otherwise legitimate programme."

In United Foods, by contrast, the principal objective of the Mushroom Act was "speech itself." All that was at stake was "a compelled subsidy" designed to "mak[e] one entrepreneur finance advertising for the benefit of his competitors." The Agricultural Marketing Agreement Act subjects the tree fruit industry to such comprehensive regulation that compulsory advertising assessments represent at most a modest marginal imposition on producers' liberty.

The Mushroom Act imposed no such constraints, and as a result its advertising programme fell before the First Amendment's razor. The contrast between Wileman and United Foods parallels the contrast between the public interest model and less intrusive forms of regulation. The less comprehensive the regulatory scheme, the greater the scope of speech rights within the industry.

The subtle slide from Wileman toward United Foods signals a larger jurisprudential shift. The argument that regulation of its own accord justifies more intrusive conduit-based restraints on speech cannot be squared with the First Amendment's commitment to expressive liberty. Chief Justice Rehnquist has suggested that compre-hensive "regulation of an industry.., might well" sanction speech-restrictive regulation in that industry. This posture is reminiscent of Justice Holmes's argument that the greater power to extinguish "the dedication" of public places "to public uses" subsumes "the less [sic] step of limiting the public use to certain purposes."

Under Justice Holmes's approach, every public forum case would follow the adage that "the State, no less than a private owner of property, has power to preserve the property under its control for the use to which it is lawfully dedicated." Chief Justice Rehnquist's suggestion also echoes his opinion in Posadas de Puerto Rico Associates v. Tourism Co. of Puerto Rico, which held that "the greater power to completely ban casino gambling necessarily includes the lesser power to ban advertising of casino gambling."This aspect of Posadas, however, has been overruled in all but name; a later coalition of four Justices, articulating what is arguably prevailing doctrine on commercial speech, explicitly rejected Posadas' "'greater-includes-the-lesser' reasoning."

From public forum doctrine to commercial speech, free speech jurisprudence has transcended simplistic lesser-included-power arguments. To the extent that it rests on the presumptive police power over private use of a conduit, the jurisprudence of conduit-based regulation is comparably suspect.

PUSH, PULL, AND PERVASIVENESS: OF SATURATION AND SOCIAL MEANING

One final factor remains: the pervasiveness and social meaning of particular conduits of speech. "Physical settings" in which speech occurs "are not significant in the abstract"; they draw meaning from "the social expectations and understandings associated with different settings, the practices such spaces foster, and the relationships of those practices to First Amendment values."

Speech does not take place in "some abstract world uncontaminated by concrete social practices," and constitutionally meaningful "communicative acts" must be distinguished from "social practices that do not carry any constitutional value."Courts fret over potential public inferences of official endorsement from the government's legal presence within a conduit.

Societal awareness of broadcast regulation supposedly invites the audience to presume official endorsement of messages in that medium, whereas the corresponding regimes governing cable and the Internet do not. Turner I cited "cable's long history of serving as a conduit for broadcast signals" in playing down the "risk that cable viewers would assume that the broadcast stations carried on a cable system convey ideas or messages endorsed by the cable operator."

Reno observed that the Internet, having remained free of the intense "government supervision and regulation that has attended the broadcast industry," would not lead its users to "infer some sort of official or societal approval" within that medium's "vast democratic fora."

Denver similarly distinguished between (traditionally regulated) public access channels and (traditionally unregulated) leased access channels. Because cable operators have historically enjoyed fewer "editorial rights" over public access channels, "the countervailing First Amendment interest is nonexistent, or at least much diminished."

The logical layer of free speech jurisprudence often invokes another factor closely related to social meaning: the conduit's putative "pervasiveness." This factor most profoundly affects indecency cases. The "uniquely pervasive" nature of broadcasting justifies temporal restrictions on sexual or scatological humour. By contrast, the FCC may not restrict nonobscene "dial-a-porn" that enters the home only when "a caller seeks and is willing to pay for the communication." Justice Stevens's observation that "the Internet is not as 'invasive' as radio or television" virtually doomed the Communications Decency Act.

At least in the realm of indecency regulation, constitutionality apparently hinges on the line between "push" and "pull" technologies, between media that deliver information passively and those that await user Intervention. For instance, Sable Communications of California, Inc. v. FCC invalidated restrictions on phone calls whose sexually explicit content, though worthy of protection, lay much further from core First Amendment concerns than did George Carlin's ribald political commentary.

The most cogent distinction between Pacifica and Sable lies in the nature of the two conduits: whereas broadcasting provides "push" communications, the telephone is the ultimate "pull" tool. Many distinctions within the jurisprudence of conduit-based regulation evidently hinge on the line between push and pull.

That line is becoming harder to draw, and its blurriness undermines the distinction's usefulness as a constitutional test. Technological flux undermines legal assumptions about the passive or interactive nature of any conduit. Indeed, to the extent that end-user technology is expanding the domain of pull, government's sphere of influence over expression correlatively shrinks.

The growing ability of "customers (in particular, parents) to limit access" to entire categories in "interactive media" should impair all types of content-based regulation, "whether it is regulation of sexual expression, violence, commercial speech, or other controversial materials."

Pervasiveness does not divide, but rather unites all forms of passive communication—audio and video, wireline and wireless, analog and digital. What Guglielmo Marconi envisioned as a "wireless telegraph," an airborne twist on an older pull technology, eventually built radio's empire of the air. Cable is at least as pervasive as over-the-air TV, and probably more so, because the presence of more channels enables subscribers to watch more and to "surf" longer before settling on a programme.

Video-on-demand "promises to transform television from a 'push' technology" at least partially into "a 'pull' technology." Now that Congress permits satellite retransmission of local broadcast signals, cable and DBS are nearly perfect substitutes.

To be sure, the biggest divide in communications law separates information viewed at twenty inches (typically a computer) from information viewed at twenty feet (typically a television). "[T]he receipt of information on the Internet requires a series of affirmative steps more deliberate and directed than merely turning a dial."

Nevertheless, anyone who has been "mousetrapped" by pop-ups while browsing the Web or whose e-mailbox has been "spammed" into submission is likely to dispute the Internet's characterization as a "pull" technology. Wireless devices, once broadly deployed, will complete the transformation of the Internet into a medium equally at home with passive push as with active pull.

If anything, telephony's status as the consummate pull technology hangs by a slender legal thread. The telephone remains a pull technology in significant part because the law so decrees. The technological trifle of sending unsolicited faxes converts fax machines into passive receptacles for information. The Telephone Consumer Protection Act of 1991 (TCPA), however, makes it "unlawful... to send an unsolicited advertisement to a telephone facsimile machine."

More recently, the TCPA and the Telemarketing and Consumer Fraud and Abuse Prevention Act of 1994 (as amended in 2003) have authorized a national do-not-call registry. States are rushing to establish their own registries or to ride piggyback on the federal campaign against unsolicited sales calls.

Unwanted faxes and sales calls combine some of the most despised traits of push technology (unsolicited communication) with the most annoying aspect of pull (the user's need to interact—in this instance, by answering a ringing telephone). Nor does technology inherently shield the traditional telephone from push uses. "Copper twisted pair" permits both push and pull; it enables digital subscriber line (DSL) service as readily as voice messages.

Broadband access via DSL is "always on," a typical push trait. Legislative classification of cable broadband and voice over Internet protocol as "information" services, "telecommunications" services, or both may further blur the already illusory distinctions between wireline telephony, broadband, and multichannel video programming delivery. In any event, legislative definitions do not control the factual underpinnings of a First Amendment claim.

Even if it did establish a bright line among conduits, however, the distinction between push and pull can carry only so much constitutional weight. Other push technologies routinely intrude upon sensitive eyes and ears. In almost any setting besides broadcasting, the usual response to unwanted "bombardment of [one's] sensibilities" is an admonition to "avert [one's] eyes" or to escort junk on the "short, though regular, journey from mailbox to trash can."

Electronic conduits equally enable an annoyed individual to "twist the dial" or push a button "to cut off an offensive or boring communications." There may be "captive audiences" worth protecting from "offensive and intrusive" messages, even at the price of invasive speakers' expressive freedom, but neither broadcast audiences nor Internet users rank among them.

Although drivers and mass transit passengers may have no "choice or volition" to absorb such messages as are "thrust upon them by all the arts and devices" of the dark science of marketing, the "radio can be turned off."

Pacifica acerbically refused to ask aggrieved listeners to "avoid further offense by turning off the radio," regarding such an instruction as a facetious pronouncement "that the remedy for an assault is to run away after the first blow." Pacifica vastly overestimated the difficulty of avoiding unwanted broadcasts. "Turning off a radio is much easier than averting your eyes from someone who is in the same room.

Just try it sometime." Efforts to "reduce the adult population to reading only what is fit for children" are eviscerated by admonishing offended viewers to avert their eyes.

Invoking "the governmental interest in protecting children from harmful materials.... does not justify an unnecessarily broad suppression of speech addressed to adults." We should not limit the "level of discourse reaching a mailbox... to that which would be suitable for a sandbox."

AGAINST A DISTINCT JURISPRUDENCE OF CONDUIT-BASED REGULATION

This Chapter rejects a distinct jurisprudence of conduit-based regulation. At best, distinguishing speech cases by conduit fails to solve basic doctrinal tensions. At worst, adopting a conduit-based approach invites unduly speech-restrictive regulation.

After describing how First Amendment jurisprudence might look if stripped of this doctrine, I advocate a unitary theory that respects no categorical distinctions based on the conduit through which speech passes.

A TRULY TRANSPARENT, "END-TO-END" APPROACH TO CONDUIT-BASED REGULATION

A separate jurisprudence on conduit-based regulation is unnecessary. A truly transparent, "end-to-end" approach that gives no weight to conduit-specific regulation would perform better. The real problem stems from the longstanding strategy of inspecting every novel conduit before fixing the appropriate level of First Amendment review. This practice, whose pedigree runs from NBC and Red Lion through Reno v. ACLU, typifies the extensive but imperfectly limned jurisprudence of conduit-based regulation.

Somewhere between the extremes of presumptive strict scrutiny for content-based regulation and the radically weaker review devoted to restrictions on the time, place, or manner of speech, the Court has sustained putatively economic regulations of communicative conduits that also affect, as they must, those conduits' underlying content. Separating conduit-based regulation's concern with legitimate economic interests from its censorial potential represents another variation on the fundamental challenge of First Amendment doctrine within track one-and-one-half.

Two of the most recent cases in this sequence, United States v. Playboy Entertainment Group, Inc., and the second case styled Ashcroft v. ACLU, illustrate an underemphasized doctrinal theme. Pacifica, Sable, Denver, Reno, Playboy, and Ashcroft H have all shown that the Supreme Court is perfectly capable of detecting—and perhaps even denouncing—content-based regulation of speech without regard to conduit.

"Regulation of content is not required to solve the technical commons problem in airwave usage" or any other aspect of the physical or logical infrastructure of communications. Physical challenges do demand some degree of regulation. "Licensing is necessary for engineering reasons; the spectrum is limited and wavelengths must be assigned to avoid stations interfering with each other."

Courts, however, must not transmogrify this narrow justification into a bootstrap by which the government can leverage licensing into unfettered content-based regulation. "Censorship or editing or the screening by Government of what licensees may broadcast goes against the grain of the First Amendment."

Though it superficially honors Red Lion's admonition to focus on conduit, the Supreme Court has never duplicated Red Lion's feat of weakening scrutiny of content-based regulation in any nonbroadcast conduit. Even within broadcasting, courts readily condemn overt, ham-fisted control of content.

Columbia Broadcasting System, Inc. v. Democratic National Committee rescued broadcasters from being forced to accept paid editorial advertisements, reasoning that mandatory carriage would degrade "the journalistic discretion of broadcasters in the coverage of public issues."

Concurring in the judgment, Justice Douglas drew a cogent distinction between legitimate and censorial regulation: "The Commission has an important role to play in curbing monopolistic practices, in keeping channels free from interference, in opening up new channels as technology develops. But it has no power of censorship."

FCC v. League of Women Voters likewise invalidated an attempt to condition federal funding of public television on broadcasters' abjuring of editorializing. Its reasoning was simple: "scarcity of air time does not justify viewpoint-based exclusion."Courts have long exhibited the ability to pierce the veneer of conduit-based regulation.

The 1952 case of Joseph Burstyn, Inc. v. Wilson invalidated a ban on "sacrilegious" motion " pictures. Burstyn merits notice for its adroit handling of First Amendment claims unique to a communicative conduit.

Burstyn confronted a technological phenomenon whose constitutional implications had previously confounded the Supreme Court. In its first look at the movies, the Court held in 1915 that "the exhibition of moving pictures is a business pure and simple... not to be regarded... as part of the press of the country or as organs of public opinion."

By 1952, however, the Court had not only accumulated extensive experience with the movie industry's stormy relationship with antitrust, but also had come to treat "moving pictures, like newspapers and radio" as part of "the press whose freedom is guaranteed by the First Amendment." The Court proceeded to extend full constitutional protection.

Although each "particular method of expression" does "tend to present its own peculiar problems," Burstyn reasoned, "the basic principles of freedom of speech and the press...do not vary." In an era not known for its dedication to expressive freedom, the Court acknowledged that core First Amendment principles "make freedom of expression the rule." Red Lion and Pacifica later cited Burstyn for the proposition that "differences in the characteristics of new media justify differences in the First Amendment standards applied to them."

Unlike either Red Lion or Pacifica, though, Burstyn found "no justification... for making an exception" to the rule of free expression. Burstyn thereby established a doctrinal model worth emulating. However nuanced the judicial approach to the physical, legal, and social vagaries of each conduit, courts should apply as much scrutiny as needed to "smoke out" official efforts to control communicative impact.

At a minimum, courts should pay closer attention to the prospect that seemingly neutral restrictions will perniciously affect content. On other occasions, the Supreme Court has dispatched content-based restrictions with nary a glance at conduit. For instance, Sable Communications of California, Inc. v. FCC bypassed the trivial ritual of determining the proper level of First Amendment scrutiny for restrictions on speech via telephone.

Decided in 1989, Sable coincided with the cable sequence that began in 1986 with Preferred Communications and ended in 1997 with Turner II. Those cases, unlike Sable, pondered the extent to which a new conduit should be analogized to broadcasting. Indeed, telephony has largely eluded the conduit-based strategy.

The "extraordinary antitrust case" in which long-distance upstart MCI sought interconnection with AT&T's local telephone networks raised no First Amendment issues besides those implicit in the Noerr-Pennington antitrust defence. The legally mediated "economic structure" of telephone companies as common carriers "has resulted in a vast regime of rate regulation" and has correlatively reduced telephone companies' First Amendment rights in content transmitted over their networks.

Congress might be able to subject even cable operators to common carrier obligations with respect to "some of their channels," if only because common carriage escapes the constitutional "defect of preferring one speaker to another." Truly neutral, generally applicable economic regulation typically survives First Amendment review, even when it targets media businesses.

The First Amendment has never shielded media businesses from labour and antitrust laws. Nor may cable operators escape franchising requirements and rate regulation. Indeed, no serious free speech challenge involving the structural regulation of telephony arose until the Bell operating companies sought to deliver video programming.

Traditional telephony and its regulation raise no serious First Amendment concerns because issues such as an incumbent carrier's ability to provide long-distance service to local customers have no expressive significance. Sometimes a medium is just a medium.

The shield protecting ordinary economic regulation from First Amendment scrutiny has worn thin. The doctrinal distinction may not withstand the sheer amount of money in contemporary communications. Partisans are determined to contest the economic structuring of communications in constitutional terms, the better to secure a legal arena for rehashing settled legislative battles.

Some of the most outlandish claims have arisen in the very market whose immunity from First Amendment scrutiny seems most secure: lingering disputes over the Bell breakup decree. In 1998 the Fifth Circuit had to spike the fatuous argument that the Bell companies had somehow become the victims of an unconstitutional bill of attainder.

In 2002 the Supreme Court dispelled "serious constitutional question[s]" over whether any ratemaking "methodology [consciously] divorced from investment actually made will lead to a taking of property." This proclamation effectively forecloses prominent arguments that mandatory interconnection, unbundling, and resale violate incumbent carriers' constitutional rights.

The weakness of strategies rooted in the contracts and takings clauses encourages partisans in high-stakes media markets to promote a distinct and robust First Amendment jurisprudence on conduit-based regulation.

First Amendment arguments tend to be more respectable than other constitutional strategies, if only because free speech represents the final redoubt of an extensive libertarian tradition that once justified vigorous judicial vindication of economic due process.

If anything, the First Amendment has apparently "become the first line of challenge for virtually all forms of regulatory initiatives." Critics warn that "[f]reedom of speech is becoming a generalized right against economic regulation of the information industry." The real trick is to preserve freedom of speech without succumbing to the First Amendment's Lochnerian potential.

In an effort to curb the First Amendment's critical power, Justice Breyer has distinguished between "pure economic regulation" and "regulation of expression": "what may count as rational where economic regulation is at issue is not necessarily rational where we focus on expression—in a Nation constitutionally dedicated to the free dissemination of speech, information, learning, and culture."

The Supreme Court "has recognized the strong governmental interest in certain forms of economic regulation, even though such regulation may have an incidental effect on rights of speech and association." Such laws are supposedly "not content related" insofar as they seek "to promote free speech, not to restrict it."

By contrast, allowing government to sort would-be speakers "on the basis of their political, economic or social views" would present a "wholly different" issue. Justice Stevens has distinguished between "policy judgments... intended to forestall the abuse of monopoly power" and laws that "regulate the content of speech rather than the structure of the market."

Many commentators likewise rely on the distinction between structural and content-based regulation. One commentator would toss "[b]roadcasting, insofar as it deals with entertainment," into "the same boat as lipstick," subject to market-driven tides determining which "brand and shade will prevail." Yet the prospect that "a majority vote" might determine public access "to information and news" is greeted with horror.

Sentiments favoring aggressive conduit-based regulation find their most powerful expression in FCC v. National Citizens Committee for Broadcasting (NCCB), the 1978 case that upheld a ban on broadcast/newspaper cross-ownership in the name of "the 'public interest' in diversification of the mass communications media." NCCB's standard of review is not perceptibly tougher than the minimal scrutiny directed at "the prohibitions imposed by the antitrust laws" as applied to media businesses.

In declaring that ""efforts to enhance the volume and quality of coverage" of public issues' through regulation of broadcasting may be permissible where similar efforts to regulate the print media would not be," NCCB also marked the apogee of the enhancement theory. Lower courts routinely describe NCCB as subjecting "'structural' regulation of the broadcast industry" to "minimal scrutiny."

At most, constitutional scrutiny in broadcasting ranges from "purely content-based" to "purely structural," while scrutiny tightens "with the extent to which a challenged provision relies on the identity of the speaker or the content of the covered speech."

Since 2002, several federal courts have invoked NCCB in cases involving restrictions on broadcast ownership. The FCC's rules on local television station ownership, national television station ownership, and broadcast media cross-ownership have all survived First Amendment attacks.

For instance, the ban on "any entity from controlling television stations the combined potential audience reach of which exceeds 35%" of television-viewing households nationwide "is not a content-based regulation; it is a regulation of industry structure, like the newspaper/broadcast cross-ownership rule the Court concluded was content-neutral in NCCB, and like the network ownership restriction upheld in NBC."

In upholding the local television ownership rules, the D.C. Circuit asked solely whether a structural rule of this nature is "rationally connected to [the] goals of ensuring a diversity of voices and adequate competition in television broadcasting."

Courts do not apply NCCB and NBC, however, when reviewing similar structural rules in other media industries. In a 2001 challenge to FCC rules on horizontal and vertical aspects of cable television ownership and operation, the D.C.

Circuit eschewed NBC and NCCB in favour of the intermediate scrutiny standard articulated in United States v. O'Brien.

These cable rules, no less comprehensive in their reach than corresponding rules in broadcasting, failed to pass the tougher test. In striking the 30 per cent horizontal limit on subscribers nationwide that any set of commonly owned and operated cable systems may reach, the D.C. Circuit found "nothing in the record supporting a non-conjectural risk of anticompetitive behaviour" among affiliated cable systems.

The court likewise struck down vertical limits on the number of channels that any cable operator may assign to programmers in which the operator holds an attributable interest. To like effect, the Fifth Circuit in 1999 invalidated a municipal fee for non-locally produced programming on a public/educational/ governmental (PEG) cable channel. The appeals court described the fee as "a content-neutral regulation which implement[ed] a significant governmental interest in promoting localism."

This is the deferential rhetoric of NBC and NCCB. The court compared the fee to Turner litigation's must-carry rule, reasoning that a fee that "subsidizes" a PEG channel "and substitutes for the local resources that could otherwise be utilized to produce programs" rests on "an independent economic basis more closely analogous to the content-neutral must-carry rule than a purely [sic] content-related localism preference."

As in the D.C. Circuit's cable case, however, this decision's invocation of O'Brien proved fatal. Given no evidence regarding "the amount of revenue generated from the fee, the number of providers who have been charged the fee, or whether the fees have actually" advanced local programming, the Fifth Circuit invalidated the fee for failure to satisfy O'Brien's narrow tailoring prong.

The contrast between NCCB's controlling effect in broadcasting cases and its inapplicability in cable cases exposes the flaw in Justice Breyer's proposed distinction between structural and expressive regulation. NCCB does nothing more than parrot Red Lion's assertion that broadcasting alone may be lawfully subjected to structural regulation whose censorial potential is unacceptable in any other setting.

Unexamined categorical distinctions between conduits offer a wholly unsatisfying alternative to the standing First Amendment trick of vacillating between strict scrutiny on track one and judicial deference on track two. "The issue would be totally different" if regulators were to rest their decisions "upon the basis of [would-be speakers'] political, economic or social views."

Yet NCCB's endorsement of enhancement theory gives the lie to the idea that structural regulation is inherently content-neutral. To the extent that government structures media markets to affect content, courts should apply strict scrutiny. Even absent lower court elaboration, the weaknesses in the jurisprudence of conduit-based regulation are evident from Supreme Court cases.

Turner provides the leading illustration. Although Turner I endorsed Red Lion's methodology in searching for a conduit-specific approach to cable, the Turner cases placed exclusive emphasis on cable's physical characteristics. This method stands in stark contrast with Red Lion's more nuanced technique. In concert, the Turner decisions represent the most emphatic rejection of Red Lion's analogical approach.

Alone among the Supreme Court's decisions, Turner I insisted that Red Lion involved nothing but physical scarcity, as though the physical characteristics of spectrum alone justified the fairness doctrine.

That assertion does not withstand a careful reading of Red Lion and its successor cases. Although Turner I declined to hinge First Amendment analysis solely on the presence of a monopoly, it also ignored the impact of the law on cable's economic structure and expressive performance.

By contrast, Red Lion counseled consideration of rivalrousness and of regulatory intensity in every First Amendment review of official efforts to structure a conduit's operative logic. Turner I's deepest pitfall, however, lay in its rendering of the balance between legislative discretion and judicial supervision.

"Deference to a legislative finding cannot limit judicial inquiry when First Amendment rights are at stake." Ceteris paribus, the Supreme Court gives far less weight to legislative flat than to individual conduits' functional peculiarities. At a minimum, Turner H evidently sought to reverse this presumption through its application of intermediate scrutiny to must-carry.

To be sure, the Supreme Court had already conceded its otherwise plenary command over the factual foundations of First Amendment disputes in FCC v. League of Women Voters, which declined to overrule Red Lion "without some signal from Congress or the FCC that technological developments have advanced so far that some revision of the system of broadcast regulation may be required."

But the Turner cases extended judicial abdication to settings beyond broadcasting. If anything, Turner calibrated judicial independence in inverse proportion to the innovative potential of the disputed technology.

What Turner I had called "substantial deference to the predictive judgments of Congress" acquires "special significance in cases... involving congressional judgments concerning regulatory schemes of inherent complexity and assessments about the likely interaction of industries undergoing rapid economic and technological change."

Of course, Red Lion also fell into the same trap. But Turner I aggravated the problem through unilateral judicial disarmament. Worse still, Turner I insisted that "Congress granted must-carry privileges to broadcast stations [solely] on the belief that the broadcast television industry [was] in economic peril due to the physical characteristics of cable transmission."

Having forsworn the portion of Red Lion which would have counseled attention to "the Government's role in allocating [broadcast] frequencies," the Court ignored how "Congress preferred broadcasters over cable programmers based on the content of programming each group offers."

Despite its centrality to this dispute, broadcasting and cable's shared regulatory past contributed almost nothing to Turner.

If Turner I's shortcomings concerned nothing besides must-carry, the resulting misalignment of cable and broadcasting would only modestly affect communications law at large. Cable's greatest competitors today are local telephone companies (in the broadband market) and satellite broadcasters (in the multichannel video programming delivery market).

But Turner's missteps matter in the same way that the larger body of broadcasting law still matters. Turner erred in two significant ways: first by stressing solely the physical differences between cable and broadcast, and second by ignoring the content-based motivation underlying must-carry. Both of these failings grew from the failure to perceive how the law structures conduit in ways beyond those dictated by strictly physical characteristics.

Conduit-based regulation of speech is a constitutional mirage. It represents no genuinely distinct category of First Amendment doctrine. Conduit-based regulation raises precisely the same issues as all other decisions reviewable under the First Amendment.

Treating conduit-based regulation as a distinct category does almost nothing to resolve the First Amendment's considerable doctrinal difficulties. Discrimination on the basis of content does not and should not acquire sudden immunity merely because speech passes through a less privileged conduit.

To be sure, distinct conduits raise distinct regulatory concerns, ranging from strictly physical characteristics to economic predictions regarding markets that exploit that conduit. Persuasive free speech jurisprudence considers differences of this sort. Condensing these nuances into deceptively convenient categories such as "broadcasting," however, blunts judicial initiative to engage in contextual analysis.

Over time, the factors that once might have justified more aggressive intervention in broadcasting may have changed or even evaporated. The mere invocation of cases such as Red Lion, NBC, and NCCB, however, effectively ends any reasoned discussion of whether structural regulation of broadcasting deserves closer scrutiny or, for that matter, whether comparable efforts to structure nonbroadcast markets warrant the deference heretofore reserved for broadcasting.

Treating conduit-based regulation as a distinct First Amendment concept invites the application of per se rules, in both directions, when what is truly needed is a constitutional rule of reason. Controversies over conduit-based regulation of speech have made two doctrinal contributions.

First, these cases have instructed courts to study the conduit in which speech is transmitted, being prepared if necessary to dilute constitutional protection for the expression of ideas. Second, these cases have concluded that one conduit among many—broadcasting—has historically merited less rigorous review on account of rivalrousness in the use of spectrum, the industry's regulatory history, and the public's interest in access to this unique but highly controlled conduit.

Almost all objections to Red Lion and the broadcast model have addressed the second aspect of the conduit-based cases. Whether Red Lion erred in its initial assessment of broadcasting and whether that analysis is obsolete today are both beside the point. It is Red Lion's apology for a separate jurisprudence on conduit-based regulation of speech whose time has passed.

Technology evolves, but the irreconcilable imperative of protecting expressive freedom while accommodating the regulation of noncommunicative concerns will endure forever.

TOWARD A UNITARY THEORY OF FREE SPEECH

"It would be convenient if there were some principle demarcating the line between those activities and resources" that directly facilitate speech "and those that do not." In reality, there is no clean division between content and conduit. The "almost metaphysical" distinctions on the continuum from the purely physical to the purely expressive provide "no clear dividing line between facilitative aspects of speech and other activities."

"It is both theoretically difficult and practically impossible to separate the uniqueness of a particular message from the uniqueness of a particular audience at a particular time and place.... The facilitative and the expressive, the media and the message, are ultimately inseparable."

The impossibility of coherent First Amendment doctrine is emerging as one of those truths susceptible of mathematical proof. "Deriving a consistent theory of the First Amendment from the myriad opinions of the Supreme Court represents a task similar to defining the inside and outside of a Mobius strip; that which appears logical at one point evaporates from another perspective."

To its credit, the jurisprudence of conduit-based regulation acknowledges the intractability of its own quest. Static technological limits, the economic rivalrousness of competing uses, the history and nature of governmental regulation, the pervasiveness and social meaning of a conduit—all of these factors inform this absurdly convoluted constitutional project.

And this is to say nothing of predicting the tortuous path of technological change. As much as the broadcast model has crippled the market for video programming and delivery, the dynamic effect of the conduit-based strategy on legal evolution and the pace of technological innovation may be even more dramatic.

"Fully to comprehend" the vast field of contemporary communications "would require an almost universal knowledge ranging from" engineering and economics "to the niceties of the legislative, judicial, and administrative processes of government." Foundationalist responses cannot encompass the full "web of values, collectively comprising our understanding of how people should live."

Yet the core of this task is simple enough to be expressed in a single sentence. Our First Amendment rests squarely on "[o]ur profound national commitment to the free exchange of ideas." What is true in popular music is equally true in constitutional law: "The hardest to learn" really is "the least complicated." Controversies over conduit-based regulation of speech cannot be resolved by traditional constitutional tools. "The Framers of the First Amendment surely did not foresee the advances in science" underlying contemporary conduit-based controversies.

Courts enjoy enormous freedom to engage in highly contextual, ad hoc judgments that hinge more on evanescent technology than on immanent and durable verities. Like any other social institution, the law must adapt to technological change. A single human generation typically provides ample time for the Supreme Court to complete a constitutional hiccough.

Yet assurances that legal change will come in a quarter-century buy nothing in this land. A polity whose modern prophet decreed that justice delayed is justice denied does not count patience among its national virtues. Law "must ultimately dissolve into a study of aesthetics and morals." We could seek cheap refuge in "new technology," invariably "the easy answer to everything."

Technological convergence among "terrestrial broadcasting, satellite broadcasting, coaxial cable," wireline telephony's "twisted pair," and other media still being refined or invented will render meaningless not only "any remaining distinctions between... various media technologies" but also "any continued effort to draw [legal] distinctions among media."

In times of technological upheaval through "constant revolutionizing of production, uninterrupted disturbance of all social conditions, everlasting uncertainty and agitation," all "fixed, fast, frozen relations, with their train of ancient and venerable prejudices and opinions, are swept away."

Architecture, it bears repeating, is destiny. The architecture of our greatest conduit teaches a vital constitutional lesson. "The Internet... offers a forum for a true diversity of political discourse, unique opportunities for cultural development, and myriad avenues for intellectual activity." The end-to-end concept animating the versatile and volatile Internet should inform First Amendment doctrine. End-to-end wisdom drives all intelligence in free speech jurisprudence to the ends—equally to speakers and to their audiences—at the expense of governmental efforts to modulate the logic of the conduit through which ideas are transmitted.

Red Lion and Justice Thomas are each half-correct. Red Lion insisted that "[i]t is the right of the viewers and listeners, not the right of the broadcasters, which is paramount." Justice Thomas has declared to the contrary that "[i]t is the operator's right that is preeminent."

These dueling propositions express a joint truth: guaranteeing expressive freedom among producers as well as consumers of information depends on minimizing the government's role in encumbering conduits with embedded expressions of official "intelligence."

"Our Constitution does not permit the official suppression of ideas." The Constitution provides scarcely more room for the official expression of ideas, especially when governmental preferences effectively marginalize private expression.

First Amendment jurisprudence has allowed certain expressive conduits to drown in a thick layer of government-initiated "code," in the stultifying structural "logic" of broadcast licensing in the "public interest." Allowing the government too much power to "tell us what to say or hear for our own good" threatens to "deform[] the entire democratic process."

Not for naught has the Supreme Court described the "right to speak freely and to promote diversity of ideas and programs" as "one of the chief distinctions that sets us apart from totalitarian regimes."

Speech, "often provocative and challenging" and invariably free by law, is intended "to invite dispute," particularly "when it induces a condition of unrest, creates dissatisfaction with conditions as they are, or even stirs people to anger." Free speech "may strike at prejudices and preconceptions and have profound unsettling effects as it presses for acceptance of an idea." Within a guarantee of free speech spanning the communicative experience, from its roots in the physical world to its transformation within the mind of the perceiver, "only a unitary First Amendment for all media will do."

The principles that have kept print media free throughout the history of the Republic should apply equally to new media. A unitary free speech jurisprudence leaves no room for a distinct logical layer, for the clumsy cluster of existing doctrines on conduit-based regulation.

The very presence of a free speech jurisprudence of conduit-based regulation invites government to shape speech according to its own vision of the good life. Normatively speaking, however, courts should stop endorsing conduit-based regulation.

Resistance to official control of the means and manifestations of imaginative expression represents the brightest of "fixed stars in our constitutional constellation." Adopting a unitary First Amendment would admittedly force us to gamble in matters of public governance. All law is an experiment, as "all life is an experiment."

First Amendment jurisprudence should err in favour of and not against the right to speak. Such is the lesson taught by the basic structure of First Amendment doctrine: we begin with presumptive strict scrutiny and then find reasons to ratchet down. From that list of excuses, conduit-based regulation should be struck. Many governmental efforts to regulate conduits and media markets would run afoul of the First Amendment.

The First Amendment's commitment to "free trade in ideas" rests on the belief that "the best test of truth is the power of the thought to get itself accepted in the competition of the market." In this marketplace of ideas, the "forum where ideas and information flourish," it is "the speaker and the audience, not the government, [who] assess the value of the information presented."

"Every year if not every day we have to wager our salvation upon some prophecy based upon imperfect knowledge." Under a Constitution that runs as a covenant across the ages, "[e]ach generation" must reject "anew... ideas and aspirations" not fit to "survive more ages than one."

A separate First Amendment jurisprudence on conduit-based regulation deserves to wither away. A generation ago, William Van Alstyne presciently "repudiated the doleful view that we are helpless captives of night riders on the air or that we need protection from every political charlatan who may seek to corrupt us with 1,000 watts of radio power." Today and tomorrow, "if we would guide by the light of reason, we must let our minds be bold."

Bibliography

Boyd, A. (2000) Broadcast Journalism,Techniques of Radio and TV News. Oxford: Focal.

Ettema, J. and Glasser, T. (2001) Narrative form and moral force. Journal of Communication, Summer 2000:8-26.

Foot, P. (2002) Who Framed Colin Wallace? London: Macmillan.

Hill, P., Young, M. and Sargant, T. (2003) More Rough Justice. London: Penguin.

Knightley, P. (2001) A Hack's Progress. London: Jonathan Cape.

Langer, J. (2000) Tabloid Television. London: Routledge.

Preston, Louisa (2001) Paul Foot: The role of the journalist in the surveillance of justice. An unpublished essay for Broadcast Practice 3, BA BJ, Nottingham Trent University.

Silvester, C. (2003) The Penguin Book of Interviews. London: Penguin.

Curran, J. and Seaton, J. (2004) Power without Responsibility: The Press and Broadcasting in Britain, 5th edn. London: Routledge.

Deacon, D. and Golding, P. (2000) Taxation and Representation: The Media, Political Communication and the Poll Tax. London: John Libbey.

Ferguson, M. (2001) Electronic media and redefining time and space. In M. Ferguson (ed.) Public Communication, the New Imperatives: Future Directions for Media Research. London: Sage.

Gurevitch, M. (ed) (2002) Culture, Society and the Media. London: Methuen.

Hall, S. (2003) Coding and encoding in the television discourse. In S. Hall, D. Hobson, A. Lowe and P. Willis (eds) Culture, Media Language. London: Hutchinson: 197-208.

Index

E

F

G

I

L

M

N

P

R

S